D1559389

Plains Histories

*John R. Wunder, Series Editor*

**Editorial Board**

Durwood Ball
Peter Boag
Sarah Carter
Pekka Hämäläinen
Jorge Iber
Todd M. Kerstetter
Clara Sue Kidwell
Patricia Nelson Limerick
Victoria Smith

OCT - - 2024

*Also in Plains Histories*

America's 100th Meridian: A Plains Journey, *by Monte Hartman*

American Outback: The Oklahoma Panhandle in the Twentieth Century, *by Richard Lowitt*

As a Farm Woman Thinks: Life and Land on the Texas High Plains, 1890–1960, *by Nellie Witt Spikes; edited by Geoff Cunfer*

Children of the Dust, *by Betty Grant Henshaw; edited by Sandra Scofield*

The Death of Raymond Yellow Thunder: And Other True Stories from the Nebraska–Pine Ridge Border Towns, *by Stew Magnuson*

Free Radical: Ernest Chambers, Black Power, and the Politics of Race, *by Tekla Agbala Ali Johnson*

From Syria to Seminole: Memoir of a High Plains Merchant, *by Ed Aryain; edited by J'Nell Pate*

"I Do Not Apologize for the Length of This Letter": The Mari Sandoz Letters on Native American Rights, 1940–1965, *edited by Kimberli A. Lee*

Indigenous Albuquerque, *by Myla Vicenti Carpio*

Nikkei Farmer on the Nebraska Plains: A Memoir, *by The Reverend Hisanori Kano; edited by Tai Kreidler*

The Notorious Dr. Flippin: Abortion and Consequence in the Early Twentieth Century, *by Jamie Q. Tallman*

Oysters, Macaroni, and Beer: Thurber, Texas, and the Company Store, *by Gene Rhea Tucker*

Railwayman's Son: A Plains Family Memoir, *by Hugh Hawkins*

Rights in the Balance: Free Press, Fair Trial, and *Nebraska Press Association v. Stuart, by Mark R. Scherer*

Ruling Pine Ridge: Oglala Lakota Politics from the IRA to Wounded Knee, *by Akim D. Reinhardt*

Where the West Begins: Debating Texas Identity, *by Glen Sample Ely*

Women on the North American Plains, *edited by Renee M. Laegreid and Sandra K. Mathews*

# Trail Sisters

## Freedwomen in Indian Territory, 1850–1890

**Linda Williams Reese**

Foreword by John R. Wunder

Texas Tech University Press

This book is typeset in Amasis MT Standard. The paper used in this book meets the minimum requirements of ANSI/NISO Z39.48-1992 (R1997). ∞

Designed by Kasey McBeath
Cover photo credits: (top) University of Oklahoma Press © 2006; (bottom) Research Division of the Oklahoma Historical Society.

Library of Congress Cataloging-in-Publication Data
Reese, Linda Williams, 1946–
   Trail sisters : freedwomen in Indian Territory, 1850–1890 / Linda Williams
Reese ; foreword by John R. Wunder.
      pages cm. — (Plains histories)
   Includes bibliographical references and index.
   ISBN 978-0-89672-810-3 (hardcover : alk. paper) — ISBN 978-0-89672-
811-0 (e-book) 1. African Americans—Relations with Indians. 2. African American
women—Indian Territory—History—19th century. 3. Ex-slaves of Indian tribes—
Indian Territory—History. 4. Indians of North America—Mixed descent. 5. Slavery—Oklahoma—History. 6. Oklahoma—Race relations. 7. United States—Race
relations. I. Title.
   E98.R28R44 2013
   305.48'896073—dc23        2013011211

ISBN 978-1-68283-015-4 (paperback) First paperback printing, 2017

Printed in the United States of America
17 18 19 20 21 22 23 24 25 / 9 8 7 6 5 4 3 2 1

Texas Tech University Press
Box 41037 | Lubbock, Texas 79409-1037 USA
800.832.4042 | ttup@ttu.edu | www.ttupress.org

The ache for home lives in all of us, the safe place where we can go as we are and not be questioned.

Maya Angelou

# Contents

*Illustrations*    ix
*Plainsword*    xi
*Acknowledgments*    xiii

Introduction    3

*Chapter One*
Living in Slavery    11

*Chapter Two*
Surviving the War    42

*Chapter Three*
Reconstructing Families    66

*Chapter Four*
Making a New Life    91

*Chapter Five*
Building Communities    114

Epilogue    141

*Notes*    149
*Bibliography*    165
*Index*    177

# Illustrations

## Maps

Pre–Civil War division of Indian Territory    15
Civil War battle sites in Indian Territory    49
All-black towns of Oklahoma    109
Land openings, 1889–1906    131

## Photographs and Illustrations

Runaway slave advertisement    20
Rose Cottage, home of Cherokee Principal Chief John Ross    47
Freedmen and Indians picking cotton    56
Cherokee freedwoman Charlotte Johnson    62
Choctaw freedwomen and -men awaiting enrollment as tribal citizens    69
Freedman log cabin home near Drumright, Oklahoma    72
John Wesley and family    75
Makeshift dress shop at Fort Gibson, Indian Territory    82
Indian Territory Emancipation Day flyer    89
Freedwomen attending a Cherokee Teachers Institute    103
Tullahassee Freedmen's School    104
Miss Eliza Hartford and Priscilla Haymaker    122
Mrs. D. C. Constant School, Seminole Nation    123
Church raising at Boley, Indian Territory    125

# Plainsword

This book—*Trail Sisters*—is a history of relationships, complex interactions that resulted from twin nineteenth-century mass movements of Americans to what is today Oklahoma. These were the unstoppable Euro-American settlements from the South Atlantic Coast westward and the ethnic cleansing of Native peoples from their homelands, a coerced westward movement now known as Removal. Also caught up in these brutal dislocations were black slaves and free African Americans. Admirably, it is the resultant multidimensional permutations of female relationships upon which Linda Williams Reese has chosen to focus.

The Indigenous women of this history include both those already residing within Oklahoma and those who were forced into mass migrations by newly formed southern states and the U.S. government. The resistant refugees came from all parts of the American South. Cherokees, Chickasaws, Creeks, Seminoles, and Choctaws—known today as the Five Tribes—were relegated to the eastern end of Oklahoma in a violent process that exacted countless lives en route. As the survivors struggled to attach themselves to new lands among existing Indigenous peoples, the Five Tribes witnessed the pouring in of Indian peoples from northern regions of the United States and from Texas and the Southwest. With the agricultural potential of the Plains still untapped by Euro-American powerbrokers, the federal government saw the Oklahoma Territory as a repository for the Indigenous from wherever white people wanted them uprooted. That ethnic cleansing had powerful appeal.

Some in the Five Tribes embraced black slavery and brought slaves with them. Free blacks found escape or sometimes legal means of migrating to Oklahoma. The Civil War brought disruption and death to the Territory's Indigenous nations, yet also the onset of freedom for all African Americans dwelling there. The post-Civil War era would see even further division of Oklahoma lands as new Euro-American settlers competed for homesteads, often on lands already occupied.

This book could not have been written without the groundbreaking work of previous historians drawn to the struggles of this nervous and claimed North American hinterland. Numerous historians of the Five Tribes and other Indian nations have helped illuminate the way. Early on, Grant Foreman, Angie Debo, Vine Deloria, Jr., and Annie Abel, among others, made seminal inroads. More modern treatments have shifted the emphasis to social history and delineated the agency of all participants. For this we are grateful to Gary Anderson, Willard Rollings, Susan Miller, Blue Clark, Daniel Littlefield, Jr., and again so many others. Of particular significance is the Southeastern Indian series edited by Theda Perdue and Michael Green and published by the University of Nebraska Press. Note also the important books on Creeks by Green and Cherokees by Perdue.

With *Trail Sisters*, Linda Williams Reese adds to the corpus a most significant contribution. Her work is particularly informed by the invaluable oral histories collected in Oklahoma during the New Deal era, rich documents that Reese has brought to life. That alone would be enough to distinguish this important book. We hear the voices of those many women who personally witnessed upheaval or became repositories for the stories their mothers and fathers, grandmothers and grandfathers, and great-grandmothers and great-grandfathers passed on so that all could learn, and remember.

**John R. Wunder**
Lincoln, Nebraska

# Acknowledgments

The origin of this book began within the initial research for the chapter on Oklahoma's black townswomen in my doctoral dissertation, *Women of Oklahoma, 1890–1920,* at the University of Oklahoma. I greatly appreciate the chair of my committee, William W. Savage, Jr., and the other members, Robert Griswold, Paul Glad, the late Paul Sharp, and the late Norman Crockett, for allowing me the latitude to explore a broad landscape of ideas that has inspired my continuing work as a historian and teacher. The Oklahoma Humanities Council provided me with a grant to pursue the research that led to an article in the *Western Historical Quarterly* on Cherokee freedwomen. Many thanks go to David W. Levy and Robert E. Shalhope for providing instructive comments on this project. The book could not have proceeded without the generous Catherine Prelinger Award from the American Historical Association's Coordinating Council for Women in History. The Prelinger Award and the cooperation of the administration and the Research Committee at East Central University allowed me the financial support and the time to research and write the book. I am especially grateful to Dr. Thomas Cowger, chair of the History Department, Dr. Scott Barton, dean of the College of Liberal Arts and Social Sciences, and to Dr. Duane Anderson, vice president for academic affairs and provost.

It would be impossible to thank each librarian individually who helped me find records and materials. I am grateful for Dr. Bob Blackburn's staff at the Oklahoma History Center Research Division; to Dr.

Donald DeWitt's staff at the University of Oklahoma Western History Collections, especially John Lovett, Kristina Southwell, and Jacquelyn Slater; and to the Fort Worth Regional National Archives and Research Center. The librarians at Northeastern Oklahoma State University and Oklahoma State University and Dana Belcher at East Central University have been very helpful. The museums and archives of the Five Nations of Oklahoma are wonderful resources, as well as the Descendants of the Freedmen organization. In addition, thank you to Jennifer Sparks and Billie Edgington for answering my advertisement and sharing their research materials with me in the truest sense of generous scholarship.

Many colleagues and friends have offered their advice, support, and encouragement along this journey. Thank you to East Central University colleagues past and present Jeff Means, Davis Joyce, Greg Sutton, Brad Clampitt, Chris Bean, Francis Stackenwalt, Sheri Spaar, Michael Hughes, Alvin Turner, Mitchelle Barton, Richard Cooper, and Kevin Lynch. I have been blessed for many years by the friendship of a large number of female academic historians and friends connected with Oklahoma. Special thanks goes to Patricia Loughlin, Melissa Stockdale, Martha Skeeters, Jacki Rand, Suzanne Schrems, and Sarah Eppler Janda. Thank you also to Darlene Logan, Barbara Million, and Elaine Rhynes. These friends never failed to encourage, to listen, and to help me find a balanced understanding.

Finally, this book is dedicated to Bill Reese, my best friend, my husband, and my north star, who shares in everything I do. Thank you for managing my life so that I could finish writing this book.

# Trail Sisters

# Introduction

**A**miniature reproduction of a painting made by the Cherokee artist Jeanne Rorex Bridges sits on my office desk. The painting depicts two women in nineteenth-century dress striding forward toward the viewer. Their faces reflect a blend of sorrow, strength, and determination. On the right is a Cherokee woman with one hand on her pregnant belly. Her other hand clasps that of an African American woman who carries a bundle. The painting is titled *Trail Sisters*. It has intrigued me for some time. Both women are tired; both are carrying burdens, yet they persevere. The two women are called sisters. So many questions arise from this work and its title. Is the sun behind them a rising sun of new possibilities or a setting sun of diminished relationships? How are these women tied to each other: by friendship, by blood, by bondage, by shared experience? What kind of hardships did they endure along the trail? What was the future for both when they arrived at their destination? These questions and more are the focus of my research.

For quite a while I have been exploring the history of freedwomen and black Indian women in Indian Territory from the Civil War until Oklahoma statehood in 1907. My interest in this area evolved initially from reading the pathbreaking work of Daniel F. Littlefield, Jr. on the freedmen of the Five Tribes of Oklahoma. Littlefield was one of the first to explore the transformation among these freedmen in education, religion, and legal and economic status through time. His work variously covers slavery, the Civil War, emancipation, and freedom up to Oklahoma statehood. It occurred to me, however, that the earlier histories on this topic assumed that the same experiences applied equally to all of the freed people of the Five Nations and so to freedwomen as well. As David A. Chang has observed about the Creek Nation, the common designator *freedmen* "both concealed and revealed much about the group." It implied that all Native peoples of African descent had been slaves, that they were all men, and that they were all discernible from their previous slave masters.[1]

More recent works, such as James Brooks's brilliant collection of essays, *Confounding the Color Line: The Indian-Black Experience in North America,* Claudio Saunt's *Black, White, and Indian: Race and the Unmaking of an American Family,* Tiya Miles's *Ties That Bind: The Story of an Afro-Cherokee Family in Slavery and Freedom,* Circe Sturm's *Blood Politics, Race, Culture, and Identity in the Cherokee Nation of Oklahoma,* Fay Yarbrough's *Race and the Cherokee Nation: Sovereignty in the Nineteenth Century,* and Celia Naylor's *African Cherokees in Indian Territory,* reveal a much more complicated story of identity, family, economics, sovereignty, and gender. The historian Joshua Piker examines each of these works and four others in "Indians and Race in Early America: A Review Essay." Piker focuses on three issues: "the Euro-American move toward racializing Indians, the Native Americans' own perspectives on difference and race, and the degree to which the beliefs of Native and Euro-Americans emerged as a consequence of cross-cultural conversations." These works have created a "newly vibrant literature" that illustrates the "messiness" and "all-encompassing" attempt to understand and embrace the history of Africans, Europeans, and Indians.[2]

Brooks's *Confounding the Color Line* is a wide-ranging book of twelve essays contributed by scholars from interdisciplinary backgrounds. The work is separated into three sections; the chapters move from first contact between Africans and Native Americans up to the turn of the twenty-first century. The majority of the chapters focus on nineteenth-century topics. In these, the lines of interaction suggest less the dichotomies of white/Indian and white/black of earlier works on race in America and more strongly a set of intertwined, complex, ambiguous, and dynamic relationships.

Nowhere are these relationships more apparent than in the books by Claudio Saunt and Tiya Miles. Each of these authors develops a history around the trials of mixed black and Indian families who attempted to navigate the white intrusion and intensifying racism of the nineteenth century in Indian Territory. Saunt presents the history of the Creek Grayson family, which began with the marriage of a Scot trader, Robert Grierson, and a Creek woman named Sinnugee. The family name Grayson resulted from the Muscogee-language pronunciation of Grierson. Two of the Grayson children, William and Katy, wed African American partners and had children. At some point Katy and her first husband separated and she married a substantial Creek man. William remained with his wife and seven children. Upon Grierson's death, Katy's new family received an inheritance, while William received nothing. When both arrived in Indian Territory, the cleavage between the two families became permanent. Saunt makes clear that the Creek Nation, in spite of its history of intermarriage with African Americans, developed discriminatory legislation that benefited Katy and her nonblack offspring and punished William and his family.

Tiya Miles's work engages slavery, Cherokee kinship norms, emancipation, and Cherokee sovereignty, bound together in multicultural conversations about racial formation. Through the family of Shoe Boots, an honored Cherokee warrior, and his wife, a slave named Doll, Miles weaves the story of their lives and those of their descendants through the nineteenth century into the twentieth. Inherent in the contradictory circumstances they faced rest the highly nuanced arguments about identity, sexuality, family, property, and Indian autonomy. Both Saunt and Miles indicate that original Creek and Cherokee attitudes toward African Americans and slavery had changed dramatically by the nineteenth century and that matrimonial and childbearing decisions held enormous consequences.

The final three books cited earlier illustrate the preponderance of new works dealing with the freed people of the Cherokee Nation. This is largely due to the early adoption of a written language developed from the alphabet or syllabary created in the early nineteenth century by the Cherokee untutored genius Sequoyah. The written language enabled the Cherokees to publish documents and newspapers from their own perspective as early as the 1820s, when they began their first movement into new homes in Indian Territory. Consequently, an abundance of written documents survive. In addition, the descendants of the Cherokee freed people have been the most articulate and unrelenting in their pursuit of the retention of their membership status and rights in the Cherokee Nation through twenty-first-century litigation.[3]

In 2002 the anthropologist Circe Sturm published *Blood Politics: Race, Culture, and Identity in the Cherokee Nation of Oklahoma*. Sturm's analysis is largely focused on postremoval Cherokee culture, but she maintains that the origins of Cherokee identity underwent social and political pressures in the eighteenth century as the people came into greater contact with Euro-Americans. Originally blood was the most critical component of their matrilineal culture and signified clan membership. Sturm identifies five characteristics (phenotype, behavior, language, religious knowledge or participation, and community residence or participation) that over time also created a race-culture continuum in which Cherokees defined themselves.

Both Fay A. Yarbrough and Celia E. Naylor build upon Sturm's work in discussing the evolution of the status of enslaved people in the Cherokee Nation throughout the nineteenth century. Yarbrough's book *Race and the Cherokee Nation: Sovereignty in the Nineteenth Century* is based on superb research in marriage records, census data, Cherokee Nation constitutional changes, interviews conducted by the Works Progress Administration (WPA) in the 1930s, case studies, and her own interviews. She traces the original designations based on kinship through the matrilineal clan structure to the eighteenth-century preference of Cherokee women for white marriage partners and the 1880s designation "by blood" for legal citizenship. This evidence establishes the rationale for the recent actions by the Cherokee Nation to remove citizenship status from the descendants of the freedmen. Her findings are twofold: first, that Cherokee officials deliberately set about to limit both marriages and rights to black partners, and second, that they established the prerogative for the designation of their own identity by determining who was not considered a Cherokee or a Native American.

In *African Cherokees in Indian Territory: From Chattel to Citizens* Celia Naylor attacks the traditional notion that slavery among the Native American tribes was more humane and lenient than white American slavery. By exploring life in the Cherokee Nation from the perspective of the enslaved people and by discussing individual and collective African Cherokee resistance, she clearly shows the fallacy of such an argument. Naylor traces the development of an African Indian cultural connection to the Cherokee communities based on shared interactions and experiences. This sociocultural dimension of belonging is the basis of the conflict with the political designation of citizenship that has troubled the Cherokees since the Civil War.

In many ways all of the books just discussed call into question the historian Theda Perdue's emphasis on cultural continuity and the belief that kinship frequently trumped race as a consideration among Native peoples. The newest scholarship broadens the context in understanding the development of racial ideology, slavery, emancipation, and citizenship in the nineteenth-century milieu of Indian Territory. What emerges is a rich texture of ideas to consider: that definitions and attitudes about race evolve over time; that they do not develop in a vacuum but are influenced by historical events; that all partners, Native American, Euro-American, and African American, contribute to the conversation; and that gender plays a significant role in unraveling this complex aspect of life.[4]

In her 1995 commencement address to her alma mater, Spelman College, the writer and activist Alice Walker honored her triple inheritance of African, European, and Cherokee ancestry. She encouraged the students to embrace the diversity within themselves as a foundation of strength. "What can I give you," she asked, "to help you know this fusion is a source not of disgrace, but of lived presence in the history of our troubled country?" This book builds upon these recent works to examine the fault lines of race and gender surrounding the Civil War and its aftermath in Indian Territory. Emphasizing less the strategies of law, politics, and sovereignty, I focus on life imperatives, choices, and actions. Gender is the first consideration in order to provide a context for the most elementary level of human life, the family. Through the voices of the freedwomen and their narratives, I explore both the unraveling of kinship, bondage, shared culture, and labor that once bound African American enslaved women and their Indian masters and mistresses as well as the knitting together of new alliances. Blood quantum analysis on the freedwomen is not considered in this discussion. Use of blood quantum as a measure of tribal membership was not in effect until the 1880 U.S. census. Government documentation was frequently carried out in an arbitrary manner and often erred in establishing levels. Most Native American peoples rejected blood quantum and preferred to establish their own standards of membership. The words of the freedwomen and -men are presented here as they appear in the documents and narratives cited, acknowledging that corruption occurred from the attempts by inexperienced white interpreters to capture the colloquialism of their subjects.[5]

Freedwomen in Indian Territory were caught among competing bases of power: a punitive Washington government, a determined Indian leadership, a burgeoning white invasion, and the demands of their own men. How did freedwomen navigate among limited alternatives to transform themselves from enslaved to free persons? Which conditions obstructed and which enabled the freedwomen as they made the journey from internalized culture, condition, place, and belonging toward a new and uncertain future?

During the years between the removal of the Five Tribes to Indian Territory and the Civil War, slavery in Indian Territory took on multiple forms as each of the tribal groups reconstructed their governments and cultures in a new environment. As tragic as the event was, removal made it possible to renegotiate the boundaries of slavery and prevent some of the sclerosis that plagued the southern states. Enslaved females understood the expectations of their roles and their positions within their own families and their tribal cultures. The cataclysm of the Civil War years, however, brought hunger, death, destruction, and dislocation. It shattered families and patterns of behavior, and it exacerbated racist attitudes. New treaties signed with the federal government at the end of the war demanded that freedmen be designated citizens of their tribal groups. In addition, government officials expected gender relationships to model those of white patriarchal society.

At the 2007 Mid-America Conference on History in Tulsa, Oklahoma, Theda Perdue appropriately distinguished her topic, "Indians in the segregated South" from the experiences of Indians in Oklahoma. She poignantly described the efforts of Indian peoples to claim their identity and rights against a white southern effort to deny their existence or to classify them in the same subservient category as African Americans.

Nearly the reverse became true in Indian Territory in the second half of the nineteenth century. A foundation for unifying whites and members of the Five Nations had been laid long before. Largely because they were residents of the land and Euro-Americans had found much to value in the tribal groups they called "civilized" tribes and because the leaders of the southeastern Indians frequently gave military aid to the Euro-Americans against foreign foes, a strong connection had developed. This in no way denies the ruthless dispossession of Indian lands, but it does help to explain the willingness of the federal government to bargain with the leadership of the Five Tribes. In Indian Territory following the forced removal of these tribal groups, all of the land was legally owned by them and developed in large part by an Americanized mixed-blood elite. Over time, white residents and Indian populations developed a unity in politics, economic development, and intermarriage as well as a racial antipathy. Freedwomen accustomed to Indian matrilineal recognition, shared circumstances, and often family relation now found themselves marginalized. They endured a continuous contest of their identity and status in the shifting social terrain of the Indian nations.[6]

In the years following the Civil War, freedwomen began to form new relationships with each other, with immigrant freedwomen, and with Native and white residents. They reconstructed family life, making choices from limited opportunities. Marriage possibilities, now more abundant, were still not entirely at their own discretion. They worked the land, alone or in continued connection to their former masters. They seized opportunities for education on their own and in every way that the Indian nations or missionary organizations made these available. And they bartered their domestic skills to provide a living for themselves and their children, often as single heads of households. Former interactions of trust, mutual benevolence, blood relation, and recognition of rights were frequently strained or permanently severed as Indian Territory rushed headlong toward statehood. The decisions they made and the lives they created provided the foundation for survival during the ensuing allotment process in the Five Nations and, ultimately, in statehood. Article 23 of the 1907 constitution of the state of Oklahoma provided that the term *white race* applied to all persons except those of African descent. This exclusionary definition represented the legal culmination of cultural, political, and economic forces at work since the Civil War. What may earlier have been an environment of sisterhood, reciprocal relations, and mutual trust between the Indian woman and the black woman depicted in the Bridges painting had come to an end. Indian women were now white, and all women of African descent were black.[7]

It has now been decades since the interpretive framework of the new western history challenged the traditional story of American westward development. The research that followed brought considerable insight into race, gender, class, labor, and sexuality in the West. Scholars have used varied and innovative perspectives to frame history less in a larger thematic or paradigm-driven analysis and more as an inquiry into the separate but significant threads that make up the complete tapestry. At the root of history are the stories of human beings. In those stories we find a reflection of ourselves and our own humanity. They also help to refine our thinking about issues from the past that continue to trouble the social fabric of the present. This exploration of the lives of African American and black Indian women as they made the journey from slavery to freedom in Indian Territory may serve to shed light on the tangled question of the rights of the descendants of the Oklahoma freed people as citizens of the former Indian nations.

Legal battles among the Five Nations, the descendants of the freedmen, and the federal government appear frequently in the twenty-first century. This book addresses in only brief and tangential ways the tortuous process of allotting Indian lands to private owners. Some scholars may find this remiss. These issues as they pertain to the contested nature of the allotment rolls and the 1866 treaties regarding the freedmen, however, will continue to be reviewed in U.S. courts for some time to come. Ongoing and future historical research into the "lived presence" of the freed people will provide some background and clarity about the shared history of Native Americans, African Americans, and European Americans as they mediated the cultural space that became the state of Oklahoma. It is my hope that this book provides a gendered lens for understanding this intricate history of multiple interactions and that it will reach beyond an academic audience to inform the general reading public.

**Chapter One**
# Living in Slavery

"Hard work was all she ever knowed."

R. C. Smith, in Baker and Baker,
*The WPA Oklahoma Slave Narratives*

T he long trail leading to freedom in Indian Territory for enslaved women and men began with the removal of the Five Tribes from their homelands in the southeastern part of the United States. Whether Cherokee, Choctaw, Chickasaw, Creek, or Seminole, this process was forced upon them by the U.S. government and became a tragic nightmare that stretched from roughly the 1820s until, in some cases, after the Civil War. The wealth of the United States in the early nineteenth century lay in its land and natural resources. Native-born Americans and European immigrants alike dreamed of the independence, security, and prosperity lodged in the ownership of a good piece of land. As the population of the United States increased, the demand for land began to impinge upon the Indian territories, held since before the arrival of the Europeans. Numerous treaties between the tribes and the federal government, in addition to philosophical wrangling over the Indian "right of soil" versus the Euro-American "right of discovery" could not hold back the flood tide of expansion.

The suggestion of removal of the eastern Indian tribes beyond the Mississippi River had been discussed since the administration of Thomas

Jefferson, but it received popular support with the advent of the admin-istration of Andrew Jackson. As early as 1825 the James Monroe admin-istration created a permanent reserve of land for tribal colonization stretching west of Missouri and Arkansas to the western boundary of the United States, and from the Platte River on the north to the Red River on the south. This came to be known as Indian Territory. In 1830 Congress passed the Indian Removal Act, a document with few concrete directives, placing authority for removal into the hands of the president. Jackson wasted no time in exercising his power to clear the Five Tribes of their land holdings in spite of their cooperation with him in the War of 1812 and abundant evidence of their acculturation to Euro-American lifestyles, including African slaveholding. In addition, the passage of the removal bill engendered a widespread surge of lawlessness. The state govern-ments and various individuals engaged in violence and unlawful seizure of Indian property. This forced removal foreshadowed the stringent poli-cies the federal government exercised toward the Five Nations after the Civil War.[1]

One by one, each of the Five Tribes defensively faced the negotia-tions with government authorities to exchange their eastern lands for new lands in Indian Territory. After the discovery of gold in 1829 on Cherokee lands, the tribe endured wholesale looting of their property by outsiders and subjection to the authority of the state of Georgia. The Cherokees brought their case for exemption from Georgia laws based on sovereignty before the Supreme Court of the United States, but Chief Justice John Marshall ruled that they were "domestic dependent na-tions," not sovereign nations. Similar to what happened in the other tribes, the prospect of removal split the Cherokee leadership, creating blood feuds that remained fierce for decades. An 1835 removal treaty at New Echota by one faction produced the migration of only a few thou-sand to Indian Territory, but by 1838 Georgia troops accompanied by the U.S. Army invaded the Cherokee lands to forcibly remove the remainder. The story of their travail as they were rounded up, placed in detention camps, and escorted overland to the West is well known in history as the Trail of Tears, an experience that would be repeated by all of the Five Tribes. Hunger, cold, disease, exhaustion, exposure, and ill treatment cre-ated a pathetic and hopeless passage of misery and persecution. These hardships were also endured every step of the way by their enslaved people.[2]

The Choctaw and Chickasaw removal negotiations followed a slightly different pattern but resulted in the same difficulties. Mississippi was no less proactive than Georgia in forcing confrontations with these two tribes. The state legislature abolished tribal governments, punished tribal leaders, and made the Indians subject to state laws. White residents looted their lands and property with impunity. Appeals to the federal government based on treaty rights were dismissed without action. In 1830 the Choctaw leadership negotiated a removal treaty at the Dancing Rabbit Creek council ground that cost the tribe all of their lands in Mississippi but gave them a much more financially favorable settlement. The majority of Choctaws and their enslaved people made their way to Indian Territory, but travel under extremely harsh winter conditions and outbreaks of cholera and smallpox produced the same great suffering experienced by the Cherokees. Some full- and mixed-blood Choctaws were allowed to remain in Mississippi and became known as the Mississippi Choctaws, but most were quickly divested of their "allotments" and, impoverished, joined their families in Indian Territory. The Chickasaws also insisted on a reasonable relocation treaty. At the Treaty of Pontotoc in 1832, they won the right to remain until they found a suitable home in Indian Territory. Their lands were to be surveyed and sold, the proceeds accruing to the tribe. They also insisted upon management of the removal process under their own control. In 1837, at the Treaty of Doaksville, the Chickasaws agreed to settle in Indian Territory with the Choctaws. They and their enslaved people began the trek westward in an orderly, if not an entirely safe and comfortable, manner.[3]

Removal of the Creek and Seminole Indians and their enslaved people was costly in lives and money. The Creeks, like the Cherokees, were deeply divided over their loss of land through earlier cessions and a recent civil war between the Upper Creeks and the Lower Creeks. In 1823 the Creek Council passed a law proscribing the ceding of land by anyone without the approval of the Council itself. A death sentence hung over the head of anyone who disobeyed. The Lower Creek leader William McIntosh believed that the tribe should accept removal while the government was willing to pay for their lands. McIntosh's Treaty of Indian

Springs in 1825 led to his assassination. Attempting to avert another civil war and to combat the same conditions of white harassment in the state of Alabama, the Upper Creek leader Opothleyoholo traveled to Washington, D.C. in 1826. With Council approval, in 1832 he negotiated land cessions, exchanging homelands for an area near Fort Gibson in Indian Territory. The final treaty extinguished the Creek Nation in Alabama. Creeks could join the Upper Creeks in Indian Territory or remain on allotments in Alabama. Most chose to stay and quickly lost their land and possessions to lawless whites. Creek retaliation for these injustices that included warriors and enslaved allies became the basis for their wholesale removal to Indian Territory in 1836–37. Their suffering was as great as that of the Cherokees. Captured warriors wore shackles and remained under guard. The severe winter weather together with disease killed the infants and elders first, then the women and men. One group of 300 perished when their boat sank on the Mississippi River. Thousands died before their arrival in the West.[4]

The Seminole Tribe proved the hardest to dislodge from their Florida lands, and in truth, the U.S. government was forced to give up the attempt in 1842. Pressure to force out the Seminoles began almost immediately after 1819, when the United States acquired Florida from Spain. Unlike the other Five Tribes, the Seminoles were loosely organized around band chiefs, many of whom were determined to remain on their ancestral land. U.S. commissioners convinced a few of the band leaders and their tributary people to migrate in 1832 in the Treaty of Payne's Landing and to reside with the Creeks. Osceola and other recalcitrant leaders, however, attacked the treaty signers and U.S. troops and pledged to fight until death. Wildcat and Bowlegs continued after Osceola's death in 1839 to make war against the army and the Florida settlements. The Seminole attacks did not cease until 1842, when the government decided to allow the Seminoles to remain in Florida. Only approximately 3,000 Seminoles were removed at a cost of $20 million and 1,500 soldiers killed.[5]

Each of the Five Tribes, with the unceasing work of the women and men they had enslaved, transplanted their people and cultures in their new western home, never forgetting but recovering dramatically from the removal tragedy. The decade of the 1850s should have been a time of celebration in Indian Territory. By then the horror of Indian removal had passed, and with great exertion a renaissance of the Cherokee, Choctaw,

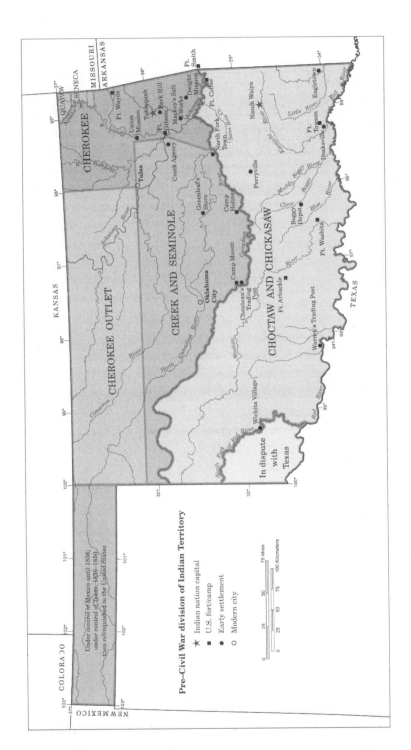

Pre–Civil War division of Indian Territory. Courtesy of the University of Oklahoma Press © 2006.

Chickasaw, Seminole, and Creek Nations had begun. The population was growing again. Small farms and ranches dotted the landscape alongside larger plantations. Steamboats moved along the Arkansas and Red rivers bearing agricultural products to the southeast and bringing passengers and consumer goods into the Territory. Little towns such as Boggy Depot and Tahlequah thrived. Newly created constitution-based Indian governments brought order. The Cherokees opened prestigious male and female academies of higher education for their children. Baptist, Presbyterian, and Methodist missionaries built small schools and churches among the tribal groups. From the outside, it appeared that by every measure the Five Nations had adapted well to their new home.[6]

This time would be remarkable, however, not only for its successes but for the mounting tension within the tribal groups concerning the institution of African slavery. They had brought slavery with them to Indian Territory, and, as in the rest of the United States, its long-term retention was in doubt. Rather than peace and progress, these years would be frightening for the entire enslaved population, but especially for its most vulnerable members, the women and children. Familiar with their roles and the structured expectations of tribal slavery, women now confronted new challenges and dangers that changed the dynamics of their lives. It would require great skill, courage, and endurance to negotiate the beginning of their journey to freedom.

Indian slaveholding existed at the time of contact with white Europeans. Initially it did not, however, contain a racial dimension. According to the historian Theda Perdue, the word for "slave" in Cherokee, *atsi nahsa'i*, referred to anything, both living and inanimate, that existed outside of the kinship system that gave the Cherokees their identity as a people. Human beings kept in this status on the fringe of Cherokee society, Perdue suggests, may have been a means to accentuate the significance and power of the Cherokee kinship system. Similarly, as Florida Indians increasingly detached themselves from the Creek Confederacy in the mid-eighteenth century, they received a new name as a separate people, *simano'-li*, meaning "wild" or "undomesticated." In other words, the Seminole Indians existed outside of recognized Creek society. One Oklahoma freedwoman, Sweetie Ivery Wagoner, explained to an interviewer in the 1930s just how complex lines of lineage could be. "My father was a slave, but he wasn't a Negro," she said. "He was a Creek Indian whom the Cherokee Indians stole long years ago and put into slavery just like he was a Negro." Wagoner's father married an African American enslaved woman and raised eleven children, all of whom became separated because of the Civil War.[7]

Originally the Five Tribes acquired slaves through raiding, warfare, and capture to replace dead relatives, and through exchange. As English and Spanish colonization advanced, they also incorporated runaway slaves into their tribal communities. War parties usually spared female captives and young children from torture and death more often than adult males. The Five Tribes, organized along matrilineal clans, recognized women as heads of the kinship lineages. Women directed and performed all of the agricultural work and owned both the houses and the fields. The senior women determined the future of slaves: whether they would be killed, adopted into the clans, or remain as outsiders until death or ransom. Slaves and their children adopted into the tribal groups enjoyed the same rights and privileges as other members of the kinship group. Women also held slaves in their own right. As a result of a battle in 1775, Nancy Ward, a Cherokee leader known as Beloved Woman, received a black male captive. By 1835 twenty Cherokee women owned collectively 120 slaves in their own names. The Seminole Culckeeeshowa went to great lengths to recover her enslaved woman, Caty, and Caty's sons and daughters and their children when they were taken by a corrupt white trader in 1835.[8]

The enslavement of African Americans, as an economic institution with attendant racial antipathy, evolved over time as the Five Tribes experienced greater familiarity with the capitalist agricultural system and racial attitudes of southern white settlers. Intermarriage among members of the Five Tribes and southern whites also contributed to the development of a mixed-blood elite who adapted the practices of southern farmers and businessmen to their cultures. African slavery came to prominence among the mixed-blood elite late in the eighteenth century and was well established by the time of their forced removal from the southeastern states to Indian Territory in the 1830s. Slavery as it evolved in Indian Territory, however, was still more heterogeneous than has been previously explored.

Numerous studies have attempted to pinpoint the causation and moment of Indian cultural change in the Cherokee, Choctaw, and Chickasaw tribes to model white slaveholding. The geographer Michael Doran traces a direct line from white fur traders who intermarried with Native women, creating offspring with tribal citizenship but broader cultural experience. "The trading establishments they operated," Doran writes, "formed nuclei for the maintenance of an alien cultural influence," in which large-scale agriculture and the value of material gain thrived. James H. Merrell, in comparing R. Halliburton's 1974 book, *Red over Black: Black Slavery among the Cherokee Indians* and Theda Perdue's *Slavery and the Evolution of Cherokee Society: 1540–1866*, examines two different interpretations. Halliburton emphasizes the easy accommodation of European economic practices and racial attitudes with existing Cherokee ethnocentrism. He maintains that Cherokee women in particular welcomed black slavery as additional manpower in the fields, work that Cherokee men viewed as inappropriate for themselves. Both Doran and Halliburton support the position that a transformation occurred resulting in a form of slavery identical to that perpetrated by southern whites. Perdue recognizes the economic changes that took place in the Cherokee way of life, but she also explores the impact of removal and growing sectionalism that hardened what had earlier been a more supple form of slavery. After removal, "capitalistic values had gradually replaced aboriginal economic values," she writes, "and Cherokee slaveholders had become increasingly more committed to the preservation of the institution." Such an evolution resonates with members in the other tribal groups as well.[9]

The tortuous process of Indian removal—overland, by boat, and by rail—may itself have afforded some slaves an opportunity to escape white ownership by hiding among the Indian peoples in the hope of reaching freedom in Indian Territory. Advertisements about runaway slaves appeared in Arkansas newspapers detailing numerous attempts by runaways to join various emigrating Indian groups. Betsy and John Reece, slaves of a white master, escaped to the Cherokees in Tennessee. According to one Cherokee, John Armstrong, they "got with a Cherokee family and made it across the Mississippi River and got to this side. . . . And they got here [Indian Territory], they come in with the Cherokee family, see." In 1838 U.S. Attorney General Benjamin Butler exempted

Indian Territory from Article 4 of the U.S. Constitution, making the capture of runaway slaves illegal without tribal permission. By the 1850s, however, Attorney General Caleb Cushing reversed that decision, based in part on the suggestion of a Chickasaw agent, Douglas Cooper, that Indian Territory might become "a great run-away harbor, a sort of Canada—with 'underground railroads' leading to and through it." Some enslaved women acted on their own behalf to save themselves and their children from separation. A woman named Fanny and her six children were on a boat bound for New Orleans to be sold. Fanny approached the maid of Elizabeth Fields Coody and asked her to convince her mistress to buy her and her children. Fanny's appeal was persuasive. Coody's husband, William Shorey Coody, bought all of them for $1,500 and removed them to Indian Territory. Fanny and one of her daughters served as cooks for the Coody family until emancipation.[10]

Using population statistics collected for Indian Territory but not published in 1860, Doran reconstructs the cultural regions where slavery increased after the forced removal of Indians from their southeastern homelands. At least part of the growth of slavery and intensifying racial attitudes among the tribal groups had to do with the geographic areas of concentrated settlement within Indian Territory and the resources available. Each tribal group removed to areas that more closely reflected the homelands they had left. The Choctaws and the related tribe, the Chickasaws, settled from the Canadian rivers southward to the fertile Red River Valley. The Creeks and Seminoles moved into the North Canadian River area, and the Cherokees established themselves northward on the Ozark Plateau and Arkansas River. By 1839 the mixed Indian-white elite of the Cherokee, Choctaw, and Chickasaw Nations owned the majority of the estimated 5,000 slaves in Indian Territory. These people put their slaves to work breaking land for agriculture and constructing homes and improvements on their new lands. By 1840 the southern Indian Territory cotton-growing regions contained ten cotton gins and exported 1,000 bales of cotton. In the northeast, slaves worked smaller corn-, vegetable-, and cattle-raising operations, contributing to their masters' profit from sales to the military posts and to westward-moving emigrants. In addition, salt springs on the Grand River encouraged some Cherokee and Creek slaveholders to purchase more slaves to employ in the salt works for Foreign Missions was held on Tuesday, the 16th, in Brooklyn, N. Y. The Hon. Theodore Frelinghuysen presided. From the several reports made to the meeting it appears that the receipts of the Board for the year ending July 31, were $254,112-97, and the expenditures, including the debt of last year, were $237,817, 07, leaving a balance in the Treasury of $18,298 89. The Board has care of twenty six missions, embracing ninety-two stations, at which 488 persons are laboring as physicians, schoolmasters, printers, bookbinders, and assistant missionaries. These missionaries have under their pastoral care sixty-five churches, embracing 24,566 members. Connected with the missions are thirteen printing establishments, having fine type and stereotipe founderies, twenty presses, thirty fonts of type, and preparations to print in more than thirty different languages, while 475,795,294 pages have been executed during the year under review. At mission seminaries, boarding and free schools, including those at the Sandwich Islands, now mainly supported by the Hawain government, though commenced and carried forward by the mission, and still receiving much care from it, there are 30,197 pupils.

— *Republican.*

*Gold mines of Guadaloupe; in the town of Cosalo, in Mexico.* — This is supposed to be the richest gold mine in the world. It belongs to Signor Yriarte, who refuses to work it to any degree of productiveness, because he could not dispose of the immense revenue it would yield, amounting to several millions of dollars. He has now far more than he wants, and says that his money is safest *under ground.*

*Ib.*

RESTRAINTS—EXERCISE.
We take the following from a Southern paper. Let a word to the wise prove sufficient.—Ea

it, does not feel at liberty to regard this as any other than a well established fact.

## Cherokee Temperance Societies.

☞ The Secretaries of the several Temperance Societies in the Nation, are respectfully requested, to forward, immediately, to the undersigned, a list of the names of all persons who have united with their respective Societies during the past year; and also any other information that may be valuable, or interesting, connected with the progress of Temperance among the Cherokees, within the same time.
WILL. P. ROSS,
Sec. Cher. Tem. Society.
Sept. 25, 1845.

## WANTED,
BY THE UNDERSIGNED.

BEEF-HIDES, Tallow, Bees-wax,

"Runaway Slave," *Cherokee Advocate* advertisement, 1845. Reprinted by permission of the Research Division of the Oklahoma Historical Society.

in order to export this valuable commodity to neighboring states. The growing disparity in wealth, lifestyle, and culture between the elite and the less adaptive tribal elements became obvious in both the size and the style of slaveholding.[11]

The development of Creek and Seminole slavery differed from that of the other three tribes. Both of these tribal groups were earlier more militant in their resistance toward the encroachment of white settlement into their lands. In addition, although matrilineal in clan organization, a far greater degree of separation and tension existed in the male and female roles among the Creeks. Adult male and female Creeks spoke different dialects of the Muscogee language, lived separately for long periods of time, and carried out distinct work roles. Within the Creek and Seminole tribes, groups of powerful full-bloods incorporated material goods but rejected much of white culture and its practices. Initial relationships between African Americans and the Creeks and Seminoles, as in the other southeastern tribes, were both contradictory and transformative. As the historian William McLoughlin observes, "Indians who were friendly to blacks at one period in their history, often later became hostile to them."[12]

Alliances with runaway slaves offered Creeks and Seminoles an avenue of cultural communication and exchange. The African Americans possessed valuable skills: they were frequently multilingual, speaking Spanish and English, making them expert negotiators and interpreters with whites; they were familiar with guns and traps and other construction and home production technology; and they were able military allies in intra-Indian and colonial North American wars. Runaway slaves represented a loss of income in times of decline in the fur trade and increasing debt to the white traders. The reward for a returned runaway slave or his scalp in Georgia in 1763 was one musket and three blankets, a sizable bounty. After 1800 the Creek agent Benjamin Hawkins paid $12.50 for each returned runaway slave. The Creeks at this time often engaged in stealing and catching escaped slaves. White colonials increased hostility and fear between Indians and blacks by using enslaved men to attack Indian communities.[13]

Over time both full-blood and mixed-blood Creeks began to acquire slaves as a means to increase their economic and political status. The value of African slaves to the Creeks can be seen during the Creek Civil War in 1813. During the attack on Fort Mims in Alabama, for example, a party of traditionalist Red Stick warriors killed approximately 500 American settlers and mixed-blood Creeks taking refuge at the fort. However, most of the enslaved African Americans there were not killed but were taken captive. Unfortunately for the Creeks, the whole tribe was held accountable for the attack. This led to severe retaliation by the combined forces of Andrew Jackson and his Five Tribes allies at Horseshoe Bend in 1814 and the cession of two million acres of Creek land. The Red Sticks and their supporters retreated into Spanish-held Florida and joined the Seminoles.[14]

At first, Creek slavery in Indian Territory continued in most circumstances to bear less resemblance to the southern white pattern. Creeks intermarried more frequently with African Americans than did the Cherokees, Choctaws, and Chickasaws. Creek Elsie Edwards remembered that her father, Tustenuggee Jimboy, had four wives: two Indian and two African American. "The Jim Crow law had not yet been made so that the whites, Indians, Negroes and half-breeds just mixed with one another," she stated, "and there was no law against the number of wives that [a] man wished to have." Creeks also granted slaves greater autonomy and freedom of movement. Slavery varied greatly among the slave owners, the size of their landholdings, and their political status. A Creek freedwoman, Nellie Johnson, recalled that she first met her master, Roley McIntosh, when he brought a minister to "the slave settlement where [they] live[d]." She remembered, "Old Chief just treat all the Negroes like they was just hired hands, and I was a big girl before I knowed very much about belonging to him."[15]

Historians have recognized the history of the Florida Seminole Indians as exceptional in almost every categorization. Similar in culture to the Creeks, they had out-migrated and intermarried with other Florida tribes and the Spanish to such an extent that by the late eighteenth century they had become a separate tribal group. The U.S. government, however, continued until well into the nineteenth century to link the Creeks and Seminoles together in spite of their frequent disputes over slaves. The Seminoles did not become a separate nation until 1856. For decades, runaway slaves had created African-led communities in Florida known as "maroons." These existed in tributary alliance with a Seminole leader but separate from the Seminoles. The two coexisted in mutually beneficial relationships. At the same time that the Seminoles became recognized as separate from the Creeks, they also began to appropriate people of African descent as slaves. In relation to the Seminoles, African Americans might exist in a complex mixture as slaves, as free persons, or as tributary allies. Seminole intermarriage with the *estelusti*, as they were called, reflected the inclusive nature of their formation as a people. Slaves lived separately but dressed and followed the culture of their Seminole masters. They cultivated land, owned herds of livestock, and possessed firearms. The increasing white settlement of Florida and pressure from southern white slaveholders and government officials further united the estelusti and the Seminoles. They aided the Seminoles in their wars against the Americans in 1813 and 1835 and in their struggle against removal to Indian Territory. The historian Daniel Littlefield estimates that between 1838 and 1843 nearly five hundred blacks were removed with the Seminoles to Indian Territory.[16]

Slavery assumed a different dynamic in Indian Territory because of increased interaction with white culture and the growing power of the U.S. government over Indian lives. Removal to Indian Territory occurred at the same time that abolition and sectionalism in the United States became problematic. Slaveholding as a whole grew to dominate all other national issues of discontent. The Five Tribes in the East in the 1830s owned collectively approximately 4,162 slaves. This figure is without doubt lower than actual numbers given that the Seminoles refused to cooperate with enumerators. By 1850, however, slavery in Indian Territory also had become the issue of greatest concern. The 1860 population statistics revealed that the collective Indian population of Indian Territory was 47,550 and that slaves numbered 8,376, or 14 percent of the total population. The largest number of slaves lived in the Cherokee Nation (2,511), and the fewest (975) in the Chickasaw Nation. Female slaves in all of the tribes represented at least 51 percent of the slave population, a sex ratio conducive to reproductive growth. Slave children belonged to the mother's owner. One freedwoman had been told by her parents, "The slave owners was always wanting more young slaves and if there was a woman on the place that didn't have no man the old masters would send to another plantation and borrow a big husky slave for the woman and when the woman was done with child they would send the man back to his own place." Statistics indicated that a small fraction of each tribe owned the majority of the slave population. Michael Doran reports that only 2.3 percent of tribal citizens owned slaves in 1860, and most of these owned fewer than five slaves. Approximately thirty of the wealthiest Indian families, however, owned significant numbers of slaves. By the Civil War, the Joseph Vann plantation included 300 slaves.[17]

Increasing numbers of slaves and the deepening racial categorization in Indian Territory, as well as the adoption of constitutional forms of Indian government, led to a more strict codification of the position of slaves in the Five Nations' legal systems than had existed in the East. The historian Peggy Pascoe has described the centrality of laws that forbade interracial marriage in the formulation of the concept of American miscegenation and the justification of white supremacy and discrimination. "By using marriage to delineate race," she writes, "lawmakers wrapped race in and around the gender differences that stood at the heart of nineteenth-century marriage, which, in turn, stood at the heart of the American state." By the mid-nineteenth century these ideas had gained a foothold in Indian Territory. Cherokee leaders in the 1840s defined and circumscribed the position of the slaves and free blacks within their nation. Earlier laws prohibiting intermarriage were reaffirmed, and a law made hanging the punishment for a black man who raped any woman other than a black woman. These laws drew sharp distinctions based on race, with the most punitive measures aimed at black men. They also had a profound impact on the safety of black women. Rape of a white or Indian woman meant death, but by excepting black women the law diminished the value of their personal security. The council passed legislation making it illegal for slaves and free blacks who were "not of Cherokee blood" or who were not entitled to Cherokee privileges to own property, trade without their master's consent, sell liquor, or own firearms. In addition, a fine of up to $500 could be imposed on anyone teaching slaves or free blacks to read or write. The new slave laws provided for the creation of armed patrols to monitor the movement of blacks around the countryside.[18]

The Choctaws and Chickasaws, always more rigid in differentiating between themselves and African Americans, also passed new legislation in Indian Territory. Intermarriage had occurred in the East; an 1834 census lists families of five men of mixed Indian and African parentage married to both Choctaw women and mixed Choctaw and African American women. The new Choctaw National Council laws included provisions that prohibited cohabitation between any member of the nation and a slave as well as intermarriage with slaves. Slaves were forbidden to own property or firearms without the consent of their masters. Slaves brought into the Choctaw lands would remain slaves, and the Council could not emancipate any slaves unless they had "rendered to the Nation some distinguished service." The owner would then be reimbursed the value of the slave, and the freed slave would be forced to leave the nation within thirty days. Hoping to deflect the missionary influence in Indian Territory, slaves could not be taught to read, write, sing, or gather without the consent of their owners. Any person with "Negro blood" was prohibited from holding office in the Choctaw government.[19]

At the more fluid end of the spectrum of Indian slaveholding, even the Creeks tightened controls over the institution of slavery. In 1840 they passed legislation denying the right of slaves to own property and carry weapons. This increased the fear among the Seminoles, who had no slave codes, of Creek control of their people, both slave and free black. Their slaves exercised extensive freedom. Many Seminoles had settled on Cherokee lands because of the tension with the sizable Creek Nation. Now large numbers of free black Seminoles and slaves clustered around Fort Gibson in fear that their status with the Seminoles would be abrogated, or worse, that they would be stolen and sold.[20]

The 1842 slave revolt in the Cherokee Nation exacerbated the situation. Approximately twenty enslaved people from the Cherokee plantation of Joseph Vann stole horses, guns, and supplies and made an attempt to reach freedom in Mexico. When they entered the Creek Nation, some of the enslaved Creeks joined them. As the group of now approximately thirty-five made their escape, they encountered two slave catchers, James Edwards and Billy Wilson, who held a group of Choctaw runaways, including two women and five children. The Cherokees and Creeks freed the Choctaw slaves, killing their captors in the process. A Cherokee and Creek posse, led by the prominent Cherokee businessman, attorney, and militia captain John Drew, caught up with the runaways near the Red River. The Cherokee National Council ordered all escapees returned to their owners, except for six men held accountable for the murders of Edwards and Wilson and two men who eluded Drew's capture. Vann did not sell the Cherokee runaways but placed them on his steamboat, the *Lucy Walker,* where they worked under supervision and were separated from their families and other home slaves.[21]

The historians Daniel Littlefield and Lonnie Underhill maintain that the presence among the Cherokees of Seminole free blacks and slaves, who were accustomed to a more lenient form of slavery, may have influenced slaves from the other nations to try to escape. Another historian, Celia Naylor, adds another dimension to the understanding of this episode. Although it was much more difficult for women, and especially women with children, to attempt an escape from slavery, the presence of the two enslaved Choctaw women and their children illustrated an orchestrated, courageous effort to free themselves from involuntary servitude. In addition, Naylor asserts that the 1842 "slave revolt" signified the ability of enslaved members of the Five Tribes to mobilize "a strategic, intertribal operation" that included a sense of mutual circumstances and interests.[22]

After 1850 Indian Territory experienced the same divisions among slaveholders and non-slaveholders, slave and free, that plagued the United States as a whole. For the most part, the Five Tribes leadership had welcomed the presence of missionaries in the East. They also appreciated their loyalty and assistance in the removal process. Now many Indian slaveholders viewed the missionaries with suspicion as agents of abolition. Cherokee Ella Coody Robinson remembered, "White men came down from the North ostensibly to preach to the Negroes, but instead of preaching they were inciting them to all kinds of meanness and deviltry." Both the American Board of Commissioners for Foreign Missions (ABCFM) and the Presbyterian Board of Foreign Missions (PBFM) had missionaries in the Indian Territory by the 1840s, but they too split over the issue of slavery. By 1859 the Boston-based ABCFM, refusing to tolerate slavery among its converts, withdrew its authority from Indian Territory, leaving its missionaries under the purview of the PBFM.[23]

Neutrality on the issue of slavery became impossible. Presbyterian workers in the Indian Territory mission field adopted a policy of compliance with slavery. In spite of this position, for five years, 1837–42, the

Creeks expelled all missionaries from their lands in response to their fear of abolitionist teachings. Robert Loughbridge convinced the Creeks to allow him to open a mission school on the promise that he would not preach in the nation or teach slaves to read. Loughbridge faced another dilemma when Celia, the hired cook at his school and a church member, was about to be sold by her master. Loughbridge purchased her for $400 with the intention that she would work out her price to freedom. Similarly the Presbyterian schools, Wapanucka Female Seminary in the Chickasaw Nation and Spencer Academy in the Choctaw Nation, employed slave labor in their initial construction, farm labor, and menial school chores. Some ABCFM Baptist missionaries also considered cultivating church membership among the Indians more important that opposing slaveholding, and they chose to refrain from addressing this issue. The American Baptist Missionary Union remained adamantly opposed to slavery, however. Evan Jones and his son, John B. Jones, missionaries to the Cherokees, honored their organization's 1852 ruling against the administration of communion to slaveholders. They also expelled from membership some Christian Indians who refused to emancipate their slaves. Branded as a dangerous abolitionist, Evan Jones was forced to flee Indian Territory in 1861. As the Civil War drew nearer, even Presbyterian ministers came under intense scrutiny. John Edwards, the northern-born and -educated superintendent of Wheelock Seminary for Choctaw girls, was interrogated a number of times about his position with regard to slavery. He was ordered out of the Choctaw Nation even after he vowed that he would do nothing to harm the Choctaw people. Warned about a plan to hang him, Edwards left his ailing wife and children behind to make his way to safety.[24]

Given the growing severity of disunion over slavery, it would seem ironic that the Baptist churches had five times more congregants in 1860 than the Presbyterians. The large number of non-slaveholding Indians and the attractiveness to African American converts of Baptist missionary teaching on this issue likely contributed to these numbers. The organizing work of Evan and John Jones among Cherokees in the creation of the Keetoowah Society, composed of the more traditional and mostly non-slaveholding members, also had an impact. Prior to the Civil War, however, schooling and church attendance for enslaved women as well as men depended on the level of the slaveholder's commitment to the Christian religion, his observance of the Indian Nations' laws, and the diversity of his economic operations. In the midst of removal, Reverend David B. Rollin wrote to the *Baptist Missionary Magazine* from Ebenezer, a missionary station between the Arkansas and Verdigris rivers in Indian Territory. He reported a church membership in 1836 of eighty-two: six whites, twenty-two Indians, and fifty-four blacks. He also mentioned that the church school had remained open for six months but attendance had been poor due to illness. The freedwoman Polly Colbert said she never went to school, but she accompanied her masters to church under the brush arbors. "We set off to ourselves but we could take part in singing," she recalled. Chaney Richardson also reported that the "Negroes" did not have schools and she could not read or write, but she attended brush arbor church meetings, where they "would sing good songs in Cherokee sometimes." Betty Robertson believed that it was the fear of jail time and fines that kept many Cherokee masters from allowing their slaves access to church services or education.[25]

For some Indian slaveholders, educating their slaves had advantages. In these cases they disregarded the laws entirely. Many of the slaves entrusted with positions of authority on the larger plantations, such as those of the wealthy Vann family, were taught reading, writing, and arithmetic in order to carry on business in their owner's absence and as a sign of the family's exceptional status. Lucinda Vann's uncle preached in the same Baptist church their master attended, but in a segregated service following the white and Indian service. He performed baptisms for the converts at the river. Phoebe Banks remembered that most slaveholders did not want their slaves to be educated but that the Perrymans did not feel this way. "They even helped the younger slaves with that stuff," she said. On rare occasions a mistress defied the law and, after the day's work was done, taught her house servants to read from the Bible and to write. Sweetie Ivery Wagoner's mother learned to read and write "long after dark" from her mistress, and every Sunday they attended a small church. Enslaved people whose owners were not inclined to the Christian religion lost this opportunity for instruction. On the Rogers plantation Nancy Rogers Bean recalled, "Us slaves didn't know much about Sunday in a religious way." Her master deliberately kept them away from such teachings. When he discovered that his own brother was surreptitiously preaching to his slaves, he beat him badly.[26]

Law codes and institutional records do not necessarily reflect the nuances and interactions of daily life. The lives of female slaves among the tribes depended on a complex matrix of variables: tribal culture, number of slaves, time, relation to owner, skill level, and age. As Indian freedwomen looked back from the vantage point of the 1930s, many of them reported to white WPA interviewers close reciprocal ties with their masters and mistresses. Careful reading of the Indian and pioneer history papers and the Oklahoma slave narratives, however, reveals sometimes contradictory testimony within the same interview as well as enormous diversity of experience. The Cherokee freedwoman Patsy Perryman reported, "The mistress and master always treated us mighty good." She heard about beatings, however, of those slaves who she was told were lazy or tried to run away. The Choctaw freedwoman Polly Colbert remarked that "Indian masters was just naturally kinder." Orphaned at a very young age, Colbert and her brother and sister were taken into their master's childless home and raised there. Still, they were Colbert slaves and not Colbert children. Polly remembered, "[Holmes and Betsy Colbert] look after us as good as dey could colored children." The Colberts later had a daughter who lived to adulthood. In her statement, Polly was most likely referencing what she recognized as the difference in her upbringing from that of the Colbert's daughter. The passage of time and economic hardship sometimes blunted the reality of previous younger lives. Chaney Richardson stated that she didn't want slavery to be over. Remembering the tragedies of the Civil War years and the hard times that followed, she compared them to the distant memory of her life as a slave on the Cherokee Rogers plantation: "I was always treated good when I was a slave . . . and my mistress give me some mighty fine rules to live by." The Chickasaw freedwoman Matilda Poe made a similar statement. "I never did know I was a slave, 'cause I couldn't tell I wasn't free," she said. "I always had a good time, didn't have to work much, and allus had something to eat and wear and that was better than it is with me now."[27]

For most enslaved women in Indian Territory, life revolved around tasks related to the workings of the farm home. Some slave women worked in the fields, but most were employed in traditionally female tasks such as cooking, cleaning, sewing, laundry, gardening, and child care. As such, the mistress usually directed the work, but slaves were always under the watchful eye of the master. The amount of time it took to complete the necessary tasks was lengthy, in that except for the very wealthy, almost everything was home-manufactured. Slave women made cloth woven from thread and spun from wool or fiber that was hand-collected and dyed with natural plant ingredients. Clothes were cut from patterns and then stitched to fit. They washed these clothes in the open in hot tubs of water and scrubbed with homemade lye soap. They made shoes, generally worn by slaves only in the winter months, from hides. They cultivated fruits and vegetables, picked them, and preserved them. They gathered eggs, milked the cows, slaughtered animals, butchered the meat, and smoked it for preservation. Daily life for slave women was determined by the work necessary for the survival and well-being of the master and mistress's home. The level of comfort for themselves and their families and the time they had to devote to their own family life depended on the size of their master's holdings, his economic stability, and the nature of their relationship with the slaveholding family.

Frequently slave women integrated Indian folk remedies with information they learned from the growing number of eastern-educated elite Indians and missionaries in order to practice medicine on the plantations and farms. Treating the sick was not a gender-specific role: both men and women with the desire and the skill used both herbal medicines and charms passed down from one generation to the next. The elderly Jane Davis Ward, identifying herself as half-Choctaw, told a WPA interviewer that she "doctored" the Indians and slaves with herbs she collected in the woods. She remembered using Cherokee cough weed, numba weed, corn root, and butterfly root. The Choctaw freedwoman Frances Banks also nursed the sick. She lived near the prominent Choctaw family of Dr. W. N. Wright in Boggy Depot, where she learned nursing skills from him and developed her own medicinal formulas. She proudly spoke of a liniment that she believed could cure just about anything. Polly Colbert also made her own medicines as late as the 1930s from long-remembered remedies. "In de old days we made lots of our own medicine," she recalled. Among these were "polecat grease for croup and rheumatism," "dog-fennel, butterfly root, and life-everlasting . . . to cure pneumonia and pleurisy," and "pursley-weed" and snake root for chills and fever. In an environment with few roads and fewer professionally trained doctors, slave women served as midwives at Indian and black births and assumed the care of the sick and the elderly in Indian Territory.[28]

Freedwomen and their children remembered these tasks in a variety of ways: some recalled them as harsh and demanding, and others found their duties relatively light. Polly Colbert said, "I never had much work to do. I helped 'round de house when I wanted to and I run errands for Miss Betsy." The Creek freedwoman Phoebe Banks described the slave quarters on the Mose Perryman plantation as two-room log cabins with a fireplace at one end. Her mother was a "house girl" who spent her days on the mistress's household tasks, and late at night she cooked and cared for her husband and twelve children. "She was always busy and worked mighty hard all the time," Banks remembered, "while them Indians wouldn't hardly do nothing for themselves." Charlotte Johnson White's mother worked in the fields. She remembered that before she was old enough to work in the master's house (usually about six years old), her mother left her a baked sweet potato to eat at lunch while she waited all alone in the slave cabin until evening. "She was sick all de time," White stated, "but dat didn't keep her out of de fields or the garden work." When R. C. Smith related his experiences growing up on the Presley Smith plantation, he recognized his mother as the only person in the family who was constantly working. He didn't remember her ever sitting down except to sew or weave. "Poor thing," he said, "hard work was all she ever knowed." Smith's aunt took care of all the babies on the farm while their mothers worked in the field. He recalled that his aunt was so miserable doing this work that she was hostile and refused to talk for long periods of time.[29]

Nearly every slave woman in Indian Territory cared for children, either their master's or their own, at one time or another. Sometimes this was their sole occupation, but more often it was integrated into other household tasks. Usually this job fell to the elderly women or to the young, unskilled girls barely older than the children they watched. Caring for the master's children carried with it both benefits and dangers. Happy households held the possibility of special freedoms, such as passes to visit relatives or special food treats, but unhappy ones often became locations of cruelty. The Taylors sometimes paid Patsy Perryman money for taking care of their children. On one occasion she had enough money to buy a doll, but she usually just bought candy with it. At six years old, Phyllis Petite joined her mother in the house to do sweeping and to look after the baby. "I used to stand by the cradle and rock it all day," she said. When she got tired she curled up and slept beside the cradle until her mother came to get her. The Chickasaw freedwoman Kiziah Love reported that she pleaded with her owners not to send her to take care of the children of one of their relatives, the Buck Colbert family. She knew that master's reputation for viciousness. When Colbert's previous nurse could not keep the baby from crying, he beat her with fire tongs until he killed her. He beat another of his baby's caretakers for the same reason, injuring her so severely that she could no longer nurse her own child.[30]

Inattention to the master's children, whether accidental or intended, carried grave consequences. Even Kiziah Love experienced a scare. On a trip with her master and mistress, Love carried a sack of clothes and their baby on a mule. She became so tired that she fell asleep and dropped first the bag of clothes and later the baby. A little farther on, she nearly slipped out of the saddle herself. "Just think how I felt when I missed the baby," she said. She raced back and found the child unhurt by the side of the road. About the time she turned around, her master appeared. Love lied to him and just mentioned the loss of the clothes, but she remained steadfastly alert for the rest of the trip. Charlotte Johnson White "somehow" dropped one of the children near some burning brush tended by her owner. As she stooped to pick up the baby, Ben Johnson grabbed her and threw her into the fire headfirst. She carried the scars from the burns on her face for the rest of her life as well as the marks of his lashings on her back.[31]

Still, many of the freedwomen associated an exalted status with their ties to the master's home. Lucinda Vann bragged about the positions that her grandmother, mother, aunts, and cousins occupied on the Jim Vann plantation: "The slaves who worked in the big house was the first class." Her grandmother was in charge of the kitchen staff and the washing crew. Vann related that her grandmother also held an exceptional position of trust. She was the only person outside of the master and mistress trusted with the keys to the family vault and commissary. The vault held the family money and valuables. When an item was needed or had to be returned, it was her job to open and close the vault. The same was true for the commissary where food and other necessary supplies for the house were kept. Vann's mother was the head seamstress and directed all the work of the black female sewing staff.

Vann and her female relatives enjoyed special status both on the plantation and when they traveled. Unlike most slave women, who always wore rough, shapeless, cotton homespun dresses, the Vann house servants wore cotton only when they were working. When they traveled—on horseback, never on foot—they wore satin dresses, bonnets with silk tassels, and gold jewelry. Master Vann "wanted people to know he was able to dress his slaves in fine clothes," Lucinda bragged. Lucinda herself enjoyed the position of house favorite. When her mother's labor pains came on suddenly, Mrs. Vann placed her on her own bed and attended the birth. The mistress kept Lucinda in the house, where she slept on a special bed. She paid careful attention to Lucinda's upbringing and gave her the winnings of one of Master Jim's prize race horses. "Somehow or other, they all took a liking to me," Lucinda fondly remembered. Such favoritism may also have been due to the fact that Lucinda and her family were both Cherokee and black.[32]

Perhaps the most difficult of relationships to untangle are those that existed between slave women who were related by blood to their masters. While intermarriage with white Americans enjoyed acceptability in Indian Territory, unions between members of the Five Nations and their slaves were officially outlawed after the legislation of the 1840s. A sense of identity among the mixed Indian-black females in Indian Territory grew more complicated with the approaching Civil War. Since the Five Nations were matrilineal, these women were significant to clan organization yet not acceptable to the acculturated factions of the Nations. To which race did African Indian women belong? Were they Indian or black? Were they free or slave? Were they to be valued as women and leaders or valued strictly as a commodity?

The most prominent example of the complex nature of these relationships involves the children and grandchildren of a Cherokee leader, Shoe Boots, and his African slave wife, Doll (Congeeloh). In 1824 Shoe Boots petitioned the Cherokee governing body to grant free status to his wife and children. The Council decided to give citizenship to Shoe Boots's daughters, Elizabeth and Polly, but not to his wife or their son, William. In this decision, gender may have played a role. Did Elizabeth and Polly's family position as female children of Shoe Boots carry more weight than their mother's status as a slave and their brother's uncertain identity as a mixed Indian-African male? After Shoe Boots's death, Doll and William emigrated as servants with the John Ridge family to Indian Territory. Elizabeth and Polly married Cherokee men, bore children, and settled in the Delaware District of the Cherokee Nation. In 1847 members of the Matt Guerring gang kidnapped two of Shoe Boots's granddaughters and took them to Missouri to be sold. Articles in the *Cherokee Advocate* newspaper demanded the pursuit and return of the girls. Sheriff Charles Landrum, accompanied by Pigeon Halfbreed, tracked the kidnappers, located the girls, and returned them to their mother. In November 1847 the Cherokee National Council allocated a reward to Landrum and Pigeon Halfbreed for their efforts in the rescue. Despite their frightening ordeal, in this instance Shoe Boots's granddaughters had every reason to believe that they were valued Cherokee tribal members.[33]

Regardless of the relationship between the freedwoman Sarah Wilson and her Cherokee family, she did not experience such acceptance. The presence of female children born of illicit relationships between slaveholders and their slaves troubled the already complex matrilineal Indian Territory lineages. Wilson shared the story of her difficult childhood among her father's family with a WPA interviewer. Her grandfather, Ben Johnson, was a white man married to Annie, a Cherokee woman. Sarah was the child of Ned, the Johnsons' son, and Adeline, one of their slaves. Both Ben and Ned, like many slaveholders, fathered children with their slaves. Sarah stated that she was uncertain about who were her half-brothers and -sisters and who were her full-, but her mother told her "they all was kin to one another." Sarah and her sister, Lottie, were given their names by their mother, but those names were overridden by the demands of their mistress, Annie Johnson. She insisted that both of the girls answer to the name of "Annie," and she beat them and the other slave children regularly. Sarah and Lottie found themselves constantly in a battle for loyalty between their mother and their mistress. "If I went when she [Mistress] called 'Annie' my mammy would beat me for answering to that name, and if I didn't go old Mistress would beat me for that," she said. "That made me hate both of them." Sarah's father's presence sometimes tempered the beatings when he would tell his mother, "Let her along [alone], she got big blood in her." The Johnsons sold Lottie to a neighboring Cherokee family when she refused to bear children according to the master's wishes. She adopted her family's surname as soon as she left the Johnsons. Ambiguity and vulnerability marked these unequal relationships.[34]

Sarah possessed a skill that allowed her some escape and acquainted her with life outside her own family circle. She became an expert at sewing; she could sew well by the time she was eight years old, and by ten she was better than any of the others girls on the Johnson plantation, she recalled. Nearby neighbors, the large Cherokee Starr family, frequently requested her to sew for them. Her talent and mediating family circumstances were recognized in this situation. "I was the only Negro that would set there and sew in that bunch of women, and they always talked nice to me," she remembered. She was also allowed to eat at mealtime in the kitchen. On one occasion another slave girl was invited to work alongside Wilson. "She didn't like me," Wilson explained, "because she said I was too white." The Starrs abruptly sent that girl away. White became the seamstress for the Johnson extended family and their neighbors until freedom.[35]

The Creek Grayson family is another example of the complications of mixed Indian and African marriages and childbearing. The Grayson family of Indian Territory descended from Robert Grierson, a Scot trader, and Sinnugee, a Creek woman of mixed ancestry. Two of their children, Katy and William, chose mates and had children with African Americans. Initially the fluid Creek society accommodated this kind of diversity among their members, but as white southern plantation intrusion changed the nature of the Creek economic life, so too did it change racial acceptance. Racial hierarchies arose that associated the identity of blacks with slavery, and the Creek government institutionalized these into law. Katy eventually left her partner and married a substantial Creek named Tulwa Tustanagee. Together they enlarged their family and followed her father's pattern of slaveholding and participation in production for wealth. How Katy and her new husband integrated her previous children and her new ones is uncertain, but as a Creek woman, all of Katy's children were born free. William remained with his wife, Judah, one of the Grayson slaves, and the two raised seven children. When Robert Grierson died, he left substantial property and slaves to Katy and his other children, but none to William. William's wife and their children were bequeathed to William's sister Elizabeth. It took more than ten years for William to secure his family's freedom from his sister's ownership.

In 1834 William and his family removed to Indian Territory and faced desperate circumstances in rebuilding their lives. The family experienced discrimination among the other Creeks. They found it very difficult to build a prosperous life, and they feared the slave-stealing reality that pervaded Indian Territory. William, however, immediately registered his family as free people in their new home. At least they had improved their position in the Creek Nation in this regard. The remaining Grayson children, including Katy and her family and slaves, arrived in Indian Territory later. They reconstructed familiar lifestyles based on slave labor and thrived. The two sets of Grayson children neither lived close to each other nor continued to relate to each other. Over time Katy's family came to deny that there had ever been any African American kindred. Once a single family, marriage choices and the hardening of racial positions in Indian Territory now split the Grayson descendants asunder. When the Civil War came, George Washington Grayson, a rising leader in the Creek Nation and Katy's grandson, fought on the side of the Confederacy.[36]

At least some slave women found ways to resist the use of their bodies according to their owners' prerogatives. When Sarah Wilson's sister, Lottie, refused to bear the children her tyrannical master demanded, she was sold. Given the brutality of Ben Johnson, it is difficult to understand how Lottie could make her refusal stand. Might she have been his own daughter or granddaughter as well, and selling her had more advantage than forcing her to have children? Freedwoman Mary Grayson's account illustrates another, more complete example. Grayson's mother belonged to a white family in Alabama. When she heard that she was to be sold to a Creek master and taken to Indian Territory, she ran away and hid in a cave. Grayson placed her mother's age at that time as ten or twelve years old. The girl's new Creek owner found her, but he decided that she was "too young to breed," so he sold her to another Creek, who brought her out to Indian Territory. Jim Perryman bought her and married her, "the way the slaves was married in them days," to one of his slaves. After waiting a sufficient time, Jim Perryman decided "she was no good breeder" and sold her to Mose Perryman. Grayson said Mose was the target of his relatives' jokes for buying an infertile slave woman, but to everyone's surprise Mose's purchase became pregnant. Ten children resulted from the union of Grayson's mother and Jacob, one of Mose Perryman's slaves. Was Grayson's mother initially too young to conceive? Did she or her first mates singly or mutually decide not to consummate their master's demands? Did she use known herbal contraceptives or abortifacients, such as teas made from the roots or leaves of mistletoe, blue cohosh, partridgeberry, or dogbane? There is no way to determine her actions, but her long union with Jacob and their progeny speaks for itself about this woman's fertility and the choices she made.[37]

Many Indian Territory slaveholders did not brutalize their slaves. Among the Creek and Seminole especially, separate living spaces ameliorated some of the worst aspects of slavery. Nellie Johnson lived on one of Roley McIntosh's many small farms. McIntosh placed his slaves on these fields much like the southern tenant farm pattern, providing them with livestock and tools. Nellie's father and mother, Jackson and Hagar, selected a site for their house and built a spacious log cabin. They and their nine children worked the field for McIntosh independently, without an overseer. They also worked land for themselves, and the subsequent harvest belonged exclusively to them. "We could work a mighty big patch for our own selves when we was all at home together," Nellie remembered, "and put in all the work we had to for the old Master, too." She said that McIntosh rarely visited the farm except to collect the harvest and issue orders for the next crop. He "just trusted the Negroes to look after his farms and stuff." Family cohesion and a level of independence reinforced their sense of pride. Betty Robertson too remembered that the Cherokee "Young Master" Joe Vann never whipped his slaves, and she believed they had a "pretty easy time," but he did sell them if they did not behave as he wanted.[38]

Among the accounts left by Oklahoma freedwomen, the names of rough masters and known abusers such as Ben Johnson and Buck Colbert were well-known. Whether belonging to a gentle master or a strict one, the threat of violence to themselves or their loved ones permeated the lives of slave women. Matilda Poe recalled that Isaac Love "punished" his slaves if they were insolent or lazy, but he never sold them. Once while he was away, however, a white overseer took a whip to old "Granny Lucy" when she couldn't keep up with the field work. "He cut her back so bad she couldn't wear her dress," Poe said. Whippings could be ruthless. Slaveholders generally had a designated area called a "bull ring" where punishments took place. Adeline Collins's master made all of his slaves sit and watch when he ordered one of them beaten. One evening it was Collins's own father. Master Jackson Kemp had a post in front of the house where slaves were tied by the hand and foot. He ordered one of his slaves to do the beatings with a large whip. Each wrap of the lash around her father's body drew blood. Watching such episodes of violence engendered both fear for their own safety and hatred of the masters. Collins said that it was her mistress who protected the "girls." Mrs. Kemp would not allow them to be beaten because, she said, they belonged to her.[39]

Slave women who worked in the fields had less protection. Charlotte Johnson White's mother was a sickly woman. White said that on many days her mother could barely get up in the morning when the work call sounded. One morning she was desperately ill, and Master Ben Johnson came looking for her at the cabin. When she was too slow in struggling to the door Johnson became enraged and he threw her into a ditch near the cabin and beat her on the back with a whip. Then he rolled her over and struck her face and neck. She died shortly after the beating. White summed up her feelings of anguish: "She better off dead than jest livin' for the whip." White ran away from the Johnson farm not long after her mother's death, but her master tracked her down and whipped her. Sarah Wilson too received beatings from both her master and her mistress. "I carry scars on my legs to this day where Old Master whip me," she said. After watching her uncle being beaten unconscious, she didn't think she could hate her master any more than she did at that moment.[40]

Slaves who attempted to run away received the harshest punishments. This was the ultimate act of rebellion where the master was concerned. It affected his economic prospects as well as his reputation in the Territory. Indian Territory slaveholders, like their southern contemporaries, used bloodhounds to track down runaways. Phyllis Petite observed the damage the dogs could inflict when one runaway was returned home. "The hounds had nearly tore him up," she said, "and he was sick a long time." As an implied threat, masters sometimes combined beatings with trips to Fort Smith, Arkansas, for the slaves to observe the hangings taking place there. Some slaves became so unruly when they changed hands from lenient masters to harsh ones that they were placed in jail until they could be sold. Slaveholders employed these scare tactics to reinforce their authority and to frighten slave families into submission.[41]

Whether related by blood or by bondage to their owners, slave women endured the possibility of the sale of themselves or their husbands and offspring by their Indian masters. Some of the larger slaveholding families in Indian Territory, such as the Vanns, Colberts, Loves, Johnsons, and McIntoshes, practiced slave trading for profit with Arkansas whites and with John Harnage, a Texas slaveholder. Others sold their slaves as the Civil War grew imminent. Nearly all of the narratives by freedwomen mentioned slave sales, if not in their own families, then in others. Slave sales dismantled families in the cruelest way. The Chickasaw freedwoman Anna Colbert reported that she had seen husbands and wives sold to separate owners and then presented with a new spouse upon arrival at their new location. The Cherokee freedwoman Betty Robertson could barely remember her brothers and sisters living with her on the Vann plantation. "I had one brother and sister sold when I was little and I don't remember the names," she said. Master Vann sold them, he told Betty's mother, because she "couldn't make them mind him." The Chickasaw freedwoman Matilda Poe remembered how sad it was when a trader temporarily deposited several slave babies he had purchased at the Isaac Love plantation. "My mammy and de other women had to take care of dem babies . . . and teach dem to nuss [nurse] a bottle or drink from a glass," she said. All the while, the infants wailed for their mothers. Frequently slaves were sold when they disobeyed or were insolent to their owners. Nancy Rogers Bean's aunt, described by Bean as a "fighting woman," chopped off her own hand with a hatchet when she found out she was to be sold. This act of defiance diminished the value of her sale for the owner, but it may also have been a desperate attempt to keep from being sold away from her family. Sarah Wilson's aunt and cousin were sold when her aunt fought back against her owner's violence. As he cursed her and approached to strike her, she lurched toward him and poked him hard in the belly. "He seen she wasn't going to be afraid," Wilson said, "and he set out to sell her." The mother of the Creek freedwoman Mary Grayson was sold to four different masters because she was believed to be infertile. Slave women could not depend on continuity of family relations when control of their own person and those they loved resided in the hands of their masters.[42]

Other slaveholders, whether from a sense of virtue or out of economic interest, attempted to keep slave families together. The Cherokee freedwoman Patsy Perryman was one of five children born to a slave owned by Judy Taylor. Orphaned at birth, her mother had been raised exclusively by the Cherokees and spoke their language. Their father was owned by another Cherokee. Perryman recalled, "[My father] would get a pass to visit with mother and us children, then go back the next day." Perryman didn't know whether her mother urged her mistress to buy Perryman's father or Judy Taylor took the initiative, but the result was wonderful: "The Taylors bought him so that we could all be together." The Chickasaw freedwoman Mary Lindsay exposed the contradictions that slaves experienced in the decisions that their masters made. The Chickasaw Sobe Love owned Mary, Lindsay's mother, but he married her to a slave named William who belonged to a full-blood Chickasaw. After Mary bore children with William, Love bought William, and for some time the family was united. While their daughter, Mary Lindsay, was still just a child, however, Love's daughter ran away and married a poor white blacksmith from Texas. Although outraged by his daughter's choice, Love sent little Mary and another slave woman to live with his daughter. "Dat jest nearly broke my old mammy's and pappy's heart, to have me took away from them," Lindsay remembered, "but they couldn't say nothing and I had to go along with Miss Mary back to Texas." Lindsay reunited with her mother and siblings after the close of the Civil War.[43]

Enslaved women in Indian Territory experienced dramatically changed circumstances in the decade of the 1850s. Theirs had always been an existence that required nimble maneuvering to survive and to flourish under slavery. Subordination of life, liberty, and future to another human being carried a heavy physical and psychic toll. They wore many faces: commodity, sexual object, humble servant, field hand, valued craftswoman, nurse, wife, mother, daughter. Some had traveled the journey of the removal process with their Indian tribal groups and suffered with them through the pain of separation from familiar home and life circumstances. Many were born in Indian Territory and knew no other life than the heavy work of building a prosperous western homeland. Originally they had developed multiple forms of accommodation within their tribal cultures. In many cases the line between slave and free black, similar to the line between slave and family member, was blurred. This decade, however, brought changes that accelerated the erosion of unity between the Indian peoples and themselves and accentuated the separateness of each. As the Indian slaveholders of the Territory adopted stronger cultural and economic connections with the power elite of the United States, their relationships with the slaves and free blacks living among them deteriorated. New laws enacted by the tribal governments and increasing marginalization defined that divergence. The battlefield would determine the future of their lives. By 1860 enslaved women and men in Indian Territory, like their counterparts in the South, lived in uncertain space, as their masters stood poised on the precipice of a war over slavery.

## Chapter Two

# Surviving the War

"Dead all over the hills when we get away."

Phoebe Banks, in Baker and Baker,
*The WPA Oklahoma Slave Narratives*

In the closing days of the decade of the 1850s, all of Indian Territory became disquieted by the rumors of war. Old feuds and political competitions within the Indian nations that had not yet healed since the days of forced removal resurrected themselves. Indian peoples experienced divided loyalties between ties to the North and the South, but most hoped to avoid entanglement in what seemed an inevitable collision. Within their families enslaved women and men quietly discussed the growing danger and the alternatives that might be open to them. Members of the slave communities held secret meetings to organize and plan for a variety of responses to their increasingly changing circumstances.

The narrative of Morris Sheppard, a Cherokee freedman, recounts the mounting pressure among slaveholders to decide the fate of their property as the Civil War approached, as well as the impact these decisions had on slave families. "When de War come old Master seen he was going into trouble," Sheppard remembered, "and he sold off most of de slaves." The sale of Sheppard's mother had cruel consequences. At the time of the sale, she was separated from her sister, three sons, and a daughter, who went to different owners. His mother was sold to an abusive master and died shortly after she left the Sheppard plantation. Sheppard's mistress told him that she died from "rough treatment," but surely this was compounded by the separation from her kindred and familiar environment. Morris Sheppard was retained on the property, but other of the plantation slaves were sold and prepared for delivery. They were placed in a pen for the trader to examine. Sheppard never forgot the sight of his relatives and companions who had to "sleep in dat pen in a pile like hogs," until they were loaded onto a steamboat at Webbers Falls to be shipped to Fort Smith. Chaney Richardson's master, Charlie Rogers, also disposed of his slaves. "Old Master sell the children or give them out to somebody," Richardson said, and she did not see her relatives again until after the Civil War. She was sent to live with a new mistress.[1]

Slaveholding became central to any discussion about the future, and these open conversations influenced the minds of Territory slaves. Many enslaved men now saw an opportunity to strike out for freedom. While Arkansas and Texas were slave states, Kansas had been admitted as a free state in 1851. Freedom depended, however, on a swift and careful escape. This made departure for enslaved women and their children nearly impossible. As the days before the beginning of military operations slipped by, slave women experienced increased violence, sales of their family members, and abandonment.

"Patrollers" had been active in Indian Territory for more than a decade, and enslaved women expressed a variety of reactions to them. In some cases, these individuals traveled throughout the Indian Nations to protect the enslaved people from outside slave catchers. Kiziah Love recalled how frightened all of the women were of any unfamiliar horsemen or wagon travelers. Now there was such an increase in strange people coming into the Territory to steal slaves and sell them that the women stayed close to the house. Free blacks and Seminole slaves were particularly vulnerable because of their more independent affiliation with their owners and freedom of movement. Citizens in Van Buren, Arkansas, had formed a company specifically to purchase captured Seminole slaves. In most instances, however, the patrollers were not there to provide safety. Polly Colbert described them as the "law." These men checked the passes of all blacks who were on the roads and far from their home plantations or farms. If the documents were suspect, the patrollers beat the slaves and escorted them back home. According to Kiziah Love, Buck Colbert was one of the worst patrollers. Even if slaves had a pass, he would claim they had stayed away too long and beat them anyway. Matilda Poe told a WPA interviewer that slaves did not leave home often for fear of the patrollers. She described them as "low white trash" just looking for any excuse to shoot blacks.[2]

In these unstable times, more slave men took the chance to run to freedom, leaving their wives and children behind. Mary Grayson's account of her father's escape provides an understanding of what this meant to slave families. Covert lines of communication among slaves from different plantations were especially active at this time. Mary remembered that her Uncle William from the McIntosh plantation brought another man to their cabin to talk to her father, Jacob. They slipped off into the woods out of fear that they would be heard by the master Mose Perryman. After this discussion, Mary's mother and father argued until late into the night, and her mother cried. Jacob brought his brother, Hector, into the plan of escape. Mary's mother instructed her children not to play with the other children, and she began to hoard food for the departing men.

The morning that Mose Perryman discovered his slaves missing was filled with upheaval, and it terrified the women and children. Trying to get information from Mary's mother, Mose threatened to beat all of them "to death" and later to shoot them. She pleaded with him that she did not know anything, but Mose demanded all of his slaves to pack up and meet at his house. Mary cried for her father, but her mother told her that Jacob, Hector, William, and "a lot of other menfolks" had all gone away. Mary said her mother "was sure scared," and she told the children not to say anything about the earlier meetings, threatening them by saying, "I'll break your necks." Mose Perryman intended to move his slaves farther south, where they could not escape. As Mary continued to cry, her mother told her not to worry about her father: "He's free now. Better be worrying about us. No telling where we all will end up!" These events foreshadowed the separation of Indian and slave families alike that accompanied the Civil War years. The rupture of family ties that included love, protection, and support bore heavily on enslaved mothers.[3]

Intertribal factionalism increased the danger to enslaved women. The division of the Cherokee Nation especially illustrated this. Violence intensified between full-blood, mostly non-slaveholding Cherokees aligned under the Keetoowah Society, sometimes called Pin Indians, and mixed-blood, slaveholding Cherokees in the Knights of the Golden Circle and the Blue Lodge. Night riders associated with all of these groups attacked homesteads, stealing and killing horses and livestock, setting fires, and injuring slaves. Rumor and uncertainty elevated the suspicion and anxiety among Indians and blacks. A Cherokee minister, Stephen Foreman, wrote in his journal, "Women are afraid to venture out on account of the negroes, and men are afraid of each other, not knowing who [is] a friend or an enemy." Chaney Richardson remembered that her master and mistress spoke in whispers about the threat of violence and that the slave children were afraid to go anywhere unless accompanied by an adult. One day her mother went out to gather bark for fabric dye, and she disappeared. Her master's family and slaves searched for her, but they did not find her decomposing body for another week. She had been beaten and shot to death and thrown under some bushes. Morris Sheppard said the Pins struck at night and would hamstring horses, set fire to barns, and murder slaves in order to punish the slaveholders. The Pins killed Sheppard's father shortly before the war. Sheppard's uncle was the overseer of the slave workers, but he believed the Pins killed his father "only to be mean." In 1859 a Choctaw slave murdered his master. Trying to get away, he blamed the cause of the murder on an enslaved woman. A mob formed and tied the woman to a stake. The angry crowd gathered around her, and in spite of her protests of innocence, they burned her alive. Violence like this affected every level of Territory life.[4]

The bombardment on Fort Sumter, South Carolina, in April 1861 had just ended when the Civil War came to Indian Territory. Seven southern states had already seceded from the Union, and by the end of May four more states would join the Confederacy. In that same month, Second Lieutenant William W. Averall delivered dispatches to the U.S. military commanders in Indian Territory to evacuate their troops to Kansas, thus leaving the Indian tribal groups to their own defense. Nearly all of the Indian agents professed Southern sympathies and suggested affiliation with the Confederacy. Confederate President Jefferson Davis, seeing the value of the resources and geographic location of Indian Territory, immediately sent an Arkansas attorney, Albert Pike, to negotiate alliances with the Indian governments. For the most part, he found the Indian peoples seriously divided in their loyalties between the North and the South and in disarray among themselves in which of their leaders to follow. The enslaved people also struggled with their loyalties to Indian families, culture, and place and their chance for freedom among strangers. The diverse traditions of slaveholding, long-standing tensions among leading Indian families, and the divergent lifeways of full-bloods and mixed-bloods intensified the decision-making process. In general the Choctaws and Chickasaws, strongly connected to the South in the cotton trade, favored the Confederacy. Large numbers of Creeks took this side, but they faced opposition from respected segments of their own people represented by the elder Chief Opothleyoholo. The Seminoles and the Cherokees found themselves most seriously fractured. Cherokee Principal Chief John Ross received Pike coolly and attempted to maintain neutrality, but the prominent leader Stand Watie immediately began to organize military units. Only a handful of the Seminole leaders led by Heniha Mikko agreed to an alliance. By the summer, Pike had secured signed agreements of support from sections of all of the Five Nations and many other smaller Indian tribal groups living in Indian Territory. He chose Douglas H. Cooper, a former Choctaw and Chickasaw Indian agent, to command the Confederate Indian troops. The Civil War shattered the peace and prosperity of Indian Territory, creating Indians loyal to the Union and Confederate Indians and engulfing the lives of slaves and free blacks in persistent danger. The devastation in Indian Territory during the war years was unmatched in any state in the union. At the same time, the savage circumstances of war required enslaved women to act beyond their previous boundaries, realize their ability to survive on their own, and reach toward freedom.[5]

Among the Creeks a division between the Upper Creeks and the Lower Creeks had existed since the days before removal. The Lower Creeks adopted more of white culture and owned the most slaves. It is this group that dominated the Creek Council in 1861. The Council passed a series of laws tightening restrictions on the freedoms their slaves enjoyed and returning free blacks among them to slave status. The Council

Rose Cottage, Indian Territory home of Cherokee Principal Chief John Ross, burned during the Civil War by Confederate Cherokee Officer Stand Watie, 1860. Courtesy of the Western History Collections, University of Oklahoma Libraries, Morris Collection 36.

then signed an alliance with the Confederacy and organized two regiments for duty. The Upper Creek leader, Opothleyohola, himself the owner of twenty-five slaves and one of the wealthiest men in the Nation, objected to these actions and rallied his allies into an encampment on his plantation for safety. He wrote to President Abraham Lincoln proclaiming their loyalty and asking for assistance in this worsening situation. Defense of the nation's capital occupied Lincoln, and no answer was forthcoming. As fall approached, more than 7,000 Indian Territory residents gathered under Opothleyoholo's leadership on the Deep Fork of the Canadian River near present-day Eufaula.[6]

All manner of Indian Territory people sought security and, for many, freedom in Opothleyoholo's camp: runaway slaves, free blacks, loyalist Cherokees, Seminoles, and frightened family groups, including white men married to Indian women from other tribes. The historian Gary Zellar estimates that there were nearly 500 Creek and Seminole slaves and free blacks in the crowd. They came together in small and large family groups—elders, couples, small children—bringing livestock, wagons, food supplies, and family possessions. Phoebe Banks's father and uncle not only prepared their own families to join Opothleyoholo, but they also encouraged other Perryman and McIntosh slaves to seize this opportunity of escape to the North. Banks said they made their getaway on horses stolen from their masters. In spite of some hesitation on Albert Pike's part, Confederate Indian leaders urged the necessity of an immediate attack on their opposition. Realizing the rapid advance of Texas cavalry alongside the Indian troops, Opothleyoholo moved the refugees northward into the Cherokee Nation. For a while they were able to elude the pursuing forces. On November 19, 1861, they came under attack at a place subsequently known as Round Mountain. The first military action in Indian Territory began with an attack on these civilians. Opothleyoholo's men, Indian and black, defended their families heroically and drove the Confederates back at Round Mountain and in one more engagement. On December 26, 1861, the Indian Confederate troops again caught the fleeing body of loyalist residents. This time they won the field, forcing the retreating families to abandon all of their supplies. From this moment on the war in Indian Territory scattered families, destroyed property, and irreparably altered the autonomy of these Indian-held lands.[7]

Although Phoebe Banks was too young to remember all of the struggle, the vivid memories passed on by her family members provide the context of the flight from the slaves' perspective. As the refugees retreated across Cherokee country, the smallest children were tied onto the horses' backs. Moving that large a mass rapidly across the rough terrain with wagons and pack horses was slow and cumbersome. When the Confederate forces caught up with them, the Creeks and the slaves fought back, but they scattered and became separated. "Some of the Negroes [were] shot and wounded so bad the blood run down the saddle skirts," Banks reported. The battle lost, the soldiers killed both Creeks and blacks and captured some of the slaves, including women and children, to be sent back to their masters. Some estimates of casualties ranged as high as 250 combatants among the loyalist Indians and blacks, and 160 women and children and 20 blacks captured. Banks recalled that her father

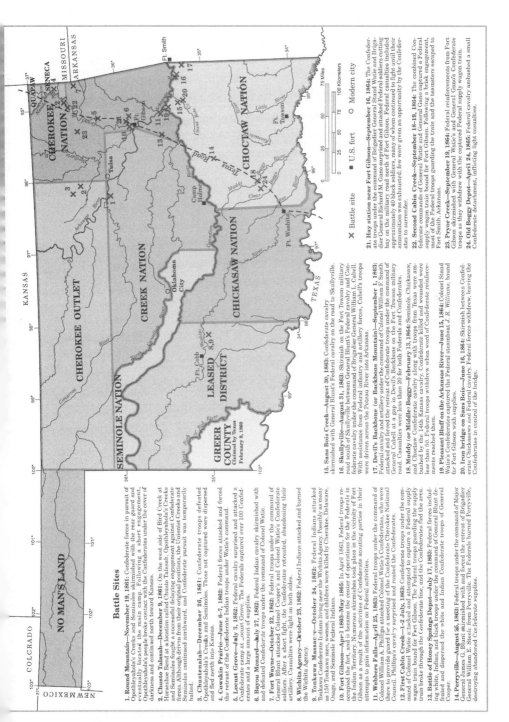

Civil War battle sites in Indian Territory. Courtesy of the University of Oklahoma Press © 2006.

and uncle kept the family together, but there were "dead all over the hills when [they] get away."[8]

Fierce snowstorms followed the refugees as they made their way into Kansas bereft of food, clothing, shelter, wagons, and supplies. They settled into a camp close to the Verdigris River. Cooper's forces harassed the stragglers, killing some and capturing women and children. The wounded and weak dropped along the route and many froze to death. Women bore children in the snow without shelter and only rags to cover their infants. One observer noted that the "women and children suffered severely from frozen limbs" and that those who survived the march arrived on the open plains with "broken constitutions" and "utterly dispirited." They straggled across Union lines to find very little comfort. The authorities had no food, shelter, or even fuel to keep them warm. Surgeons amputated frostbitten arms, legs, and toes. Many sickened and died from hunger, exposure, and pneumonia. Southern Superintendent of Indian Affairs William G. Coffin declared, "The destitution, misery, and suffering amongst them is beyond the power of any pen to portray; it must be seen to be realized." It would be another month and 240 more deaths before a meager supply of food and blankets arrived. This was only the beginning. Hundreds of other Indians and blacks migrated into the area as conditions worsened. Several hundred ponies died of starvation, and the refugees resorted to eating raw horsemeat and dogs. When warmer weather arrived the whole area was contaminated by the rotting animal decay. By spring the total number of exiles had reached approximately 7,500.[9]

The tattered, sick, and weary exiles moved north again to what was supposed to be a better location on the Neosho River, but white settlers complained about them and protested their use of firewood. Many of the young went naked; the others had scarcely any clothing. Hunger, disease, and death haunted the camps. In the summer of 1862, the Sac and Fox Tribe offered a part of their reservation for the suffering Indian Territory people. Many would remain there until the end of the war. The winter weather of 1862, 1863, and 1864 tortured the people with freezing cold. Corrupt suppliers cheated on deliveries of clothing and food. The government issued the camps condemned bacon unfit for consumption and cast-off army tents worthless for shelter. Intestinal problems joined the list of illnesses that plagued them along with the bitter cold, and a smallpox epidemic spread quickly after they received faulty inoculations. For every year in Kansas, more than 200 new graves marked the encampment. Most of these were for women and children.[10]

Many of the enslaved women endured the Kansas years alone, holding their families together as best they could. Sarah Wilson's uncle "went to the North and never come home." Most of the women's husbands joined with the Indians and Union forces in 1862 to launch an invasion into Indian Territory in order to speed their return home. Whenever possible, the soldiers sent their wages to their wives in Kansas to help sustain their families. Phoebe Banks's father stayed in Kansas with the family and worked as a blacksmith at Fort Scott, but her Uncle Jacob joined the Union forces. Her uncle's stories about the battle for Fort Gibson terrified her. "He killed many a man during the war," she said, "and showed me the musket and sword he used to fight with." Two regiments from the refugee camps plus two brigades of Wisconsin, Ohio, and Kansas troops composed the Indian Expedition commanded by Colonel William Weer. In June 1862 the black and Indian forces defeated the Confederate Indians at Locust Grove and marched deep into the Cherokee Nation to take Tahlequah and Fort Gibson. Confederate guerrilla attacks and a conflicted Union command made this victory only temporary, however. It would not be until 1863, when Colonel William A. Phillips took command, that the combined Union forces secured control of the Fort Gibson area. Emily Walker, an African American, served as Phillips's scout and interpreter. The Indian Expedition drew under its protection more runaway slave families and loyalist Indians escaping the lawless looting and pillaging across the Territory.[11]

Cherokee Chief John Ross disavowed support of the Confederacy and left Indian Territory with Union troops. Acting Cherokee Principal Chief Thomas Pegg led the council assembled at Cowskin Prairie in Indian Territory in abrogating the agreements with the Confederacy and, on February 21, in signing an act emancipating the slaves in the Cherokee Nation. The act declared all "Negro and other slaves within the limits of the Cherokee Nation" to be "forever free" effective June 25, 1863. A fine between $1,000 and $5,000 could be imposed on offending parties "holding any person in slavery" within the Cherokee Nation after that date. This document is extraordinary for many reasons, not the least of which is that the Cherokees were the largest slaveholding group among the Five Nations and their 4,000 slaves represented a complicated tradition of intermixed kinship and identity. Additionally the words *forever free* entitled the Cherokee freed people to the use of Cherokee common land, thus giving them a means of earning an independent livelihood. They became the only one of the Five Nations to do so until the end of the war.[12]

Indian Territory slaves sought out the protection of Union troops when they came into proximity to them. When the prominent Cherokee William Penn Adair was taken prisoner, Union officers ordered all of his slaves to pack up and follow the army to Fort Scott, Kansas. Some of his slaves remained on the farm, and others joined the procession northward. One of Adair's slaves, ten-year-old Chaney McNair, remembered the activity of the journey. "They take us in wagons and on horseback," she said. "They went to different plantations and take as many slaves as they could get. They did a lot of robbin' too; took an awful lot of stock." McNair did not remember being hungry on the trip, but she recalled sleeping under the wagons at night and how tired she became on the march. Federal soldiers also escorted a large group, with several hundred head of cattle and wagons of furniture and stolen goods. At the Kansas border the troops instructed them to go on alone. The freed slaves were so frightened of being caught that they turned the cattle loose and destroyed most of the furniture. Some black women sought the opportunity to flee with the army all on their own. The Cherokee Hannah Worcester Hicks wrote in her diary about two of her women servants who took off on horses and "left [her] without any help." Only one of the women managed to get away, however; the other had to return when she lost her horse.[13]

In the summer of 1863, General James G. Blunt assumed personal command of Union troops in Indian Territory, and the largest and most significant battle took place at Honey Springs. The outcome of the battle returned the northern half of Indian Territory to Union oversight, if not peace, and allowed many of the Kansas refugees to return home. Male Indian Territory runaways and refugees enlisted in the First Colored Volunteers Infantry Regiment immediately after the Emancipation Proclamation. They had proven their mettle on July 2, when they successfully defended a federal supply train and, along with the Indian Home Guards, defeated the Creek and Cherokee Confederates at Cabin Creek. Two weeks later the Colored Volunteers and Indian and Union troops overwhelmed the combined forces of Cherokee, Choctaw, Creek, and Chickasaw soldiers accompanied by three units of Texas cavalry. General Blunt praised his command and singled out the Colored Volunteers, stating, "Their coolness and bravery I have never seen surpassed; they were opposed to Texas troops twice their number whom they completely routed." In September the First Colored Volunteers Infantry Regiment was joined by the Kansas Second Colored Volunteers Infantry Regiment. These two regiments and the Indian Home Guard continued to patrol Indian Territory against Cherokee Stand Watie's guerrilla attacks until the conclusion of the war.[14]

For the freedwomen and their children still waiting in Kansas or surviving alone in Indian Territory, the circumstances of their lives were compounded by the loss of their husbands and sons. R. C. Smith's father served with the Kansas Regiment. "He and Mother never saw each other again after he enlisted," Smith reported. "He died with pneumonia. Never got to enjoy his freedom after he fought so hard for it." Finally, in May 1864, Congress appropriated the necessary funds to transport the African American and Indian exiles back to Indian Territory and to provide for their temporary subsistence. Once again the estimates of needed wagons and supplies proved inaccurate. Hundreds of the refugees walked beside the wagon train that spread out for six miles. Five thousand travelers arrived at Fort Gibson by June, leaving behind in Kansas 500 Seminoles quarantined with smallpox and a few hundred from other, smaller tribal groups. The number huddling under the protection of Colonel William Phillips and the soldiers at the fort reached approximately 16,000.[15]

The refugees celebrated their return to familiar territory. Remembering their suffering, they immediately set about to plant crops and establish shelter. Unfortunately Stand Watie's raiding in the Creek and Cherokee lands was ceaseless. He and his troops stripped the area of livestock and tools, burned the crops and houses, drove the people back into the fort, and disrupted the federal supply lines supporting this population. Whether in Kansas or in Indian Territory, adequately supplying the desperate Indian and black civilians became a constant source of conflict between the U.S. military, the suffering people, Southern Superintendent of Indian Affairs William G. Coffin, and unscrupulous contract suppliers. Coffin's secretary, Henry Smith, wrote that the women and children huddled outside the fort were "exposed to the hot sun, half starved and naked and a great many of them sick with dysentery and diarreah [sic]." A census of the loyalist Cherokees taken in 1863 revealed that one-third of the adult women had been made widows and one-fourth of the children were orphaned. Black women and their families, while undocumented, surely sustained similar if not greater losses. Agent Justin Harlin distributed garden seeds and potatoes, but he reported that since the able-bodied men were nearly all in the army, the planting and cultivating fell almost entirely to the women and children. This work was done with only the crudest of implements. Conditions became desperate when a cholera epidemic swept through Fort Gibson, killing hundreds of refugees and soldiers. By the final year of the war, more than 20,000 Indians and blacks who were camped around Fort Gibson were dependent on the federal government. Secretary of the Interior James Harlan reported, "Thousands of them must inevitably perish during the present winter, unless timely provision be made by the government for their relief." [16]

Although the relocation of Indian refugees with Confederate sympathies out of the war zone was somewhat easier, the same could not be said for their slaves. As enslaved men ran away to join the Union forces, they left their families in the crossfire. Mose Perryman, so enraged by the desertion of large numbers of his slaves, told the remaining women and children, "We're going to take all you black devils to a place where there won't no more of you run away!" Bereft of protection, black women had few alternatives. In the early years of the war, when the Confederates militarily controlled Indian Territory, many of the Indian slaveholders moved their slaves to the forts for protection. Rachel Aldrich Ward's master, Joe Beck, left his elderly wife on the farm but moved all of the slaves to Fort Gibson. Ward remembered that her mistress cried mournfully as her husband and slaves departed. Ward stated that there were hundreds of slaves at the fort from all over, "cooking in the open, sleeping most anywhere, . . . digging caves along the river bank to live in." For some, the only shelter came from worn-out blankets, scraps of cloth, and brush. Ward said there were so many people living together that "there was no way to keep the place clean." Other Confederate Indians left their wives in charge of their lands and slaves when they went away to fight. Many black women maintained their ties to the women and elderly Indians left behind. They clung to the only people they had ever known rather than risk the dangers of abandonment and exposure to violence from both sides. Much of the war was fought in Cherokee and Creek country, and the looting and destruction was devastating. Union commanders, desperate to provision their troops, confiscated livestock, burned houses, tore down fences, and stole anything of value. With thousands of stray cattle at large, enterprising rustlers drove them north to sell in Kansas. Agent James Harlan claimed that "white men, loyal or pretending to be so, have taken five times as much" livestock and crops as "rebels, bushwhackers, and guerillas." Kiziah Love hid the chickens under the floor of her cabin in the slave quarters, hoping to protect them, but the soldiers found them and took them anyway. Some of the freedwomen interviewed in the 1930s resented the actions of the Union soldiers and held President Lincoln personally accountable.[17]

The return of the Union, Indian, and black troops in 1863 to Indian Territory changed the whole dynamic of existence. A mass exodus of Confederate Indians and their slaves proceeded southward to the Red River on Choctaw and Chickasaw lands and on into Texas. Frequently slave families faced a brutal separation. Creek judge G. W. Stidham sent some of his slaves to Texas but retained others at home. Jim Tomm, an enslaved man, remembered that after his father had been taken south, his mother and the other children remained unprotected on Stidham's land. They and others hid in the cellar beneath the house, terrified of the cannons that roared at the Battle of Honey Springs. Fortunately the women and children were discovered as the Union soldiers were about to burn the house down. They sent them to join the other refugees at Fort Gibson. Some slaves ran away and hid during the confusion of the war; others were stolen or captured and sold in Arkansas and Texas. Women sometimes acted out of the urgency of the situation to find a way to escape. When the mother of the Cherokee Martha Phillips found out that Martha's half-brother and owner intended to sell her, she gathered Martha and her two brothers together and made a run for the Grand River. They were able to evade capture by their Cherokee relatives with the help of a

Freedmen and Indians picking cotton near Tulsa, ca. 1885. Reprinted by permission of the Research Division of the Oklahoma Historical Society.

local man, and they eventually made it to Fort Gibson and safety. The Cherokee Rogers family sold all of their slaves, including Chaney Richardson, who was taken by her new mistress, Hannah Ross, to Texas. "All the slaves was piled in together and some of the grown ones walking," she said."They took us way down across the big river and kept us in the bottoms a long time until the War was over. We lived in a kind of camp."[18]

Lucinda Davis remembered well the journey south with her elderly master's family after the Battle of Honey Springs. During the battle, only the enslaved women and children were left because the male slaves had all run away or joined the fight on the Union side. They hid in a cave near their home until the battle ended. Then they packed the wagons and moved carefully south, encountering both Union and Confederate soldiers. They stayed in deserted cabins until they reached a large body of refugees on the Texas road. Lucinda remembered how crowded and muddy the road was, "people all moving along in bunches," helping each other dig wagons out of the mud. At night the women and slaves made a communal supper in big pots, but there was not a lot to go around. Lucinda told a WPA interviewer, "De men so tired dey eat everything up from de women and de niggers, purty nigh." By the time Lucinda reached the Texas border, she was the only slave left in her master's family. One by one, all of the others had slipped away to freedom.[19]

Along the Red River border and in Texas, conditions were somewhat better than those surrounding Fort Gibson. Chaney Richardson remarked that she was too young to remember "where they got the grub to feed [everyone] with." Some aid came from Stand Watie's successful guerrilla raiding, some from the sale of the slaveholding family's personal possessions, but most came from slaveholders hiring out their slaves to work for others. At least some of the support came from the Confederate government. The office of the Confederate superintendent of Indian affairs was created to oversee the welfare of the civilians from the tribal groups who furnished military units. Assistant Superintendent Colonel R. W. Lee supervised most of the assistance to the Confederate refugees. Although he did not designate racial or gender composition, in 1864 he reported that 14,790 dependents from the Five Nations, Osage, and smaller tribal groups received subsistence from his office. Lee's records outlined the problems inherent in this situation. The people were scattered widely over the land, there was conflict between tribal groups, transportation was inadequate and irregular, supplies were insufficient, and dishonest contractors swindled the government.[20]

Lee believed the Choctaws and Chickasaws to be more fortunate than most in that they were still on their own lands. Some, however, had been driven from their homes, and the loss of the men to the battlefront created a "destitute condition." The Creeks had the largest numbers of dependents and had received only half of what they needed. Another group of Creeks and Seminoles received infrequent supplies near Fort Washita. The Cherokees appeared to be adapting well. Government-established workshops and blacksmiths manufactured spinning wheels, looms, and wagons. Lee stated that they lived in a "moderate degree of comfort" and were reasonably healthy "since the subsistence of the smallpox which prevailed amongst them." Still, Sarah Watie, wife of Confederate Colonel (later Brigadier General) Stand Watie, managed her large extended household with the help of some of her slaves. Ill and discouraged, she wrote to her husband in 1864 inquiring whether he could secure "a negro woman if she is a good one" and send her to help with the heavy work in caring for the family.[21]

In 2000 the historian David LaVere documented a little-understood aspect of the Civil War in Indian Territory that affected not only the people of the Five Nations but the freedmen as well. The Prairie and Plains Indians who had occupied areas of land contiguous with the Five Nations were drawn into the conflict between the Union and the Confederacy. Both sides, at one time or another during the war, solicited alliances with these tribal groups. One of the many consequences of the war was a disruption of the usual life patterns of these Indians. Trade networks and access to food supplies, manufactured goods, and guns and ammunition were undependable as the Union and Confederate Indians fought each other. Necessity, combined with opportunities for valor and distinction for young warriors, created the perfect environment for raiding against both sides. Comanche Chief Ohopeyane told the Creek Confederates that Union officials had instructed them to "kill all the men and boys and take the women and children prisoners and drive off all the cattle and horses." They had taken the advice of their close friend, the Cherokee Jesse Chisholm, and refused to follow this suggestion. In the latter years of the war, however, Kiowa and Comanche warrior bands would carry out frequent raids into the Chickasaw and Choctaw Nations.[22]

The warrior societies of Plains Indians terrorized the Chickasaws and Choctaws, stealing horses and cattle and taking captives, but they at least had the resources to fight back. The freedmen lacked horses and guns to defend themselves. The Comanches and Kiowas traded horses and furs with Kansas merchants for revolvers, breech-loading carbines, and ammunition. The U.S. government negotiated the Little Arkansas Treaty in the fall of 1865, establishing peaceful relations and granting the Kiowas and Comanches a sizable reservation west of the Chickasaws. The raids did not cease. In 1867 a black Seminole child was taken captive near Fort Arbuckle. Several blacks were killed and scalped in 1870. Immigrant wagon trains of freedmen and white families entering Indian Territory encountered the Kiowa, Comanche, and Apache warriors and lost their lives, their possessions, and their children to capture. In spite of numerous councils, negotiations, and treaties, the attacks by the Plains Indians on the Five Nations did not end until 1875, when they were defeated by the U.S. Army in what became known as the Red River War.[23]

The war divided the loyalties of black families as well as Indian. As many as 1,000 enslaved men in Indian Territory are estimated to have joined the Union or the Confederate forces. In many cases, the slave supported the side of his Indian master, following him to the battlefields, driving supply wagons, acting as a messenger, and performing personal services. Chaney Richardson's father fought beside the Confederate Cherokees and died in Arkansas, leaving her orphaned. After he had been sold, the Cherokee slave Wash Sheppard ran away and joined the Union Army in Kansas, but his nephew Morris remained by his master's side in exile on the border of Texas. Victoria Taylor Thompson's father went with his master to fight with the Confederate Cherokees and returned home with stories of how the soldiers had suffered from cold and starvation. Some slaves, like some Indians, began the war on the side of the Confederacy and changed sides after 1863. Henry Henderson, the enslaved son of Martin Vann, went to war and left his wife, Mollie, at home. He later described himself as a "strong Southern soldier," but after capture by the Federals he fought on the Union side. Henderson was captured, but many others, unwilling to fight against their own people, quietly deserted Confederate commands for the Union side.[24]

Runaway and abandoned slaves drifted across Indian Territory searching for safety. For the black enslaved women and now Cherokee freedwomen left behind, regardless of their location, the most immediate concerns centered on the essential needs of survival: food, shelter, and clothing for themselves and their children in the midst of war and destruction. Unlike Indian women, black women lacked the kinship networks, literacy, access to transportation, and freedom of movement available to others. Black family connections had been shattered by the slave sales, Indian flight, and male military enlistments. Wagons, oxen, and horses had all been requisitioned by their owners to transport their own families or were stolen by campaigning forces. Unable to read or write, the freedwomen were at the mercy of those left behind or those who assumed authority over them. In addition, their color alone left them open to violence and kidnapping by Indian and white alike. They bargained the skills they had acquired in slavery—weaving, cooking, cleaning, gardening, washing, sewing, and child care—in exchange for food and shelter. Chaney McNair and others worked as house servants for Kansas families. Many women and children went to work in the fields for whatever resources they could acquire to sustain themselves. J. W. Stinnett's mother told him that in Texas she plowed and planted the ground with a team of oxen and performed all the work in both the house and field after his father ran away.[25]

The Cherokee Nation document that abolished slavery followed by six weeks the date, January 1, 1863, that President Lincoln's Emancipation Proclamation was to become effective. From then until months after the war's end in 1865 both the Cherokee enslaved women, unaware of their government's position, and most of the other enslaved women of Indian Territory remained ignorant of the fact that they had been set free. Just as Stand Watie refused to surrender his Confederate command until June 1865, becoming the last Confederate general to lay down arms, so too did Indian slaveholders retain their slaves as long as there was any hope that they could negotiate some form of favorable settlement with both their loyalist kin and the federal government. For many enslaved women, freedom became a reality only when it was safe enough for their masters to return to Indian Territory or when their master's financial circumstances made it impossible to support them any longer.

Some enslaved women, such as Charlotte Johnson White, found out that they were free only when soldiers passed through their area. She remembered how she rejoiced when the men on horseback in blue uniforms told her the news, and she promptly declared for everyone to hear, "I is a free Negro now!" Sarah Wilson, taken by her master, Ben Johnson, to Texas early in the war, described how her owner announced her new status. They were still in Texas when Johnson received a letter informing him about the peace settlement. "He went wild," Wilson remembered. "It was a long time after he knew we was free before he told us. He tried to keep us I reckon, but had to let us go." Wilson told a WPA interviewer, "It near about killed him to let us loose, but he cooled down after a while and said he would help us all get back home if we wanted to come." Patsy Perryman's mistress also prepared to return to Indian Territory after the war, but she planned to leave her slaves behind in Texas. She relented when Perryman's mother cried and begged her to take them with her. They were shocked at what they saw when they arrived. Perryman remembered, "We found the old house burned to the ground when we got back and the whole place was a ruin. There was no stock and no way for any of us to live." At that point Perryman's mistress told the slaves "that [they] were free anyway and to go wherever [they] wanted to." Phyllis Petite's family was set free in Texas after the war, but they had to find their own transportation to leave. Her father bargained with a white man going to the Cherokee Nation. He would drive an ox-drawn wagon in exchange for a ride home for his family. Petite later told a WPA interviewer that, after they had settled on a piece of land, "[she] seen negro women chopping wood and asked them who they worked for and [she] found out they didn't know they was free yet."[26]

For young children, like Lucinda Davis, news of freedom brought many changes to their lives. Davis had been sold as a very young child by her mother's master to a Creek man named Tuskaya-hiniha to provide care for his grandson. She spoke only the Muscogee language growing up, and at that time she did not know when she was born or who her parents were. Tuskaya-hiniha and his family fled to the Choctaw bottom lands after the Battle of Honey Springs. Lucinda was the only slave that remained with the family, and she helped them put in a corn crop. "I don't know when de War quit off, and when I git free," she said, but she remained with the elderly and near-blind Tuskaya-hiniha for "a long time after [she] was free." Eventually three men came to the cabin and spoke English to Tuskaya-hiniha. He told her to go with the men, who would take her to her own family. At the Creek Agency, her parents reclaimed their daughter. Lucinda happily explained, "My mammy and pappy git me after the War and I know den whose child I is." Her very identity and family connection had been disguised by the dislocation of both slavery and freedom until that moment.[27]

Few of the freedwomen in Texas wanted to remain in the unfamiliar and dangerous territory. Most wanted to return to Indian Territory to

A Cherokee freedwoman, Charlotte Johnson, eighty-eight, at her home at Fort Gibson, Oklahoma, 1938. Reprinted by permission of the Research Division of the Oklahoma Historical Society.

rebuild their lives. Lifelong relationships, however unequal, were not easily severed. Women in other parts of Indian Territory also sought to return to the areas consistent with the Indian cultures they had grown up in. All struggled to make the return journey through their own resources and to reunite families separated by slave sales or the circumstances of the war. Sarah Wilson's mother refused Ben Johnson's offer of help and chose to devise her own way home for herself and her daughter. The difficulties of the trip remained vivid in Wilson's mind years later. She described the journey as "hell on earth." "We had to straggle back the best way we could," she told an interviewer. They were desperately hungry, and no one would give them a ride. Wilson stated that it took them two weeks to walk the distance, but she must have been referring only to the last, approximately sixty-mile part of the trip from Fort Smith, Arkansas, to Fort Gibson. The journey from where the Red River crosses into Arkansas alone would have been close to 120 miles. "We was skin and bones and feet all bloody when we got to the fort," she remembered. They first went to Fort Smith, and then pushed on to Fort Gibson, where they collected some rations. Sarah's mother sold pictures of President Lincoln for an itinerant photographer in order to make some cash. They then moved out to a community known as Four Mile Creek, where other freedmen were settling. Her mother soon died, and Sarah married a freedman.[28]

Mary Grayson's mother also took the initiative in bringing her children home from their wartime displacement near Fort Washita. When the war ended Creek Mose Perryman told his slaves that they were free, and they would have to "root for themselves after that." Grayson's mother and the children set out walking a short distance each day. Every day she would try to bargain for some kind of work for their food. Sometimes she was paid in money and could afford to purchase a ride for the smaller children on a horse belonging to other freedmen returning on the same route. Often they waited all day for a wagon to come along to take them across a river. At the Creek Agency, they encountered someone who had seen Grayson's father. They sent word to him, and he quickly found them. He had seen action with the Union army and had tried to locate them around Fort Gibson. Reunited, the family cleared land and began to farm. Grayson's successful story illustrates the strength of a long-standing communication network among the enslaved people as well as the powerful identification with place that drew the freed people back to their roots.[29]

There is no way to measure the number of orphans taken in by freedwomen or Indian women who stayed in Indian Territory or encountered them after their return. During the Civil War, the Creek Milley Fish Gilroy's grandmother discovered two little girls hiding in a hollowed-out tree in the Creek Nation. They were so young that they could not provide her with any information about their identity. She gave them names, Nancy and Patsy, and kept them until they were grown. Phyllis Petite's mother and father both died shortly after they settled the family back in Indian Territory. Her aunt raised her and her youngest brother until she married. Another younger brother had been sold by their master, a slave trader, to a member of the Vann family. She always wondered who took care of him and what his fate had been. Phoebe Banks found an infant left on her doorstep. She told a WPA interviewer, "[I] raise him like he is my own blood." She enabled him to get a good education and was proud of his job as a teacher. Acts of kindness and generosity such as these characterized the women of Indian Territory during the harshest of times.[30]

After the suffering and displacement of the war, some freedwomen simply wanted the security of the Indian families they had known all of their lives. Frances Banks told a WPA interviewer in 1938, "[I] stayed on wid de fam'ly after the war. I'se allus lived on this land which jines the Ole Master's and I'se never stayed away from it long at a time." Others were so young that they remained with their mistresses for security. Chaney Richardson, sold when the war started and orphaned when her father died in battle, returned with Hannah Ross to Indian Territory after their sojourn in Texas. "Miss Hannah take me to her place," Richardson remembered, "and I work there until I was grown." Richardson was never paid for her work, but she explained, "My mistress give me some mighty fine rules to live by to get along in this world." Rochelle Allred Ward continued to have a close relationship with her former mistress after the war. "The mistress always get us anything we need, even after the war," she said. On one occasion her former mistress brought fabric to Fort Gibson, where they lived, and helped to make dresses for her. It would take time for everyone in Indian Territory to find stability, to form new methods of relating to each other outside of the confines of slavery, and to create independent lives.[31]

The tragedies of slavery and war had ended. Freedwomen had suffered great hardship and loss, but they had not been defeated, and they had discovered new strengths that had enabled them to survive. The possibilities for the future were enormous, but so were the challenges and responsibilities that lay ahead. The freedwomen in Indian Territory faced the task of building homes and families in a new and much more convoluted environment that included not only the Native peoples familiar to them but Plains Indian tribal groups, freed people escaping the South, a larger military and U.S. government establishment, and enterprising white intruders. Familiar communities remained but were restructured by the inclusion of the new arrivals. Their lives would be shaped by a greater complexity of forces than they had ever known, but at least they had the freedom to make choices about their own destiny. The freedwomen would be integral to the creation of new communities that for the first time offered them alternatives in employment, religion, education, and political participation.

## Chapter Three

# Reconstructing Families

"I am glad slavery is over and I do not want to see any more wars."

Patsy Perryman, in Baker and Baker,
*The WPA Oklahoma Slave Narratives*

Reconnecting families was the first crucial step in rebuilding the lives of the freedwomen and their dependents. So much had happened since the outbreak of the war to remove them from familiar surroundings. Slave sales, abductions, forced migrations to Kansas and Texas, and deaths from disease and battle had all contributed to the disarray of the families of the freedwomen. Searching for their loved ones became their priority. Jim Tomm and his mother and siblings had been reunited with his Union soldier brother at Fort Gibson, but he remembered the day his father returned from Texas: "Daddy came back to the Stidham plantation after the war and we all got together again and not one of the family was killed. We sure was lucky." Not all Indian Territory freed people were so fortunate. Chaney Richardson's mother was killed by feuding Indians shortly before the war began and she and her sisters and brother were sold to different individuals. "I never see my sisters and brother for a long time until after the Civil War," she remembered. Her father was forced to join the Confederate side and died in Arkansas. Richardson's memories of the war were very painful. She told a WPA interviewer, "All that trouble made me the loss of my mammy and pappy."[1]

For many freedwomen there was no joyful reunion. They had lost fathers, mothers, sisters, and brothers during the war and had to make their own way alone. For others, only fragments of their families remained. Mary Lindsay, taken away from her family as a child, stayed with her mistress in Texas for some time after the war ended. When her mistress informed her that she was free but failed to pay her for work done, she left in search of her family. "My pappy done died in the time of the War and I didn't know it," she remembered. She located her brother, Bruner, who told her where her mother and sisters were living on the Red River boundary. He took her by wagon, and she lived with them until her mother died. R. C. Smith's mother never saw her husband again after he joined the Kansas First Volunteer Colored Regiment. He died at the end of the war, and she took her two girls to Fayetteville, Arkansas, where she supported them as a cook. Smith and his brother worked as cowboys in the Cherokee Nation. They used their earnings to buy their mother a house and traveled back and forth to see her. The 1870 census of Indian Territory listed 6,378 black citizens, a loss of 1,998 people in this category since the census of slaves taken in 1860. Considering the postwar births, the returning refugees, and the number of blacks fleeing the South who were entering Indian Territory after the war, such a large deficit indicates a devastating loss.[2]

The federal government and the leadership of the Five Nations, however, were not preoccupied with the needs of freedwomen at this time. Not unlike the mid-nineteenth-century white women of the United States, women of color in Indian Territory had no voice, no vote, and very little security in personal property ownership. Black women and their children were subsumed under the generic term given to all former slaves, *freedmen*. The officials were much more interested in brokering a peace agreement that met the goals of each side. The federal government entertained the idea of settling large numbers of freedmen in Indian Territory and incorporating the Indian lands into eventual statehood. The leadership of the Five Nations was divided among themselves between those who had remained loyal to the United States and those who had allied with the Confederacy. Both sides were determined to retain autonomy over their tribal lands. The most controversial and critical issue concerned the fate of the former slaves. The Choctaw and Chickasaw leaders wanted some form of restitution for the loss of slave property. Major

General John Sanborn, sent in 1866 to oversee the conditions there, reported that the Chickasaw governor Winchester Colbert had told the slaveholders to hold onto their slaves until they learned whether or not Washington intended to reimburse them. If not, "then they would strip them naked and drive them either south to Texas or north to Fort Gibson."[3]

Intense negotiations took place at Fort Smith, Arkansas, in September 1865, but the severity of the federal demands so shocked the Union Indians and infuriated the Confederate ones that confusion and disagreement prevailed. The Five Nations sent representatives to Washington, D.C. in 1866 to petition for better terms and to complete the final treaties. The primary focus of the treaties revolved around federal sovereignty, land, and citizenship for the freedmen. Among the demands was a north-south and east-west railroad right-of-way through Indian Territory and the unification of the tribes under a single government. The Seminoles concluded their treaty first, in March 1866, followed by the Choctaws and Chickasaws, the Creeks, and finally the Cherokees in July. The treaties required the Indian nations to cede millions of acres of their lands back to the government for settlement by other Indian tribes, to abolish slavery, and to incorporate the freedmen into their nations with equal rights as citizens.[4]

The Seminole and Creek nations acquiesced to these conditions with little resistance. Theirs had always been a more open environment for inclusion. A few of the interpreters participating in the negotiations were clearly black Indians. Some Confederate Creeks, however, continued to harass the freedmen. The Cherokees placed a time limit on citizenship. Only those former slaves who resided in the nation at that time or who returned to the nation by January 19, 1867, would be considered citizens. This stipulation caused enormous hardship, especially for freedwomen who were destitute and still stranded in Kansas, Arkansas, Texas, and as far away as Mexico. It would also complicate the later claims of both legitimate Cherokee freed people and counterfeits from outside Indian Territory who wanted Cherokee land. Both the Choctaws and Chickasaws were adamant in their refusal to admit freedmen to citizenship. Their treaties allowed them a period of two years to incorporate their freedmen on an equal basis, or the United States would use money from the cession

Choctaw freedwomen and -men awaiting enrollment as tribal citizens, 1899.
Courtesy of the Western History Collections, University of Oklahoma Libraries,
Phillips Collection 3070.

of their Leased District lands to remove the freedmen from their nations. Inaction from both sides made the conditions of the freed people in the Choctaw and Chickasaw Nations intolerable. It would be another seventeen years before the Choctaw Nation finally admitted its freedwomen and -men to citizenship and granted each forty acres of land. Except for a brief, failed effort in 1873 to legislate the status of the freedmen, the Chickasaw Nation never allowed their former slaves citizenship.[5]

Conditions in Indian Territory for the freed people during these proceedings grew increasingly dangerous. The black Cherokee families who had stayed in the Cherokee Nation throughout the war now found themselves confronted by returning Confederate Cherokees who were militarily defeated and resentful of them because they were freed slaves. Once the Cherokee Nation was under the control of the federal troops, black Cherokees moved onto the farmland previously owned by their masters that was confiscated by loyalist Cherokees during the war. The peace negotiations recommended the return of the confiscated lands to their original owners, and conflict inevitably ensued. Eliza Daniel Strout, a Cherokee, shared her reminiscences with a WPA interviewer in 1937. Similar to some eastern white families, one of Strout's brothers fought for the Confederacy and one fought for the Union. Her family went to the Choctaw Nation during the war. She explained what happened when they returned home: "We found our farm house occupied by negroes who had been freed during our absence. . . . The negroes did not want to give up our place, and my father was afraid they would make trouble, and possible cause bloodshed, but my brothers were not afraid of the negroes." Her brothers bargained with the black Cherokees, offering them "some little trifle" to move away. When the black family left, they took three horses belonging to the Daniel family. Eliza's brothers tracked them during the night, recovered the horses, and "sent the negroes on the road to where all horse thieves went in those days." Vigilante activity such as this carried few penalties. Eliza's father and one of her brothers later served in the Cherokee Nation government. The Canadian District of the Cherokee Nation, which was recommended during the treaty negotiations as a postwar settlement area for the freedmen, quickly filled with Confederate Cherokees who had no intention of sharing their lands with former slaves. They used violence and threats of violence to push the black Cherokees north into other districts and west into Creek lands.[6]

U.S. Secretary of the Interior James Harlan dispatched Major General John B. Sanborn to Indian Territory in 1866. Sanborn, a Minnesota attorney and politician, experienced a rapid rise in military rank during the war. He had organized three regiments of volunteer Union infantry from Minnesota and became their commander in 1861. He served under General Henry Halleck and General Ulysses S. Grant in the Mississippi campaigns. Following the fall of Vicksburg, Sanborn and his troops stood garrison duty there. His command later aided in the defeat of General Sterling Price's forces in Missouri. Promoted to brevet major general in 1865, Sanborn served several missions related to Native peoples on the western frontier until his military retirement in 1869. His orders for Indian Territory were to acquaint himself with the condition of the freedmen and "the state of feeling, relations, prejudices or difficulties existing between them and their former masters."[7]

Sanborn headed the commission for regulating the relations between freedmen of Indian Territory and their former masters. His initial reports in January 1866 revealed the different levels of accommodation in the Five Nations that had been made with their former slaves. He reported little distress among the Seminole and Creek freedmen, although some of the Confederates were hostile toward them. The Cherokees preferred that the freedmen be located in a specific area of their nation. But regarding the Choctaw and Chickasaw environment, he was appalled. On January 8 he reported that freedmen were being "shot down like dogs," and "a woman has been whipped nearly to death." On Choctaw lands the freedmen were being driven away from their homes and murdered with no action taken to punish the guilty. The Chickasaws were still holding their slaves in bondage and entertained "a bitter prejudice against them all." Any black man who fought for the Union was prohibited from returning to Chickasaw lands. According to Sanborn, the former slaves had no rights in these two nations, and it would require federal supervision to alleviate these problems. He requested that a military force be posted immediately in the Choctaw and Chickasaw lands.[8]

The condition of destitute single freedwomen and their children became a matter of record when Sanborn took notice of their circumstances. He issued his administrative orders through several circulars to the Indian agents. Sanborn exercised wide latitude in the execution of his duties as he instructed the Indian agents who at that time were military men. These circulars reveal his intent to impose a strict, patriarchal definition of the values and laws of the United States into Indian affairs, especially those issues related to freedwomen.

Sanborn took particular interest in Americanizing the institution of marriage in Indian Territory. He was offended by the accepted practice of polygyny among the Indians and ordered its immediate discontinuance. He was further appalled that freedmen had also adopted this practice, and he sent a circular to the agents detailing his orders regarding its abandonment: "No Freedman will be allowed hereafter to take to himself more than one wife and shall be bound to live with her as long as both live." Marriages solemnized after the custom of the Indian Nations were to be considered binding. He commanded the agents to issue certificates to those couples desiring to marry only after the officials had investigated to their satisfaction that no other spouses were involved. Sanborn also instructed the agents to keep a record of the names of the parties and the dates of marriage, to be presented for review at the end of their terms.[9]

Sanborn became especially concerned about the plight of freed-women with numerous children and no husband, not recognizing that his previous order may have contributed to the numbers of single female

Freedman log cabin near Drumright, Oklahoma, 1900. Reprinted by permission of the Research Division of the Oklahoma Historical Society.

parents. He reported, "The large number of children of this class of females is a bar to their receiving good husbands, and unless some provision is made for them their case and that of their children is most hopeless." He requested a special provision to be included in the ongoing
negotiation of the peace treaties among the Five Nations in Washington.
Each single freedwoman with one or more children should be granted a
homestead of 160 acres of land. Ownership of land would have two positive benefits, he believed: it would improve the marriage prospects of
these single mothers, and it would give their children a future. Sanborn
recognized the previous pairings of Indians and blacks, whether voluntary or forced, by the presence of their offspring. "Many of the children
are mixed bloods, and, with a home, may become quite valuable citizens," he suggested. This recommendation never received approval.[10]

Sanborn also addressed the disposition of the children of the freedwomen and the work they did. In some cases this may have been helpful,
but in others it challenged the integrity of families and hindered the ability of families to reconnect with each other. Circular Number 4 directed
that contracts for the labor of minor children must be made with the
parents or guardians and that any person refusing to deliver a child upon
the request of the parents would be subject to a district court suit. Sisters
Victoria Taylor Thompson and Patsy Perryman, whose master brought
them back home from Texas at the end of the war, lived with their mother near Tahlequah. She supported them as a cook for the prisoners at the
jail. A local judge took eight-year-old Victoria into his home to do housework. When Victoria's father arrived after the war and tried to reclaim his
daughter, the judge's wife objected. "She didn't like my father," Victoria
said, "and kept him off the place." Victoria had been stolen once before,
in slavery days, by a white man. He kidnapped her, branded her on the
cheek, and kept her prisoner at his home until she escaped. The family
feared that even in freedom, their powerlessness might prevent them
from protecting their daughters.[11]

The freed people's connections with the Indians sometimes proved
more trustworthy than those they had with the government officials. Sanborn's instructions included an additional interpretation with his official
decree: "In some instances, children will be better off, living with their
former masters than with their parents, until their parents secure a home,

and more means of supporting them, and it may be better that parental affection in such cases, should for the time being, yield to policy." Since Victoria's father was afraid to go near her on the judge's property, a Cherokee agreed to lure her away from the judge's home, hide her, and return her to her father. Patsy explained, "We was all worried about her for a time, until we found out she was with him." Victoria and her father worked for the Cherokee man to pay him for reuniting her with her parents.[12]

Another Cherokee freedwoman related her own, similar experiences. "When I was freed," Nancy Rogers Bean told a WPA interviewer, "my mistress was Mrs. O'Neal, wife of a officer at Fort Gibson." Nancy was strongly attached to Mrs. O'Neal because she treated her better than her previous mistresses and because she had given her a rag doll, the first Nancy had ever owned. O'Neal allowed her one hour a day to play with the beloved doll. She wanted to take Nancy back to Virginia with her at the end of their tour of duty, but her parents stepped in and refused to allow her to go. Economic necessity, as Sanborn suggested, might have prevented some black families from living together. The Rogerses accepted their child living with and working for Mrs. O'Neal, but they would not tolerate O'Neal's assertion of rights over their daughter and her future after emancipation.[13]

Since economic security and family stability were closely associated with marriage in nineteenth-century America, the question of suitable marriage partners for Indian freedwomen became an issue of public discussion and policy. Marriages and sexual relations between Indians and African Americans had been common during their lengthy relationship with each other. Separating these classifications in the aftermath of the Civil War created a complex, superimposed structure of race that more often reflected white American values and racial attitudes. In many of the Five Nations, family relationships, individual actions, and community far outweighed an artificial racial designation. As the historian Fay Yarbrough writes in her study of the Cherokee Nation, "Questions of racial identity involved a complex interplay of self-identification and community reputation, as well as blood, descent, and clan membership." A person might be accepted or excluded by the citizens of the nation regardless of racial mixture.[14]

As time went on, however, public recognition of mixed Indian and

John Wesley, Seminole interpreter, and family, 1909. Courtesy of the Western History Collections, University of Oklahoma Libraries, Seminole Nation Collection 137.

black ancestry more frequently complicated family relationships. Pairings occurred in the Seminole and Creek nations more regularly, but they were not unheard of in the Cherokee, Choctaw, and Chickasaw nations. Many freedwomen acknowledged their mixed heritage openly. Rachel Aldrich Ward mentioned her Cherokee grandmother, a member of the prominent Downing family. Lucinda Vann, another Cherokee freedwoman of mixed ancestry, told a WPA interviewer that "a bunch . . . that was part Indian and part colored" had been well-provisioned by the Vanns before they retreated to Mexico for the duration of the war. Sometimes, however, these mixed Indian-black relationships were denied after the war, and this led to estrangement within the extended families. After emancipation, for example, Patsy Perryman's brother married a full-blood Cherokee woman and refused to associate with his freedman family any longer. Perryman characterized her brother this way: "He's just like an Indian, been with them so much, talks the Cherokee language and don't notice us Negroes any more." Cherokee unions with their freedmen lay at some point along a spectrum between two extremes, with the Seminoles and Creeks on one side and the Choctaws and Chickasaws on the other.[15]

Acceptable intermarriage among the Seminole and Creek people with the freedmen continued until Oklahoma statehood. Among the Creeks, the female population outnumbered the males by about 1,500 following the war. Unions with freedmen of their nation or other freedmen may have seemed a choice advantageous for security. In 1907 L. J. Abbott visited the principal towns in Indian Territory and reported that blacks "were accepted as an integral portion of the Creek and Seminole tribes." He made the claim, undoubtedly exaggerated, that there were few Seminole and Creek families without "negro blood." In a study of African American relationships with the Native Americans in the Creek and Cherokee Nations, the ethnohistorian Katja May explores a case sample of 531 families in the Creek Nation from the 1900 census, of which 24.9 percent were black Indians. Out of this group, 5.3 percent were married to full-bloods, 65.9 percent were married to other black Indians, and 9.8 percent had black immigrant marriages.[16]

Some scholars have equated the relative peace between the Seminole Indians and their freedmen with widespread intermarriage between the two. The historian Kevin Mulroy argues persuasively, however, that the cooperative relationships had far more to do with Seminole cultural factors than intermarriage. His research indicates that Seminole and black unions were rare. "Far from being one society of mixed heritage," he maintains, "the Seminole Nation became a place where clearly distinguishable Indian and freedmen communities peacefully coexisted." He identifies five additional, and more significant, influences. Each played a primary role in the destiny of both groups.[17]

First, Mulroy asserts that the Seminoles had not developed a capitalist economy similar to that of the South before the Civil War. They had not engaged in building large-scale plantations and sizable business enterprises. Second, they had been less inclined than other of the Five

Tribes to incorporate a mixed white elite within their leadership structure, eliminating some of the severe southern racial attitudes. Maroons had exercised considerable freedom in land use, ownership of weapons and horses, and free passage in the East. As more Seminole tribal members arrived in Indian Territory, African Americans assumed a traditional and comfortable, if separate, place and were easily incorporated as advisors and interpreters. In addition, Mulroy maintains that the Seminoles were more accommodating to incorporation of the freedmen because they were less acculturated than the other four Indian tribes. Their political, social, and cultural structures continued to reflect a traditional model with hereditary *mikkos* dominating the leadership positions. More than the others, the Seminoles continued to reject the acculturating influences of American education and religion.[18]

Third, the destruction of their many and prolonged wars with the U.S. government made the people anxious for stability. They had faced a brutal removal to Indian Territory and settled on land that remained in contention with the Creeks for years, only to see their families, homes, and possessions destroyed during the Civil War. Loyalists and Confederates suffered alike, and neither side wanted a continuation of racial conflict. As the Confederate Seminole leader Heniha Mikko stated in 1885, "Our people in the past have seen enough of turmoil and strife and greatly desire peace."[19]

Fourth, it was the loyalist Seminoles who largely negotiated the 1866 peace treaties and oversaw the incorporation of the freedmen. John Chupco, who became principal chief after the Civil War, had fought alongside maroon supporters in Florida and in the Civil War. The freedmen supported Chupco until his death in 1881. Even after the former Confederate supporters reasserted power in the 1880s, their objections were directed less toward the freedmen than toward Texas maroons who had left the tribe years earlier and now wanted to migrate to Indian Territory. When they arrived, the maroons gravitated to the existing separate freedmen communities.[20]

Fifth, the continuing separation of Indian and black townships in the Seminole Nation reduced conflict between the two. Although freedmen were accepted into the nation, they were not adopted into the clans. Mulroy maintains that only a very small elite with long-standing marriages and ties to the Seminoles moved within the inner circles. The freedmen population rose 150 percent between 1870 and 1905, while the Seminole population increased less than 10 percent. This large increase Mulroy attributes to intermarriage with Creek freedmen, not Seminole Indians.[21]

The Choctaws and Chickasaws were the most emphatically opposed to racial mixing with African Americans. In 1885 the Choctaws passed a law making intermarriage with blacks a felony. The Chickasaws insisted that their people maintain "racial purity," which really meant no marriages with African Americans, but it did not exclude widespread intermarriage with white Americans. Choctaw and Chickasaw relationships with African Americans existed much more widely than recognized and appeared in multiple forms. Milley Franklin, according to her son, was one-quarter Choctaw and three-quarters black, but she had not been reared as a slave. She was born in Mississippi, the daughter of Tim Colbert. She grew up in her Choctaw household, spoke Choctaw, and was educated at Armstrong Academy along with a relative of Governor Winchester Colbert. She married David Franklin, a former Chickasaw slave whose father had bought the whole family's freedom. The couple wed in Mississippi in 1856 and returned to Indian Territory, where they raised a large family and developed a sizable ranch. After the war, the Chickasaw Nation refused to recognize Chickasaw-black marriages when they occurred and deemed the children of those marriages "illegitimate." In 1884 one freedman stated, "There may be a few of such cases, but as a general rule, we of African descent do not intermarry with the Chickasaws; we intermarry amongst ourselves." In 1885 the Chickasaw Nation required freedmen from outside the nation who married Chickasaw freedwomen to buy a permit to stay in the nation.[22]

The devastation of war to both races and the impositions of Reconstruction created circumstances wherein interracial unions could take place. Formal wedding ceremonies were not common. The usual custom for marriages among nonelite Indians and African Americans at this time was a brief announcement followed by a feast. Separations were just as informal and easily followed by another marriage. Evidence of the continuation of these pairings existed long after Indian Territory became part of the state of Oklahoma.

Statehood, however, made such informal marriages less viable due to legal definitions and strictures. The Oklahoma State Constitution defined members of the white race as anyone not of African descent, thereby making the Native peoples white. One of the first actions of the new state government was to pass antimiscegenation laws. In a study of early statehood miscegenation cases, the historian Charles F. Robinson maintains that all of the court cases involved couples from the Five Nations and usually centered on property issues. In two cases the defendants challenged the state court by arguing that their marriages, contracted as citizens of Indian Territory, overruled the Oklahoma laws.[23]

Many decades after their marriages and, for most, the death of their spouse, the freedwomen remembered the happiness surrounding their weddings. Their joy came at least in part from knowing that at last this life event was of their own choosing and their bonds held legitimacy. The black Cherokee Sarah Wilson married her husband, Oliver, in 1878. She remembered the "white and black checkedy calico apron" she wore, especially since it had cost her a whole day of washing for a woman near Fort Gibson. Her husband's former master gave the couple a pear tree that still lived at the time of her interview. "I was sure a happy woman when I married that day," she told a WPA interviewer. Some freedmen also remembered their wedding clothes. Johnson Thompson wed his first wife in wool pants and a blue striped shirt. Thompson's sister, Phyllis Petite, probably had the most elaborate wedding. A minister performed the ceremony for her and George in the home of a friend at Fort Gibson. The bride wore "black high-top shoes, and a large cream colored hat." "And on top of all I had a blue wool dress with tassels all round the bottom of it," she remembered. The Chickasaw freedwoman Polly Colbert had a big wedding as well. Her former mistress came to the ceremony and stayed for dinner. "We danced all evening," she recalled, "and after supper we started again and danced all night." Of course, not all freedwomen were as well-positioned as these. Betty Robertson wed in her old work clothes, and Lucinda Vann refused to take her husband's name because she was proud of the Vann name. She claimed her husband never gave her anything and that she had enjoyed fine things only when she was a slave.[24]

Sometimes freedwomen entered into marriages hastily, out of a sense of desperation and loss of the security if not of a family, then of a familiar home. The Cherokee freedwoman Betty Robertson and her mother settled and worked a small patch of land near Fort Gibson after the war. When her mother died, Betty got married "to have somebody to take care of [her]." Her new husband was eighty-nine. For the freed-women there were likely many marriages of convenience such as this. Not all marriages contracted at this time endured for life. Patsy Perryman had a series of husbands from different backgrounds. Her first husband was a full-blood Creek Indian, and her second was a "black African." According to Perryman, they were not compatible: "So I let him go, and married Randolph Perryman." In one family, a story survives into the twenty-first century of a brave freedwoman who seized an opportunity to secure a safe place for herself. From a place of hiding, she saw a fight between two Indian men. In the course of the struggle, one of the men killed the other. She revealed herself and negotiated a pledge with the survivor: if he would marry her, she would keep the secret until her dying day. They married and raised several children who were considered by his nation Indian rather than black. She kept her promise and revealed her story only to her closest relatives on her deathbed. It remains a carefully guarded secret within this multiracial family. The mixed descendants of this couple do not recognize their black kin.[25]

Katja May's study of the Cherokees and African Americans in the census of 1900 contains 862 families. Black Indians constituted 18 percent of these cases. A striking statistic lay in heads of household: thirty-five years after the close of the Civil War, black Cherokees still had a higher ratio of female-headed households, 19.4 percent, than full-blood, mixed-blood, and black immigrant groups. Their population also contained the highest ratio of widowed household heads, 21.9 percent. From the sample, 5.2 percent were marriages between black Indians and full-blood Cherokees, 61 percent were black Indians married to black Indians, and 9.1 percent were unions between black Indians and black immigrants.[26]

Rivalry among freedwomen for suitable mates also existed. In Boggy Depot, Choctaw Nation, two freedwomen rather publicly competed for the affection of a dashing black teamster with "eel-skin covered braids." Johnson Cline was an attractive, popular citizen of the town who hauled ox-drawn wagons containing packets of money and merchandise over the Fort Smith Road to be sold by the local merchants. He was held in high esteem by the Choctaws for his "honesty and trustworthiness." According to a Boggy Depot resident, Malvina and Polly, housemaids in the area, were very jealous of each other. The locals watched in amusement to see which young woman appeared to be in the courting lead at the moment. Both women hoped to gain his favor by paying on Cline's account at the flour mill. The competition was finally settled when Malvina won his heart.[27]

Major General John Sanborn could not possibly have foreseen the multiple options freedwomen in Indian Territory would have over time. In addition to marriages with their freedmen and with Indian men, the war also brought other possible partners. Since June 1863 the Kansas First Colored Volunteer Regiment, commanded by Colonel James M. Williams, had been active in the campaigns in Indian Territory. The regiment first functioned as scouting patrols across the Kansas border. After successful battles at Cabin Creek and Honey Springs, they joined the garrison at Fort Gibson. The Kansas Second Colored Volunteer Infantry Regiment arrived in September, and both regiments were attached to the Second Division, Army of the Frontier, at Fort Smith, Arkansas. These regiments included runaway slave volunteers from all of the tribes of Indian Territory as well as black men from other states. Throughout 1864 both outfits had made frequent sorties into Indian Territory, where they engaged the Confederate raiding forces of Stand Watie. Following the war, Colonel Benjamin Grierson commanded the all-black Tenth Regiment of cavalry and made his headquarters at Fort Gibson in 1872. These soldiers patrolled the Indian lands, removing whiskey peddlers, outlaws, and intruders.

Freedwomen encountered these young men on a personal level during the course of their military assignments. The soldiers were often the first to tell the slaves that they were free; they provided escort to safety away from the battle areas; they also dispensed food, clothing, and supplies provided by the U.S. government and those they had scavenged from raids. The presence of large numbers of black soldiers and black female refugees around Fort Gibson provided new opportunities for social encounters. Much has been written about the drinking, gambling, and prostitution around the fort, but it was also a site of more respectable diversions. Church services, dances, piano recitals, horse races, sailboat rides, and dinners gave black soldiers and freedwomen opportunities to meet and become acquainted. Just as white troops married young Indian women in Indian Territory, so too did black troops marry freedwomen.[28]

A prominent example of such a marriage was that of George Goldsby and the freedwoman Ellen Beck. George was a sergeant in the Tenth Cavalry Regiment. While stationed at Fort Concho, Texas, in 1876 the couple had a son, Crawford Goldsby. When the child was only two years old, George became involved in a dispute with some white Texans and was forced to flee. Ellen Goldsby moved from place to place to find work and support her son. She returned to Indian Territory and eventually remarried. Crawford did not like the new husband and soon struck out on his own. Ellen's advice to her son was this: "Stand up for your rights. Don't let anybody impose on you." He must have adopted an aggressive form of that advice. As he grew older, he formed his own gang and became a ruthless outlaw known as Cherokee Bill. He was so attractive and

Makeshift dress shop at Fort Gibson, Indian Territory, ca. 1900. Reprinted by permission of the Research Division of the Oklahoma Historical Society.

charming that freedwomen often provided places for him to hide. It was a black Cherokee girlfriend, however, who eventually turned him over to her relative, a U.S. deputy marshal. Cherokee Bill was hanged at twenty-one in Isaac Parker's Arkansas court.[29]

Indian Territory became famous for lawlessness during the postwar period. It was impossible for the small number of federal troops to patrol the 74,000 square miles. It also took some time for the Indian governments to unify and to provide law and order through their Indian police, called the Lighthorse. Postwar resentment toward the former slaves frequently resulted in violence. Freedmen as well took advantage of the uncertain situation and looted homes, stealing horses and other livestock. Government reports often referred to the "unsettled conditions" of the Territory. The Reconstruction treaties with the Five Nations created a complicated and frustrating system of law enforcement. U.S. marshals had jurisdiction over all cases involving noncitizens of the nations and cases that included both citizens and noncitizens. Those persons arrested were taken to the Court for the Western District of Arkansas at Fort Smith. The Indian police dealt with lawbreakers who were citizens of their own nations. This situation particularly impacted the freed people of the Choctaw and Chickasaw nations whose citizenship was left in limbo. Their cases would not be heard in local courts, and they had to appeal for and pay the expense of justice dispensed all the way from Fort Smith.[30]

The historians Daniel Littlefield and Lonnie Underhill identify ten black law enforcement officers in Indian Territory who gave distinguished service, although there were undoubtedly more than these before the end of the century. B. R. Colbert, Crowder Nicks, and John Garrett were Indian policemen. Bass Reeves, Edward D. Jefferson, Robert Love, Grant Johnson, Isaac Rogers, John Joss, and Dick Roebuck were U.S. marshals. These black officers enjoyed better relations with the Native peoples and other freedmen than the white marshals. Black marshals, many of them freedmen themselves, understood the cultural ways of the Indians better because of their long history together. In addition, Reeves and Johnson spoke the Creek language, and Rogers spoke Cherokee. Marriage to freedmen in this line of work, although prestigious, could not have been easy for the freedwomen. Besides the danger, their husbands could be away for as long as thirty days at a time, ranging far and wide across the

Territory. Meanwhile the wives stayed at home tending the children and protecting their own property. Marshals were paid on a fee system that included provisions for their prisoners and mileage plus expenses, but the fee was paid only upon the successful delivery of the prisoners. Depending on the frugality and perseverance of the man, this may or may not have been an adequate income. It could also be heartbreaking if an officer had to arrest a relative, as was the case for Bass Reeves, who had to bring in his own son for the murder of the young man's wife.[31]

After the Civil War an industry arose that had an immediate impact on Indian Territory and brought additional marriage partners into contact with the freedwomen. The expanding size of eastern cities and a burgeoning population of immigrants dramatically increased the demand for beef in the United States. Indian Territory and Texas were fertile areas for the development of cattle ranches. Choctaw Wilson N. Jones and Creek George W. Stidham developed large ranges for their herds of cattle. By 1882 at least 140,000 head of cattle grazed on Chickasaw lands. But until the railroads reached westward, the cattle had to be driven to the closest market. The trail drives brought numerous cowboys into the area to accompany the herds making their way up to Kansas. They also provided employment for numerous freedmen, such as R. C. Smith and his brother in the Cherokee Nation. It has been estimated that approximately one-third of the western cowboys were black. Three of the major cattle trails running from Texas up to Kansas pass through the Five Nations' area of Indian Territory. The earliest were the East Shawnee and the West Shawnee, but the most famous was the Chisholm Trail, named for the Cherokee Jesse Chisholm.[32]

In 1868 a Chickasaw rancher, Montford Johnson, hired the freedman Jack Brown to supervise a new ranch he had built near what is now Washington, Oklahoma. Brown had recently married Eliza, the former slave of one of Johnson's relatives. Jack brought some horses and Eliza brought some chickens and hogs to their new home. Johnson's agreement with Brown was that he was to receive every fourth calf in pay. Brown in turn hired two other freedmen, Ed Cohee and Henry Cole, to help him with the ranch operations. Although Jack and Eliza could not become citizens of the Chickasaw Nation, they enjoyed a long and productive relationship with Johnson.[33]

Without doubt, the provision of the 1866 Reconstruction treaties with the Five Nations that affected the Territory and the freedwomen the most was the one providing for the construction of railroads through the Indian lands. In 1872 the MK&T (Katy) Railroad was the first to complete a north-south line all the way to Texas. The railroads allowed outsiders to recognize the bountiful opportunities of these previously closed-off lands. Indian Territory's natural resources of coal, timber, cattle, agricultural products, and later oil attracted all manner of interested immigrants. Elite members of the Five Nations recruited cheap contract labor, black and white, to develop their lands and natural resources. For most, the lure of thousands of acres of quality agricultural land, seemingly underdeveloped, held the greatest attraction. Freed black citizens of the Five Nations, just as any other citizen, could claim land and develop it as long as no one else owned it. Because of the matrilineal structure of the Indian families, marriage to Indian women had more security, but marriage to freedwomen also offered the advantage of a fresh start on good land. While the arrival of white immigrants dramatically outnumbered the black, the growth of the black population was significant. By 1890 the black population had grown to 18,636. In only twenty years the presence of African Americans, mixed-blood freed people, and immigrant blacks in Indian Territory had increased by 12,258 individuals.[34]

The rapid economic development of the railroads had both a positive and a negative impact. As in all other areas of the United States, railroads accelerated the development of the mining and timber industries, agriculture, and shipping. During the 1880s railroad construction crews created temporary communities all over Indian Territory. Some of these became permanent communities. The railroad workers included freedmen from the South, white workers from all over the United States, and European immigrants. One Cherokee petition to President Rutherford B. Hayes asked him to prevent unauthorized individuals from entering Indian Territory. They claimed that the MK&T Railroad had dumped a whole "load of Negroes" and that this was happening everywhere in the Territory. On one hand, the crews provided not only marriage partners but opportunities for employment for the freedwomen. They earned money with the skills most familiar to them: cooking, cleaning, and washing. On the other hand, the rail camps and towns, known as "Hell on

Wheels," were notorious for crime and violence. One reporter from Ohio commented on the danger along the Katy line in 1872, "The records of Muscogee are bloody." He reported sixteen murders in five weeks. The violence was not directed at travelers but at "their own class, and new-comers who are weak enough to mix in, drink and gamble with them." Within eight miles of Muskogee he encountered a community of freed people. "We entered a region of rude log cabins and gaunt farm stock, where black faces peered at us through the cracks of 'worm fences.'" (wooden fences with no upright posts). The flow of whiskey into these areas was unstoppable; peddlers sold their wares to the construction crews and recruited gamblers and prostitutes. The safety of freedwomen and their families was at best questionable.[35]

The combined stipulations of the 1866 Reconstruction treaties doomed any chance that Indian Territory might remain under the author-ity of the Five Nations. They also flung the door wide open for the en-trance of resident non-Indians. Each of the new industries and the devel-opment of for-profit cattle and agriculture needed additional workers in order to increase production. White, black, Mexican, and European im-migrants moved into Indian Territory to fill the need. Besides employ-ment opportunities, black immigrants also noticed that the racial compo-sition in Indian Territory created an environment less rigid and violent than they had known in the South. Interest in Indian Territory settlement was also spurred by an 1879 article in the *Chicago Times* written by a Cherokee lawyer, Elias C. Boudinot, who claimed that millions of acres of unoccupied public land existed in the Territory. By the 1880s national black leaders were organizing pressure groups to lobby Congress for a black state to be carved out of Indian Territory. Others, such as Hannibal Carter, James Milton Turner, and Edwin P. McCabe, formed immigration societies to encourage freedmen to colonize and create a sizable pres-ence in the area. Twenty-five all-black communities, some as old as re-moval and some newly created, existed in Indian Territory.[36]

Soldiers, cowboys, miners, lumber men, railroad men, government officials, and farmers came singly and in families to participate in the development of the area. Uninvited gamblers of all varieties looking for a big break also intruded into the Indian lands. In spite of efforts by the leadership of the Five Nations to legislate the noncitizen status of the newcomers and to place limitations on marriages to citizens both Indian and black, the numbers overwhelmed them. Time ran out in 1889, when President Benjamin Harrison opened the "Unassigned Lands" in the middle of Indian Territory to white settlement. These lands had not been allocated after the Civil War to either the Five Nations or the Plains Tribes. This action led to the creation of Oklahoma Territory adjacent to Indian Territory. By 1890 the Indian people were the minority on their own land. The 1890 census reported white residents as the largest concentration in Indian Territory: 61 percent of the population. Indians and blacks together constituted only 39 percent of the population.[37]

The arrival of large numbers of immigrants created an entirely new dynamic for the freedwomen living in Indian Territory. Initially the new black arrivals, whom freedmen called "state Negroes," were not welcomed. Native-born freedmen feared both loss of lands to these outsiders by fraud and the further deterioration of their own status as the number of black newcomers increased. They blamed increasing racial antipathy from both Indians and whites on these new freedmen, who they believed to be poorer and more subservient. Native-born freedwomen quarreled with "state" women over the meaning of freedom and their seemingly backward behavior. When a woman refused to take a progressive attitude toward the new freedoms, as compared to the security of slavery, she was called a "rag-head." Alafair Carter Adams expressed the resentment by commenting wisely that a number of the intruders "claimed they were natives that weren't, just to latch onto a free piece of land here."[38]

Fees, regulations, restrictive rights, and discrimination, imposed by Indian government leadership and sanctioned by the federal government, sometimes hindered alliances between freedwomen and noncitizens. When Rachel Aldrich Ward married a "state" man from Texas, she had to have Cherokee witnesses to vouch for the marriage before the Fort Gibson judge would issue the marriage license. "I got seven signers," she remembered, "all of them Cherokee Indians who know I was a good slave woman." Although quite unusual, immigrant white men also married freedwomen from the Nations. Silas Smith, a blacksmith sent into the Creek Nation to teach farm implement construction and repair, married twice; each time he chose a black Creek woman. A white surveyor who met them wrote in his journal, "The colored people in the Creek nation are upon an equal footing with the Indians. A man who marries a colored woman becomes a member of the Nation the same if he had married an Indian woman." Katja May's demographic work found little intermarriage between whites and black Indians. In the Creek sample, 59.1 percent of black immigrants married other black immigrants. In second place, 19.5 percent of the black immigrants had native black Creek spouses. For her sample in the Cherokee Nation, this type of intermarriage was in first place: the figures for 1900 indicated that 23.6 percent of the black immigrants were married to black Indians.[39]

Indian Territory celebrations illustrated the need for the freed people to reconstruct families and a shared sense of culture and community in the midst of such rapid transition. For a time in Indian Territory freedwomen played the central role in an event commemorating the most important moment of their history. Between 1870 and 1900 the black Indians held an annual celebration on August 4 in memory of emancipation. Full-blood and mixed-blood Indians and white people also attended. Some of the celebrations included speeches by Indian and black politicians about the importance of strength in unity. There were calls for better education for the freedmen. They sang songs and held parades and marches, the celebration sometimes lasting several days. The activities were always accompanied by feasting and dancing.[40]

A committee of freed people chose a site for the celebration, erected an American flag, and placed a cannon nearby. Days before the event, the finest horses were groomed and fed; when the day arrived, they were decorated with fringe, ornaments, and colorful draping. The people wore traditional dress of bright calico and multicolored streamers. The various bands organized themselves in separate locations. As the freedman Aaron Grayson remembered, "They came on horses at a gallop, laughing, joking and yelling and were heard miles away." Each band circled around the flagpole individually, and the cannon was fired. Several young freedwomen competed for the role of queen of these festivities. By majority vote, a committee presented the winning girl with a divided riding skirt and a silk crown. She was placed on the finest horse and escorted for the day by two mounted attendants who catered to her every need. It must have been quite rewarding for the freedwomen to see their daughters

# Emanciption Day ✗ ✗ ✗

### Will be Celebrated with a Grand Street Parade in which all the Colored Citizens will Participate, with

# John Porter

### As General of the Day, and

# Miss Emma Brown

### as the Queen.

# *FREE BARBECUE*

### in the afternoon. Everbody invited. Speaking by celebrated orators. Dancing day and night.

**WILEY McINTOSH,**
           **President,**
    **LOUIS SANGER,**
                  **Clerk.**

Times Job Print, Muscogee, I. T.

Indian Territory Emancipation Day flyer, 1882. Reprinted by permission of the Research Division of the Oklahoma Historical Society.

honored for their beauty and grace. "At the end of the day," Grayson said, "everyone felt that this was a day that had been well-spent in good fellowship."[41]

Freedwomen witnessed dramatic changes in Indian Territory during the postwar period. Calling on enormous reservoirs of strength, hope, and determination, they searched for loved ones separated from them by the war. Sometimes they were able to reunite families, and sometimes they mourned their losses and continued on alone. Women of marriageable age found themselves in an environment they had never experienced before. The Reconstruction treaties and the postwar economic development brought a whole new population into the area. No longer constrained by the demands of their former masters, it appeared that they could choose partners from a broad spectrum of alternatives. Instead they found themselves caught in the middle of a contest between officials of the U.S. government determined to regulate their marital relations according to white American values and officials of their Indian governments resentful of the freedmen citizenship rights forced upon them and fearful of an invasion of their lands. Both of these authorities attempted to place restrictions on their choices. Even so, freedwomen and -men reestablished intimate relations according to their own needs and desires and set about creating new families to inhabit Indian Territory. The priorities of the freedwomen changed. No longer looking back at the past, they now sought economically viable positions for the future. They hoped to create peaceful, comfortable, productive lives for themselves and their families by any means at their disposal.

## Chapter Four

# Making a New Life

"I'se always been a workin' woman, no matter where I is."

Chaney McNair, in Baker and Baker.
*The WPA Oklahoma Slave Narratives*

Chaney McNair's remark in 1939 to a WPA interviewer makes a universal statement about the lives of freedwomen in Indian Territory. Working both inside their homes and in outside employment became a necessity. To support their families as single heads of households or to sustain and supplement the income in two-parent families freedwomen used every skill they knew and grasped every opportunity they could to acquire new ones. If their children were ever to survive and prosper, it would take the strength, energy, and drive of both mother and father to create opportunities for them that they had never known under slavery. As freedwomen sought employment, they had to mediate the gendered imperatives of the postwar settlements between the U.S. government and their Indian nations, and sometimes the authority of their own husbands. There was freedom and hope in the ability to make money, but there was also great vulnerability in the negotiation of this new economic status.

The transition from slavery to paid work for Indian freedwomen required numerous adjustments in Indian Territory, just as it did in the South. Finding a suitable economic replacement for slavery that recognized an independent relationship between worker and employer was not an easy process. As in so many other issues related to freedwomen, General John Sanborn laid out the particulars of their paid labor in Circular Number 4. Sanborn attempted to define the economic relationship between husband and wife with regard to paid labor by granting authority and power to the male in the household. Item 3 of the circular stated, "The husband is entitled to the compensation for the labor and services of his wife, when parties are living and cohabiting together." In other words, he placed fiscal ownership of family resources, even those earned by the wife, into the hands of the husbands. Item 6 added, "Contracts for the labor of the wife, must, in all cases, when possible, be made with the husband." With these two directives, Sanborn transferred the control of the freedwoman's economic productivity from her slave master to her husband.[1]

It is unlikely that these instructions were followed with any regularity or for very long, especially given the disarray of the black family structure at that time. They revealed Sanborn's efforts, however, to impose a white American patriarchal gender model upon a weakened Indian cultural system that had previously granted wider economic prerogatives to women. He insisted that Native peoples recognize the rights of the freedmen, but he cautioned the freedmen about making any kind of rapid change. He viewed slavery chiefly as an economic arrangement between master and slave and suggested that former slaves remain with their "present employers" until they could provide for their own subsistence. Sanborn closed his circular declaring that everyone had an interest in making "the greatest efforts to harmonize what seems conflicting; to bring system and order out of confusion; to elevate and enlighten the laboring masses; . . . and to secure protection, competency, and happiness to all classes of men." The system and order proposed was largely that of white America, not that of the Native peoples.[2]

When freedwomen were first told that they were free, they were frequently also told that they would receive wages for future labor. Many continued to work for their former masters and mistresses for some time but never received any payment. Mary Lindsay explained that she stayed with her mistress in Texas after emancipation "'cause [she] didn't have no place to go." Her mistress told Mary that she was supposed to pay her, but she had no money. If Mary would stay with her, she said, she would give her a good home. Mary carded and spun cotton and wool and worked in the fields. Sometime later Mary's mistress traveled back to the Chickasaw Nation to see her father, Sobe Love, of the successful and politically important Love family. When her mistress returned with a sack of money, Mary asked her about payment for her duties. Her employer refused to give her any of the money. "Den I starts to feeling like I ain't treated right," Mary remembered. She felt even worse when she met a freedman who told her that he made a dollar a week working in a nearby town. She bundled up her few possessions and, without saying goodbye, set out alone to find her family. Chaney Richardson also remained with her mistress, Hannah Ross, until she was grown. She later remarked, "I didn't git any money that I seen," but she appreciated the good home Ross provided.[3]

Freedwomen's ignorance of the types and value of money and inexperience with the appropriate ways to transact business complicated their new status as wage earners. On some of the larger prewar plantations, enslaved women were allowed to raise chickens and sell eggs to the mistress, but these exchanges were rare. With the exception of the Creek and Seminole freedwomen, most remembered working a common garden that raised food for the whole farm, the Indian families and the slaves alike. They were issued rations of other food supplies such as flour, coffee, and molasses, and they supplemented their diet with the wild game they hunted. Betty Robertson claimed that occasionally her master, Joe Vann, gave her some money in appreciation for how hard she worked. "I couldn't buy anything in slavery time," she said, "so I jest give the piece of money to the Vann children." Another freedwoman remembered that she occasionally received a little money and bought candy with it.[4]

Many freedwomen had never possessed money of their own. In addition, several different kinds of money circulated in Indian Territory. There was gold, silver, tokens, and paper scrip, similar to U.S. currency, that fluctuated in value depending on the liquidity of the Indian national treasuries. The influx of Confederate currency during the war years and U.S. greenbacks later also complicated financial transactions and understandings. Sarah Wilson explained, "Lord, I never earned a dime of money in slave days for myself but plenty for the Old Master." She remembered that he often sent her out to work in a neighbor's field and later collected the money himself for her labor. She described the first time she ever had any money that belonged only to her: "We was free, and I found a greenback in the road. . . . I didn't know what it was." When her mother explained that it was money, Sarah took the bill to a store, placed it on the counter, and exchanged it for a pretty pitcher that she had admired earlier. She had no idea what the trinket cost or how much the bill she put down was worth.[5]

Deciphering the types of work freedwomen pursued is more difficult than it would seem. The assumption that they just continued to follow the patterns of labor they had known under slavery limits the possibilities that opened for them in freedom. For the first time, freedom of movement, family connections, open communication networks, and access to education allowed them to transition into occupations inaccessible before. In addition, the narratives left by many freedwomen often conflate their labor under generic phrases, such as "I went to work for a family" or "I nussed the children." What did these expressions really mean? Certainly many did assume the primary responsibility of child care and housework. But under this umbrella statement undoubtedly lay numerous chores unrelated to either children or homemaking. The phrases also assume that freedwomen had only one occupation over the course of their lives. Many worked the land on farms and ranches. With greater familiarity with white immigrants and a larger governmental presence as well as citizenship status within their tribal groups, freedwomen pursued all of the options open to nineteenth-century women. For example, the Choctaw freedwoman Phoebe Banks became a nurse for her local community, other women became community teachers, and others started their own businesses.[6]

Some of the freedwomen began paid employment at a very young age. Polly Colbert worked for the prestigious Chickasaw Nation Bloomfield Academy, one of the finest educational institutions for Indian women in the Territory. It was not at all unusual for the wealthier girls at the school to have personal black maids. After the war ended, she began to "take care of a little girl" at the school. She left the academy after two years and returned to the home of her former mistress, who had just given birth to a child. She cared for the child and remained with the Colbert family until she was fifteen, helping her mistress through the grief of her husband's death. Polly returned to Bloomfield and stayed another three years. She then married and began her own family.[7]

While Polly Colbert's experience at Bloomfield offered a young black girl a secure employment environment, other schools were not so safe. During slavery missionary women and enslaved girls rose early to prepare breakfast at the boys' schools in the Choctaw Nation. An incident during prewar days at the prestigious Spencer Academy illustrates the possible dangers. School leaders became embarrassed by a "slave chore-girl" because of her "very loose notions" and hoped that she would leave. Little else is known about the circumstances, but the brief records inspire many questions: Was she criticized because of her own moral failings? Were the "loose notions" simply examples of a freer social interaction among Indian peoples and their slaves? Might the situation also have been one of a young girl placed in a subservient position among a group of privileged Indian males who were accustomed to liberties with enslaved women? The rules became more strict after emancipation. One Choctaw freedwoman went to work at Spencer at age thirteen immediately after the Civil War. Her chores included washing, ironing, and assisting the seamstress in making the boys' clothes. She reported that she was occasionally given permission to go into the church, but she was never allowed to attend the parties and dances. It is unlikely that the school leaders were trying to protect the young freedwomen employed there. Rather they intended to enforce segregation and prevent any personal interaction with the male students.[8]

An occupation easily accessible to single freedwomen was domestic service in the homes of the numerous white families moving into Indian Territory. Some freedwomen also found work with the military and government agencies on hand to resolve the postwar settlements. A cultural collision of Indian, white, and black experience immediately became obvious. Many of the freedwomen secured whatever domestic work they could find with both prominent Indian families and whites—washing, ironing, sewing, cooking, or caring for children—often earning no salary beyond room and board. Sometimes they earned a small sum supplemented by "totin's," that is, leftover or surplus food and cast-off clothing. Language differences, an uncertainty about money, insecurity about ex-

pected racial etiquette toward the new white families, and lack of knowledge about the rudiments of private ownership of property all created
initial confusion.

Many freedwomen knew only the language of their former masters,
or perhaps the Native language and a little conversational English.
Chaney McNair worked in white homes while in Kansas during the exile
and later in the Cherokee Nation after the war. She shared the following
humorous story with a WPA interviewer. Her employer dismissed her
from her first position after only a few hours because she did not know
how to make a fire with coal in a stove. McNair's only experience was
with a wood fire in a fireplace. When her employers told her to fill the
stove "reservoir" with water, "malgamate" the eggs, and clean the "bal-
cony," she just stared at them in puzzlement. "I didn't know white folks
language," she said, "They used so much different language, those north-
erners, I thought I'd never learn it." McNair believed that this story exposed her ignorance. In fact it illustrated the challenges of crossing the
boundary lines of race and culture in this type of domestic arrangement.[9]

Another former enslaved woman remembered learning an important
piece of racial etiquette. In addition to a certain social distance, white
homemakers demanded physical distance as well. "White folks now don't
want you to tech 'em," she said. "You kin cook for 'em and put your hands
in they vittles and they don't say nothing, but jest you tech one!" Most
freedwomen, even in unequal status, were accustomed to living in close
proximity, frequently sharing the intimate spaces of homemaking with
the Native people. Now the shared environment of woman's work no
longer seemed appropriate. Georgia judge W. O. Tuggle traveled through
Indian Territory in 1879, stopping at the church of a Creek minister, R. A.
Leslie, to attend the service. Later he and other white boarders dined at
Leslie's home, and Tuggle met his wife, whom he described as "coal
black." Tuggle complimented Mrs. Leslie in his journal on the excellent
meal she prepared but concluded his entry with, "She did not sit at the
table." Little did Tuggle realize that Nellie Ann Leslie was a northern free
black woman who had been educated at Oberlin College. Even she did
not challenge the racial etiquette with white guests. Widening experience
with whites acquainted Indian freedwomen with these new demands
about physical as well as social separateness. They backed away from

displays of familiarity and developed a new reserve around their employers and all white people. Those distinctions often had to be learned the hard way, through experience.[10]

Another occupation in which freedwomen could find employment was cooking for both the resurrecting Indian government facilities and the U.S. military and government installations. Freedwomen were familiar with the local produce, the location of edible plants in the wild, and varieties of available meats. They also knew the suppliers of goods. From long experience, they intimately knew the recipes of the favorite Indian dishes. More than a half-century later, the Creek freedwoman Lucinda Davis remembered how to make the corn dish *sofki*, adding crushed hickory nuts to give it even more flavor. Most cooking was still done out in the yard in big pots rather than in kitchens. Davis spoke rapturously about roasted corn, "all kinds of greens from out in the woods," and chopped deer, pork, turkey, and fish. Patsy Perryman too recounted the instructions for making the corn-based dishes, and opossum, raccoons, and squirrels that made up their diet. "Hit sure was fine eating dem days," she stated. Patsy and Victoria Taylor Thompson's Cherokee freedwoman mother cooked for the prisoners in the Tahlequah jail, in addition to her household duties. Prior to that, she had earned a living for her children cooking at Fort Gibson. Phyllis Petite's family returned to Indian Territory from Texas and stayed for a time with her grandmother, who was cooking for the soldiers at Fort Gibson.[11]

Younger black girls worked as assistants in the kitchens, doing the menial chores of stoking the fires, hauling water, cleaning the vegetables, and washing dishes and pots and pans. Nancy Rogers Bean reported that she peeled potatoes and helped the main cook. Rachel Ward's sister cooked for one of the officers at Fort Gibson. Rachel took care of her sister's children while she worked. She also ran errands to the commissary for her. Rachel spotted huge piles of sugar there; she would occasionally filch some and trade it for other necessities. She said the commissary officials knew that she took the sugar, but they liked her and never challenged her about the theft.[12]

When freedwomen found work at the military and governmental agencies on hand to resolve postwar settlements, they were exposed to dangers beyond those associated with former Indian masters and mistresses. Forts and posts in Indian Territory with large numbers of black and white soldiers who performed tedious, repetitive work were notorious as sites for gambling, alcohol, and violence. Although it was illegal to sell alcohol to Indians, abundant supplies made their way into Indian Territory throughout its history. Sometimes the liquor was hauled in from surrounding states and sold by freedmen, on whom there were no restrictions. Fort Gibson in particular became known as "a 'tough' place, infested with outlaws, fortune hunters and riff-raff of all creation." Positioned on the Grand River, Fort Gibson was an ideal location for debarkation. Taverns and brothels surrounded the fort. In addition to imported spirits, large supplies of intoxicating homemade "Choc" (Choctaw) beer were also available. An uneducated, homeless, and impoverished black woman might easily be enticed into occupations at these establishments where drunkenness and racial violence occurred frequently. When construction of the railroads began after 1870, they became moving locations of vice. Gibson Station was one of the worst. Black women made easy targets for rape, beatings, and murder that went unpunished. Freedwomen who became caught in these dangerous locations were no different from single, unskilled Indian and white women in the Territory who attempted to survive as best they could.[13]

A frequently overlooked role that the freedwomen played in Indian Territory was that of primary medical caregiver. Much has been written about Indian medicine women and *curanderas*, but little attention has been paid to black women who were proficient in the use of homeopathic medicines and the treatment of injuries and diseases. Prior to the Civil War, trained doctors were extremely rare in Indian Territory. Long after the war, except for military corpsmen and agency doctors, they continued to be in short supply. The commissioner of Indian affairs in 1878 ordered that all physicians employed at agencies had to be "graduates of some medical college and have the necessary diplomas." Sometimes, however, unaccredited doctors came into Indian Territory to practice because official oversight was lax. Others came long enough to earn money to return to medical school for a degree. The first organized meeting of medical doctors in Indian Territory was held in Muskogee in 1881; there they agreed to write a resolution expressing their views on the state of medical practice and the doctors in Indian Territory. The group soon dissolved, however, and a formal medical association did not begin again until 1890. Often the missionaries provided whatever medical skills they possessed along with religious instruction at their mission stations.[14]

In 1871 Henry Breiner, an Indian agent at the Seminole Agency in Wewoka, expressed particular alarm about the health conditions of the Seminole Indians. Wewoka and its surrounding area was largely populated by bands of black Seminoles. He believed that exposure, lack of seasonal clothing, inadequate housing, insufficient diet, and "the promiscuous intercourse of the sexes" would lead to their eventual extinction. Breiner requested appropriations for a hospital, inasmuch as there was no physician within sixty miles of Wewoka and both Fort Gibson and Fort Sill were more than 100 miles away. He asked not only for an experienced doctor but also for "a careful white, or other experienced, intelligent and obedient nurse." A smallpox epidemic spread throughout Indian Territory in 1882–83, causing many deaths and the demand for widespread vaccination. In the absence of doctors, black women were the first resource for nursing care in Indian Territory for most families of all races and classes.[15]

Freedwomen had grown up side by side with their Native sisters and, in spite of their unequal status, had learned the craft of making medicines and treating the sick and wounded. The Creek Nancy Grayson Barnett discussed her mother's abilities as a medicine woman with a WPA interviewer in 1937. Although Barnett was not trained as a healer and did not remember the healing words and actions her mother performed that went with the herbal cures, she detailed the preparation and uses of a vine called redroot and broom weed for curing numerous illnesses. Members of both the Grayson family and the Barnett family had owned slaves and intermarried with blacks in the distant past, and it is probable that those female descendants also knew the same information Barnett did. Plants, roots, berries, weeds, and herbs were frequently mentioned as medicines by numerous freedwomen in their 1930s narratives.[16]

The Chickasaw freedwoman Polly Colbert stated, "In de old days we made a lot of our own medicine and I still does it yet." The most common symptoms that freedwomen discussed were chills and fever, which might accompany any number of illnesses, from the common cold to tuberculosis. Colbert enumerated a long list of traditional homeopathic plants used to cure chills and fever, rheumatism, and croup. The Cherokee freedwoman Rochelle Allred Ward recounted that the older men and women dug roots and gathered herbs to use as medicine. They also created some compounds for strength and energy. The Choctaw freedwoman Kiziah Love explained, "Balmony and queen's delight boiled and mixed would make good blood medicine." The black Choctaw Jane Davis Ward continued to grow certain herbs in her yard as late as 1937 in order to treat sick patients. According to Ward, in slavery days she treated both Indians and blacks. The WPA interviewer wrote that Ward was still active and that "colored people all over Oklahoma bring their babies to her when they are sick for her to treat."[17]

The Choctaw freedwoman Frances Banks had the rare experience of both Indian cultural healing methods and a professionally trained doctor. After the Civil War, Banks's family remained with the Choctaw family who had previously enslaved them. Banks was proud to relate that she had lived close to the Choctaw Chief Allen Wright's family for sixty years and had taken care of all of his children, grandchildren, and great-grandchildren. She said that she had always enjoyed good health and had been able to do any work she wanted to do. She spent a great deal of time in the home of Dr. W. N. Wright, a leading Choctaw Nation physician, where she learned about medicine and professional nursing practices. Banks used those skills to help others. "I'se allus been willing to go an nuss de sick an 'flicted," she said, "but I allus come back home for a while." She had never been taught to read, but she created her own medicinal compound that she used on her patients. She declared that her "liniment" worked well on snake bites and was "good for nearly everything that ails you."[18]

Possession of this specialized knowledge of folk medicine empowered freedwomen within the white, Indian, and black communities of Indian Territory. Their ability to recognize appropriate plants, harvest them, preserve them, and process them into teas, potions, and liniments gave them a status higher than that of other black workers. These freedwomen were allowed the freedom of movement and shared intimate space denied to others. The ability to treat injuries and nurse the sick back to health placed them in great demand in rural areas. For other women, the presence of a black woman during the birthing process of a child created a meaningful bond not usually extended to members of another race. The familial designation "Aunt" was frequently prefixed to their first names. While this may seem belittling in present times, it carried weight greater than expressions such as "mammy." Black women commonly stayed with the family two weeks after the birth to care for the mother and child. Conversely, this same knowledge empowered freedwomen to limit their own births and to help other women control their reproduction or to escape social condemnation for births outside acceptable relationships. Cotton root, tansy, pennyroyal, camphor, and cedar berries were frequently combined into potions to bring about miscarriages.[19]

Perhaps the exemplar of a freedwoman folk doctor was Eliza Brown, wife of a Chickasaw freedman rancher, Jack Brown. Eliza handled the illnesses and emergencies for the related Chickasaw Nation Campbell and Johnson families. Neil Johnson wrote that Eliza was the "doctor and nurse combined for most of their troubles." Eliza was an expert at devising innovative ways to deal with difficult situations. One of Montford Johnson's sons lived only a few months after birth. Mary Johnson had been nursing her baby, and after his death, her breasts became painfully engorged. "Aunt" Eliza took a pup from a newborn litter of dogs on the ranch, wrapped its feet, and allowed it to suckle. The innovative breast pump worked well, and Mary became fit again. Eliza treated toothaches by placing tobacco on the infected tooth and holding a bag of hot ashes against the jaw. She soothed burns with molasses and baking soda, made poultices out of tobacco and earwax for insect bites, and a chest cold received a hot foot bath and a heated flannel wrap coated with a mixture of lard, kerosene, and turpentine. She even operated as a last resort on one of the Campbell men who had a raging fever. After she made a small incision, she used a cow horn to suction out the blood. In spite of her best efforts, however, this patient did not survive. Even after her marriage to Jack Brown, Eliza continued to be sought after in illness and emergencies. No longer enslaved by the Campbell family, she held a position of trust and respect as a free woman.[20]

Along with the ability to treat the sick, freedwomen also assumed the responsibility of Christian funeral services in their communities. They washed the body of the deceased, anointed it with fragrant oils, clothed it, and prepared the inside lining of the casket. They then sat with the body in prayer and sang hymns until it was time for a religious service and burial. Gendered religious history and understandings prevented freedwomen from becoming ordained ministers of the gospel. Although some of the Indian Territory freedwomen recounted Native burial practices, none of the freedwomen in this study mentioned a female preacher. However, the freedwomen presided over the most critical human moments, those of the beginning and the ending of life. By the turn of the century, freedwomen had transformed this cultural responsibility into a business. Mrs. O. H. Bradley and Mrs. Mattie Armstrong, for example, were part owners of the Burial and Funeral Association of Boley, one of the larger all-black communities of Indian Territory.[21]

Teaching was another prestigious position open to freedwomen with literacy in English or some education. The greatest desire of the freed people in Indian Territory was for schools for their children. In a letter to the U.S. secretary of war, Assistant Commissioner J. W. Sprague wrote, "The freedmen of the territory as elsewhere show a desire for schools to enable them to educate their children, that from the first has seemed to me remarkable." Education represented an avenue of escape from drudgery and poverty and a yardstick of their advancement within their Indian nations. Families struggled to build and operate local schools and to keep their children attending. More often, black parents attempted to keep their daughters attending school longer than their sons. Boys could find employment and earn higher wages than girls, but having a daughter in the family become a teacher held high prestige. Teaching offered their daughters a respectable vocation and a brighter future for their grandchildren. The black Choctaw freedwoman Milley Franklin, educated at Armstrong Academy, taught school to all of the local children, including her own ten children, on her husband's ranch in what is now Carter County, Oklahoma. The one-room schoolhouse, built and funded by David Franklin, who could neither read nor write, overflowed with pupils.[22]

The effect on the lives of freedwomen and their children of having educated black teachers was incomparable. The Cherokee freedwoman Patsy Perryman remembered, "[I was] a big girl when I learn the letters and how to write." She tried to teach her mother but was unsuccessful. Perryman became the person who wrote to Washington for her family and many others in her community when the Indian lands were allotted to individual owners at the turn of the century. Elzora Lewis, the daugh-

Freedwomen, top left, attending a Cherokee Teachers Institute, 1890. Courtesy of the Western History Collections, University of Oklahoma Libraries, Ballenger Collection 22.

ter of a Choctaw/Creek freed couple, also related how important her "academic training" was. She told a WPA fieldworker in 1937 that she had attended a Baptist missionary school opened by a Creek minister, Robert A. Leslie. Leslie's educated black wife, Nellie Ann, taught at the Evangel Mission. "Her services were invaluable in the training of the students," Lewis said. Nellie Ann Leslie also operated a boardinghouse in their home where female students were taught home economics. The school was associated with Minister J. S. Murrow of Bacone College, and Lewis's grandmother Susie Bruner Scott was the treasurer of the school. Educated black teachers provided the building blocks of respectability and success for generations of the children of freedmen. Clara Vann lived out that model of generational improved circumstances. She worked as a matron and laundress for the Cherokee Nation Colored High School when it opened in 1890. She watched with pride her granddaughter, Lelia Swepston Ross, graduate from the school in 1908.[23]

Tullahassee Freedmen's School, near Muskogee, Indian Territory, 1890.
Reprinted by permission of the Research Division of the Oklahoma Historical
Society.

Agriculture constituted the backbone of Indian Territory prosperity, and the sooner it could recover from the war, the better it would be for everyone. Freedwomen in great numbers began farming and ranching either on their own or with their husbands. They went into the fields with their husbands and children in a seasonal cycle of backbreaking labor. Betty Robertson's master, the wealthy Joe Vann, told his slaves they were free, but all he offered if they stayed with him was food and clothes. The first thing Robertson's widowed mother did when she was told that they were free to leave was to get a wagon and two oxen. She and the children went to Fort Gibson first, then moved a short distance away and began farming. "We worked a good size patch there until she died," Robertson remembered. Robertson then married and began her own family. Freedwomen recognized their disadvantage when selling the crops they had labored so long to produce, so they sometimes sold their harvest to their former masters or negotiated through them rather than outsiders, believing they could trust them to make a fair deal.[24]

Small farms of ten to twenty acres characterized the agricultural pattern in Indian Territory after the Civil War. Most of the land was devoted to self-sustaining crops such as corn, oats, hay, vegetables, fruits, and sorghum. The exception to this pattern was the large plantations along the Red and Arkansas rivers that had been developed by the mixed-blood Indian elite who engaged in large-scale cotton production using slave labor. Since slavery was now abolished, those plantation owners turned to noncitizen workers from the surrounding states who were allowed to enter the Territory to work for the Indians under a permit system. Freedmen families began to cultivate areas of the tribal common lands on their own. Indian agents, as they had prior to the Civil War, encouraged the development of cotton as a cash crop. After the 1870s diversified agriculture remained predominant, but cotton production grew into a major enterprise, increasing dramatically in acreage every decade. Cotton, corn, and livestock became the three principal agricultural pursuits of the people of Indian Territory through the end of the century. The 1900 census counted 535 black female farmers, 474 female farm laborers on home farms, and 196 female laborers working outside their own lands.[25]

Black women, like their Native sisters who farmed the land, embraced the work not as an occupation but as a life. They contributed their labor to every aspect of the farm and home production as well as bearing and raising the children and creating a comfortable home. Along with their husbands, they marshaled the help of both male and female children from the time they could do simple chores such as feeding the chickens until they were capable of more elaborate work, such as fence building and plowing. Women tilled the family garden and canned and preserved the harvest. They cooked, washed, sewed, and cleaned with limited resources. They went into the fields and plowed, planted, chopped, and picked cotton and corn, always conscious of the weather and the market prices. They held on tightly to the hope that the following year would produce a better crop and better circumstances. In 1988, at 100, Emma Rentie Harrison discussed her early life in Indian Territory with a reporter from the *Oklahoma Eagle*. Harrison's Creek freedman father operated a ferry on the Arkansas River. She told the reporter that her mother, Rebecca, raised the children and helped her husband farm 160 acres of cotton, corn, hogs, chickens, ducks, geese, and "everything like that."

In the interview she said, "I was a home girl. . . . I helped mother with my twin brothers. . . . I'm no 'goodtime' woman. . . . I came up the old way." While still in her teens, she married and replicated her mother's role of farmworker and wife to her husband.[26]

Unlike their native sisters, freedwomen could never feel entirely secure about retaining the resources they worked so hard to accrue. While the Cherokee, Creek, and Seminole Nations fulfilled the 1866 U.S. treaty demands to incorporate their freedmen as citizens with equal rights, the Choctaw Nation acquiesced to that rule only in 1885. Over time they allowed their freedmen and women forty acres. The Chickasaw Nation never bent to the government's will on citizenship, although they too eventually allowed their freed people forty acres. Regardless of the nation the freed people belonged to, however, their rights as developers of the common lands were frequently abused. Indian citizens and white permit holders, now flooding Indian Territory, often fenced-off lands already improved by the freedmen, cut down their trees, or lawlessly raided and burned out black settlements. Inasmuch as Chickasaw freedmen were not citizens, they had little redress for their losses. In 1874 Commissioner of Indian Affairs Edward P. Smith reported that the freedmen "are obliged to expend their labor upon farms to which they have no title, and which once well improved are not infrequently taken from them." Years of hard work and careful tending could vanish overnight.[27]

Conflicts like these many times led to violence and bitter reprisals or, just as tragically, created transient families of freedmen seeking safety in all-black communities. The strong-willed Queenia Z. Rouce took action even though her husband refused to defend their property. James Rouce, an Arkansas immigrant, developed a successful farm, bought part ownership in a mill, and became active in black politics. According to family memories, he could reach these heights of success because his wife managed the children and the farm single-handedly. On one occasion some white men stole the Rouce horses. James refused to chase after the thieves, but Queenia would not be so easily duped. She tracked down the horse thieves and set up an ambush. When they agreed to surrender the horses, she took home only those belonging to her and let them keep the ones that belonged to her husband.[28]

Kiziah Love and Mary Lindsay represent examples of freedwomen who worked the land along with their husbands and endured the conflicting currents of Indian Territory as the lands filled with permit holders and intruders both black and white. Kiziah managed to retain her land and continued to live on it at the time of her WPA interview in the 1930s. She had been enslaved by Frank and Julie Colbert. Before the Civil War she married Isom Love, then enslaved by Sam Love, a neighbor on adjoining land. They had one child when the war came. They built a log cabin halfway between the two farms and went back and forth daily to work for their masters. Kiziah thought this freedom of movement was available only because both of their owners were Indian. She remembered, "They let us do a lot like we pleased jest so we got our work done and didn't run off." In her elder years Kiziah remained on her forty acres with her son, one of fifteen children. Mary Lindsay was not so fortunate. She returned to Indian Territory in 1887 with her husband, Henry, and together they farmed land in the Creek Nation with their four children. When the Indian lands were allotted, Mary and Henry's land was given to a Creek Indian. "After while he makes us move off," she said, "and we lose out all around."[29]

Mary Lindsay was one of the freedwomen who discussed the work she had done as a young girl that prepared her for life as a farmwife. She had extensive experience with livestock and the rigors of farm labor. During slavery she had been responsible for numerous outdoor chores. Besides chopping and hauling firewood, "[she] got to feed all the stock and milk the cows and work in the field too," she remembered. On one occasion her regular team of oxen refused to pull the plow. When she tried another team, the oxen charged her, forcing her to run for her life. Another time she suffered a broken arm when she attempted to juggle a full pail of milk, a barn gate, and her horse's reins. When the wind slammed the gate shut, her arm became entangled in the reins of her frightened horse, which ran away, dragging Mary behind him. The Creek freedwoman Mary Grayson remembered that her mother, in addition to many other tasks, herded cattle. Those freedwomen who lived on the land outside of the small communities growing up in Indian Territory became more than helpmates to their husbands; they had to function as extra farm hands and ranch hands in order for the family to survive and prosper.[30]

Milley Franklin's life and death best represent the demands, both public and private, on the freedwomen. From outward appearances she seemed the epitome of success. She had been raised as a Choctaw, loved and educated by her Choctaw father. She was married to a successful rancher whose father had bought his family's freedom years before, and was beloved by her children. Her community and church respected her and cherished her as the local schoolteacher. While on a trip attempting to gather evidence of her citizenship by blood in the Choctaw Nation, she came down with a fever. As she lingered in bed during the weeks of fall, she could only instruct her husband and nine older children on the chores that needed to be done. Her son, Buck Colbert Franklin, later wrote, "This was the busiest season of the year at home. It was hog-killing time and there were a thousand chores to do."

She kept insisting that she would be better, but as she grew weaker, a series of doctors were called in to assess her illness. Buck overheard the family doctor tell his father, "Millie will not recover. She is literally worn out. Teaching school, going from dawn to dusk, and many times far into the night, having babies, . . . and doing a thousand and one other things, have used up her strength." The family was devastated by the news. She seemed to rally as Christmas approached, but on Christmas morning she gathered all of the children around her. She asked her eldest daughter, Dolores, to be a mother to the new baby, and she urged the rest to remember the lessons she and their father had taught them. She died on Christmas day 1886. Earlier, when the doctor delivered the news that she would not survive the illness, he had attempted to console her husband, telling him, "She knows she will not recover, and don't you feel bad about it. She would not have had it any other way." Millie Franklin represented the strength, character, and perseverance that life in Indian Territory demanded of the freedwomen, and her death illustrated the human cost.[31]

Not all freedwomen lived in isolated rural areas, however. Wewoka had always been heavily populated by black Seminoles and Muskogee by black Creeks. Small communities of blacks had existed before the Civil War, but postwar conditions caused them to grow into sizable all-black settlements and towns. The desire for protection, mutual interests, a shared history, and feelings of kinship created an environment for the freedmen to unite their resources and to experience an independence they had not known before. Approximately twenty-five all-black towns existed in Indian Territory before Oklahoma statehood in 1907. The oldest town, Tullahassee, dated as far back as 1850. Soon after the Civil War, Creek freedmen organized three such towns, known as North Fork Colored, Arkansas Colored, and Canadian Colored. Although the greatest growth occurred after large numbers of noncitizen freedmen immigrated into Indian Territory, many of the black towns emerged out of earlier Indian freedmen settlements. Twine (later renamed Taft), for example, began originally as a small community of Muscogee Creek freedmen.[32]

Indian freedwomen and immigrant freedwomen mingled in these all-black communities, but relationships were not always cordial. Immigrant freedwomen considered the Indian freedwomen backward and lazy. As Alafair Carter Adams reported, the Native freedmen expected an easy life and "lived up everything before they wanted to do anything." Indian freedwomen, however, had experienced a position of belonging within

All-black towns of Oklahoma by 1907. Reprinted by permission of the Research Division of the Oklahoma Historical Society.

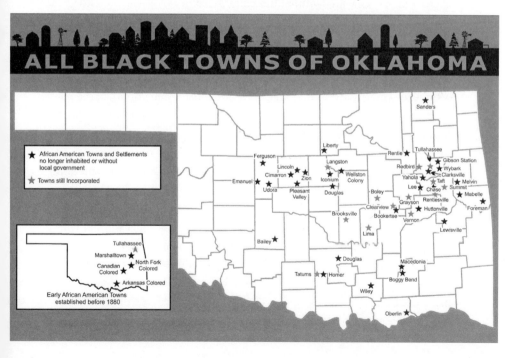

their Indian nations and had access to land, allowing them a moderate standard of living. They feared the loss of their lands to these outsiders through fraud and the deterioration of their own status as the number of black newcomers increased. The new immigrants had not been part of the long history with the Five Nations and were now either permit holders on the Indian lands or considered intruders. In both cases they had lived a different form of slavery than the Indian freedwomen. In addition, the Native freedwomen were a minority. In the early days, Native-born blacks in Boley and Clearview constituted only 10 percent of the population. At the same time, white officials, businessmen, permit holders, and intruders also invaded the Indian lands. It seemed to the freedwomen that the black immigrants were not only poor, ignorant, and dishonest but lacking in self-respect and too subservient to whites. As one Creek freedman commented, "I was eating out of the same pot with the Indians . . . while they were still licking the master's boots in Texas." Immigrant blacks were given the name *Watchina*, meaning "white man's Negroes." In addition, as the flood of newcomers increased over time, both the Indian peoples and the Indian freed people were overwhelmed by resident aliens, black and white, without the cultural history of Indian Territory.[33]

Still, Indian freedwomen and immigrant freedwomen took responsibility for providing for their families and educating their children by whatever means possible. They overcame their differences for the benefit of the whole group. Where there were concentrations of population, there were also opportunities for female entrepreneurs. Freedwomen in the all-black communities opened shops and businesses in conjunction with those of their husbands or as sole proprietors. Interestingly the WPA slave narratives provide scant information about these enterprises. Their emphasis reflected the desire of the fieldworkers to capture information about Indian folkways, slavery, and the Civil War. But it is also likely that the enterprises were barely mentioned because the Indian freedwomen had fewer liquid capital resources than the immigrant black women who came as part of families or in community groups. A careful review of the black newspapers published by the larger black towns reveals the network of black freedwomen's business initiatives. Women married to prominent black businessmen or professionals, the wives of Indian nation officeholders, and schoolteachers not only set the cultural tone for the black towns but promoted and patronized the shops of their male and female residents. Married women, widows, and daughters engaged in businesses to supplement their income and to increase the prestige and prosperity of their communities.

Boley and Clearview were two of the largest of the all-black towns. Among the early female-run businesses in Boley were Mrs. J. H. Bagby's drugstore, Mrs. M. W. Brown's grocery store, Mollie Robinson's grocery store, and Mrs. A. E. Stephenson's general store. Mrs. Nodie Tieuel and Mrs. Annie Cowan both ran millinery shops. Nodie Tieuel also taught school in Boley. Several women, such as Mrs. Mary Reynolds Ashley and Mrs. Clara Boykin Williams, were independent dressmakers operating out of their homes. Mrs. Maymie Morris Jones taught music at the Creek and Seminole school and gave private music lessons to Boley residents. Francis B. Berry owned a "first class" café, with meals ordered from menu folders. Many of the Boley women worked several jobs simultaneously as teachers, homemakers, and managers of their husbands' mercantile stores. Hilliard Taylor owned the Boley Cotton Gin and marketed lumber, while his wife sold hair care products as the local agent of the French System of hair straightening. California Taylor Turner managed the drugstore owned by her banker husband. Booker T. Washington's inspiring rhetoric and example of "uplift" moved west with the migrants and unified the women in their efforts to build prosperous, independent communities of black pride and self-determination.[34]

The female-run businesses were less grand than the banks, lumber yards, and cotton gins, which required large amounts of capital, but their services to the growing communities were just as important. Newspapers in the black towns gave equal space to advertisements for the female-run enterprises, and in editorials frequently applauded the efforts of the working women. The *Clearview Patriarch* praised Miss Rebecca Grayson for her work in the grocery store. Maggie Aikens's boardinghouse and Mrs. B. Goen's ice cream parlor also received extensive advertisement space, as did Mrs. J. H. and Miss Amanda Cummings's sundry store. The newspapers were especially pleased to report on new arrivals with strong educational backgrounds; these were the women who worked as stenographers, notaries, secretaries for local law firms, the town site manager's office, and the post office and, of course, in the schools. Miss Scott Herriford, a recent graduate of the business course at Western University in Kansas City, assisted the Boley city attorney in rewriting the city's ordinances. A front-page article in the *Boley Informer* praised Herriford as "quite an intellectual young lady" and assured her of Boley's patronage. Most of the women mentioned here joined together to organize the Boley Ladies Industrial Club in 1908. They took on the responsibility of serving the social, economic, and benevolent needs of the community. Members not only stimulated financial growth through their investment and labor, but they also united to provide social services for the aid of less fortunate Boley residents.[35]

For the first time, the freedwomen in Indian Territory made their own decisions about where, when, and how to support themselves and earn a living. They brought to freedom all of the employment skills they had performed during slavery, but the circumstances were far different. They had to learn immediately how to navigate the uncertain terrain of a country that contained powerful white people and, in some of the nations, resentful Indians. The U.S. government intervened in their lives to secure for them access to Indian land so that they could be self-sufficient. Many of the officials, however, were ignorant of their relationships to their former masters and the cultural roles assigned to women of the Five Nations. They insisted on regulations that conformed to traditional white American standards of female submission, not realizing that in many circumstances these arrangements fit neither Native patterns nor black family conditions.

Many freedwomen were forced to learn quickly the English language of eastern Americans, the types and value of the money circulating in Indian Territory, and the ability to negotiate skillfully labor agreements with their employers. The short period of transformation in their lives was remarkable. They seized every opportunity to improve the quality of their lives and to prepare their children for a world of new opportunities. Freedwomen entered employment familiar to them, that of cooks, domestic workers, and child caregivers, but they also perfected roles in high demand by the rapidly changing environment. In the absence of trained doctors, they became the chief source of medical assistance in Indian Territory; with improving opportunities for education, they stepped into humble rural classrooms and brought literacy to red, white, and black children.

Most freedwomen performed a combination of labor. They worked on farms alone and with their husbands, raised the children, taught school, and nursed the sick. There was some gendered division of labor on the farms of Indian Territory freed people. Men were less likely to perform housekeeping and child-rearing chores except in cases of emergency. Women were just as likely as men to shoulder outdoor and agricultural tasks. Women worked side by side with their husbands to dig wells and build fences, plow and harvest, as well as feed the chickens, milk the cows, and tend the garden. They became accustomed to their roles as both productive and reproductive workers. They worked for more than just the present; they were earnest in establishing a future for themselves and their children.

In the growing all-black communities of Indian Territory, the Indian freedwomen encountered a new kind of freedwoman, one without the cultural heritage of a lifetime spent with the Indian nations. The Indian freedwomen and immigrant freedwomen learned to work together to create showcases of independence, pride, and prosperity. Concentrations of population brought opportunities for female business ventures. The freedwomen embraced all of these new possibilities to work toward the accumulation of assets. They adopted the ethic of incipient capitalists.

More than opportunities for steady employment and economic solvency, however, directed the lives of the freedwomen. As early as the 1870s both positive and negative forces affected their views of the world. The influence of Christian missionaries and the increasing possibilities for education shaped a new understanding of their potential for independent lives in Indian Territory. Suddenly they found themselves socially linked no longer with the Indian peoples but with the escalating numbers of black immigrants from the southern states. The racial composition of Indian Territory changed so rapidly that they became overwhelmed by white Americans and their racial prejudices. National demands for the opening of Indian lands to non-Indian settlement and incorporation into the United States made the freed people more conscious than ever of the need for self-preservation in stable, close-knit communities. Freedwomen directed their energies toward building the social foundations of those communities.

## Chapter Five

# Building Communities

"The good Lord knows I'm glad slavery is over.
Now I can stay peaceful in one place."

Nancy Rogers Bean, in Baker and Baker,
*The WPA Oklahoma Slave Narratives*

Immediately after the Civil War, the most important concerns for the freedwomen, regardless of their location, centered on the essential needs of survival: food, shelter, and clothing for themselves and their children in the midst of postwar scarcity. Next came the desire to reestablish family ties and kinship networks. Finally, they sought to find sustainable work and to build homes and communities. By the last decades of the century they were to realize, however, that the ongoing clash of interest groups, government policies, and immigration into Indian Territory caused momentous changes to their lives, some nearly as significant as emancipation had. These forces would completely redefine their relationships, their freedom of action, and their identity. The Reconstruction treaties signed with the Five Nations in 1866 precipitated the conditions that opened Indian Territory to examination by the larger population and institutions of the United States. Indian Territory and its natural resources were "discovered" by business interests caught up in the accelerating industrialization process forging the growth of the United States. Religious and educational organizations now considered all the people of Indian Territory fertile ground for mission work. Baptist, Presbyterian, and Methodist denominations were predominant in this field. Black leaders and freedmen from the South, disappointed in the violent environment and limited freedoms of Jim Crow racial policy, looked west to the possibilities of a new and less rigid frontier. Freedwomen watched the world they had known slip quickly away, to be replaced with a world of larger opportunities and greater dangers. In this process new relationships and connections with immigrant freedwomen were consummated.

Christian missionaries had been active in Indian Territory since the time of the removal of the Five Nations from their southeastern homelands. Some of the missionary families made the overland journey with the Indian peoples and experienced the hardships of rebuilding homes and mission stations in a raw, undeveloped area. Indian, black, and white people worshipped together in these early times. For example, Ebenezer Church, the first black Baptist church in Indian Territory, was organized in 1832 by Rev. and Mrs. David Lewis, white missionaries to the Creeks. Charter members included three black slaves and one Creek Indian. By 1836 the church had grown substantially. Rev. David Rollin wrote an account of the church's work that year for the *Baptist Missionary Magazine*. He reported that services had been held every Sunday except one, and he had instituted a temperance pledge, which all members had signed. Church membership, including himself, his wife, and one female assistant, totaled eighty-two: six whites, twenty-two Indians, and fifty-four blacks. By 1842 black pastors known only as Jack and Jacob held a revival and baptized 100 Indian, black, and white congregants. The question of Christianizing the enslaved people of the Indians grew more contentious in the 1850s, and with the onset of the Civil War many of the missionaries were forced to flee their churches for safer ground elsewhere in the United States.[1]

Peace brought renewed interest in Indian Territory for religious propagation not only among the Indian peoples but among their emancipated slaves as well. Now missionaries had no restraints placed upon their efforts by overly cautious slaveholders. By 1870 there were three black Baptist churches in the Cherokee Nation, and in 1872 two churches from the Choctaw and Chickasaw Nations formed an association in Atoka. All of these churches were integrated, but as time passed, a racial divide became more apparent and pronounced. The North Fork Church proved typical of the process. The congregation, ministered by Harry Islands, a former Cherokee slave, saw their racial composition slowly change. One observer wrote that the church continued to prosper as a black church, "but the Indians shied off from it, since the Blacks were in the majority, and now free." The original Baptist leaders fought against segregation as long as possible, hoping to retain one body of faith in Indian Territory, but by 1891 the Baptist Missionary and Educational Convention set formal division in motion. Their message, addressed to "Our African Brethren," recommended that they "organize themselves into a territorial convention" since the older states had "deemed [it] wisest and best" for the black churches to have their own, separate conventions. Freedwomen who attended these churches lost long-standing friendships, sometimes relatives, and sources of mutual support as these congregations became segregated.[2]

While Baptist churches represented the majority among the freedmen in Indian Territory, other denominations also began to develop followings. The attorney Buck Colbert Franklin outlined the role his mother and father, Milley and David Franklin, played in the arrival of a Colored Methodist Episcopal Church (CME) minister in the little community of Homer several years after the Civil War. One of the Franklins' relatives accompanied the arrival of the new minister, and quite a disturbance followed. The African American Baptist minister, Reverend Davis, refused to allow the new CME minister access to his church building for services. He loudly proclaimed that he was sure the "Negroes" in the Chickasaw Nation had never heard of a church other than the Baptist church. He was certain that they would not believe there was any other kind of church and that the Bible said there could not be any other. The news of the new CME church spread quickly beyond the Chickasaw Nation borders and appeared in a few of the Territory newspapers. "It was sheer temerity for this new and strange sect, or for any sect, to challenge the 'faith' of Negroes in the Territory," Buck Franklin later wrote. Buck's father faced a serious dilemma. Although a Baptist himself, and a deacon in Reverend Davis's church, David Franklin believed in freedom of worship. Any help he gave to the new minister, however, risked his removal from the Baptist church leadership. Milley Franklin therefore took the lead. She

quietly provided counsel to the CME minister, and through her interven-
tion the new church took root. Women frequently worked in interior ways
such as this to accomplish what men believed they could not publicly do.[3]

The Presbyterian denomination had also been very active in Indian
Territory from the time of Indian Removal. By the Civil War, Presbyterian
missionaries had established sixteen churches among the Five Nations in
Indian Territory. In addition, they had built six boarding schools and six
day schools. The same issues that rent the nation apart also split religious
denominations. All of the Territory Presbyterian churches closed during
the war. Rev. Alexander Reid, the superintendent of Spencer Academy, a
well-known male boarding school in the Choctaw Nation, stayed on
through the war years and became increasingly concerned about the desperate conditions of the freedmen. He took the lead in promoting the
cause of the Indian Territory freed people to national church officials. It
was through his transmission that the hymns sung by Wallace and Minerva Willis, former Choctaw slaves, made their way into the songbook
of the famous Jubilee Singers. While visiting New York in 1871, Reid re-
hearsed the singing group in the songs he had heard from "Uncle Wallace" and "Aunt Minerva," such as "Steal Away to Jesus," "The Angels
Are Coming," "I'm a Rolling," and "Swing Low, Sweet Chariot." Through
the Jubilee Singers the music of the Indian Territory freedmen became
famous all over the world.[4]

At his headquarters in Atoka, Choctaw Nation, Reid took charge in
1882 of the mission work among the freedmen. The southern branch of
the church had continued some work after the war, but it would not be
until 1879 that the Presbyterian Board of Foreign Missions sent four ministers out to the Choctaw, Creek, and Cherokee Nations. In 1883 the Pres-
bytery of Indian Territory was re-created with eleven churches. The next
year the Presbyterian Board of Missions for Freedmen received the records of the work accomplished by the black minister Rev. Charles W.
Stewart since 1867. Stewart had established five churches among the
freedmen settlements; the following year he added two more churches to
his circuit. It was also in 1884 that the Presbyterian Church hierarchy recruited their female members to work on behalf of the freedmen and
their families. In the first three years, the contributions from the Women's
Missionary Societies increased fivefold and led to the creation and sup-

port of numerous boarding schools and day schools and salaries for their teachers.[5]

When the Indian freedwomen shared their reminiscences to the WPA fieldworkers in the 1930s, many of them mentioned their Christian faith. Victoria Taylor Thompson told the interviewer, "I been belonging to church ever since there was a colored church." Betty Robertson remembered her baptism in the Grand River. Her master, Joe Vann, allowed his slaves church and singing but no instruction in reading or books. After he freed her, she left with her mother for Fort Gibson. A large group of freedmen were gathered at a camp meeting there. It was wintertime with snow on the ground and ice in the water, but Betty was baptized. She proudly remembered, "The Cherokees and the soldiers all come down to see the baptizing." Charlotte Johnson White said that she joined the Baptist church "a long time after the war is over and everybody is free of dey masters." Phyllis Petite settled along with many other families in an area she referred to as Four Mile Branch. She reported that her grandmother had helped to start the church there and added, "I think everybody ought to belong to some church."[6]

The freedwomen narratives revealed a fascinating blend of African, Indian, and white cultural reflections with regard to religion and beliefs. Some of their customs reflected the influence of African indigenous customs; in addition, the women were familiar with both Native American religious practices and the Protestant observances followed by some of their former Christian masters. The freedwomen sometimes integrated all three into their practices. Many of them reported that they believed in visions, spirits, and ghosts, at the same time professing traditional articles of Christian faith. Sometimes these visions had overt racial overtones. Some of the freedwomen also wore special charms or carried tokens for safety, good luck, or prevention from harm. When Chaney McNair was asked if she believed in spirits, she replied, "Sure I do. Sometimes the spirits of folks what's dead come back." She recounted the vision of a beautiful little white girl who had died while McNair was in exile in Kansas. At the time McNair wondered why "God made [her] black and ugly and that little girl so white." The little girl appeared to McNair in dreams several times over the years, and she believed that when her time to die came, the little girl would come back and accompany her to heaven.

Kiziah Love said that she had not seen many spirits, then added, "But I've seen a few." Once, when she was very ill, she talked with a ghost who came into her home and wanted her to leave with him. He seemed so real to her that she made her brother hunt for tracks around their property. In preparing for her own future death, Frances Banks spoke of rejoining her old friends in heaven. "If our skins here are black, dey won't be no colors in Heaven. Our souls will all be white," she said.[7]

Betty Robertson told the fieldworker that she had been a good Christian since her baptism. "But I keep a little charm here on my neck anyways," she admitted. The charm contained a buckeye and a lead bullet that she believed would ward off nosebleeds. Kiziah Love kept a butcher knife under her mattress for protection against intruders and spirits. Matilda Poe said that she no longer believed in charms, but she knew of people "keeping all kinds of things for good luck charms." As a child she had worn necklaces she called "charm strings," with buttons on them that different people had given to her. Her grandmother told her ghost stories, and she remembered that when the children misbehaved, they were threatened with stories of "Old Raw Head and Bloody Bones" coming for bad children. Many of the freedwomen maintained an internal syncretistic faith.[8]

In addition to these churches, hundreds of small community churches grew up in the settlements of the freedmen. Many of them came together after camp meetings where preaching might go on for days. The Cherokee freedman Dennis Vann outlined a series of camp meetings held in 1867 by lay preachers up and down the Grand River, at Saline and Webbers Falls, and on Spavinaw Creek. In addition to the religious services, Vann said, church members would contribute beef, hogs, and chickens free to those in attendance to be used for communal meals. Religion, community, and social welfare, traditional among the Indians of the Five Nations, combined to improve the circumstances of all who struggled after the war.[9]

For most of these small rural churches, there was no formal affiliation, and services often consisted of singing, praying, and professing without trained ministers or written liturgies. Lay leaders led the congregants in hymns and Bible verses and sometimes highly emotional services that included shouting, crying, falling to the ground, and fits. More educated and proper white clergy found these meetings embarrassing, if not very frightening. Eliza Hartford, Presbyterian missionary to the Choctaws at the Oak Hill Church near Valiant, Oklahoma, described one of her first services at the primitive log church in a letter to a friend in 1887. After a full morning of Sunday school and two hours of afternoon singing and preaching by the black church elder, he issued the call for membership. A woman fell into a swoon, Hartford wrote: "It occurred to me they were getting up one of their 'feelin' meetin's' as they call them, and I was frightened half out of my wits." Thinking things would only get worse, Hartford ran out of the church. She called the preacher to her room later and gave him a stern lecture. She also told her amused schoolchildren that "shouting and falling in fits is not religion." Explaining to her friend, she wrote, "They have had enough preaching to make them think they are religious, but have had no real Bible teaching."[10]

The missionary work among freedmen in Indian Territory concentrated in certain areas, especially those with large populations. The most active region lay in the Creek Nation, with many churches in and around the Muskogee area. In the Cherokee Nation, freedwomen continued to attend Cherokee-language Christian services for quite some time. Chaney Richardson told a WPA fieldworker that she had been an active "church-goer" all her life, until she became too feeble to attend. She could still speak and understand the Cherokee language, and she loved "to hear songs and parts of the Bible in it": "It make me think about the time I was a little girl before my mammy and pappy leave me." The Seminole freedmen received the least attention. The Baptist leadership in the Seminole Nation was controlled by highly acculturated Seminole ministers. Membership peaked in 1883, but according to the historian Kevin Mulroy, "the great majority of Seminoles remained unaffected by Baptist influence." The Presbyterian churches appealed to the more traditional Seminoles, but as a numerous denomination they fared even worse than the Baptists. At the time of Oklahoma statehood in 1907, only 20 to 25 percent of the Seminole population was Christian.[11]

Missionary schools developed side by side with the churches, and here the response was overwhelming. The Oak Hill Presbyterian Church was organized in 1869 in the Choctaw Nation. This was one of the churches administered by the Choctaw freedman Rev. Charles W. Stewart, who had been educated during slavery by the missionary Cyrus

Kingsbury. The Choctaw Nation provided some funds for a school at the log church until 1886. In addition, between 1885 and 1886 the Choctaw Nation established thirty-four schools for their freed people. A series of Native-born teachers, both male and female, taught three-month sessions. They daily witnessed the disparity between their inadequate training and resources as compared with the nearby prestigious Spencer and Wheelock Academies for Choctaw children.[12]

In 1886 the Choctaw freedmen appealed to the Presbyterian Board of Missions for Freedmen for a boarding school to train their young people to become teachers. Eliza Hartford arrived in February of 1886 and immediately set to work. A week after her arrival she held her first Sunday school at the church house and opened a school with seven students. One week later her class had grown to fourteen, and by April twenty-four students were boarding with her at the school. At this point she organized a women's prayer meeting that resulted in building a kitchen at the west end of the church. By the following year, Hartford needed an additional teacher, and Priscilla Haymaker joined her. She and Haymaker solicited funds during the summer to furnish the schoolhouse. Lacking any available labor except for a small boy, together they wielded hammer and saw to make the bedsteads and tables themselves. When school opened in September, sixty students enrolled. The heat, limited supplies, and arduous work took their toll on both of the women. Hartford wrote to a friend, "I am not so strong, in fact feel ten years older than one year ago. . . . It is the constant hard work and miserable way of living that makes it so bad."[13]

By 1888 Eliza Hartford could no longer physically continue her labors, but she had permanently established what became Oak Hill Industrial Academy. Mr. and Mrs. James McBride replaced Hartford in 1889, and a number of new female assistants, including Bettie Stewart, a black teacher, joined their school. One of the first actions the new administration took was to build a Girls' Hall. This building represented the first truly comfortable living quarters for teachers and students at the school. Oak Hill School educated numerous Choctaw freedmen children and sent them on to higher education outside of Indian Territory and to careers in the ministry and teaching. Many of the young women, including Celestine Hodges, were sent to Scotia Seminary in North Carolina and returned to teach at Oak Hill. Two of Rev. Charles W. Stewart's daughters

Eliza Hartford and Priscilla Haymaker at Oak Hill Industrial Academy, n.d. From
Robert Flickinger, *The Choctaw Freedmen and the Story of Oak Hill Industrial
Academy* (Fonda, Iowa: Journal and Times, 1914).

became teachers after they returned from Allen Seminary in Texas. Even
those who did not become teachers, however, received the gift of literacy,
which enabled them to achieve a better quality of life than they would
otherwise have had.[14]

Neither the Cherokees, Choctaws, nor Chickasaws allowed freedwomen to attend the modern, well-provisioned boarding schools, such as
the Cherokee Female Seminary, Wheelock Academy, or Bloomfield
Academy, that they had established for their own daughters. An act of
fate, however, transferred one of the oldest and most prestigious missions in Indian Territory into the hands of the freedmen. A Presbyterian
missionary, William Schenck Robertson, established the Tullahassee
Mission and Manual Labor School for the Muscogee Creeks in 1849. He
brought his new bride, Ann Eliza Worcester Robertson, daughter of the
esteemed Cherokee missionary Samuel Austin Worcester, to the mission
station in 1850. Together they built an important educational facility for
the Creeks that inspired respect and ultimately led to the preservation of

Mrs. D. C. Constant School, Seminole Nation, ca. 1900. Reprinted by permission of the Research Division of the Oklahoma Historical Society.

the Creek language and traditions for posterity. Near Christmas in 1880, in the midst of a long and especially cold and snowy winter, a third-floor chimney caught fire and badly damaged the main building. Exhausting efforts to save the school and rebuild some of the damaged buildings compromised Robertson's health, and he died later in the spring.[15]

The Creek Council offered the remaining structures and 100 acres of land to the black Creeks and provided funds to rebuild the school. With help from the American Baptist Home Mission Society the school re-opened in 1883 as the Tullahassee Manual Labor School. John P. Lawton, the first superintendent, reported that the trustees had considerable dif-ficulty choosing the first students because of "the greater number presenting themselves." The school fields and buildings expanded over time, and eventually Tullahassee stood as one of the few schools to educate Indian freedmen above the elementary school level in Indian Territory. The Freedwoman Phoebe Banks sent her adopted son to Tullahassee and proudly told a WPA interviewer that his education there qualified him for his teaching position at Taft, Oklahoma. Tullahassee continued to provide education to black Oklahomans until 1924.[16]

Mary Allen Dawes and her husband, Hiram, came to Muskogee, Indian Territory, as Baptist missionaries in 1886. When her husband died in 1889, Mary raised $1,000 and opened a school for Chickasaw freedmen near what is today Gene Autry, Oklahoma. Although it was intended for freedmen, Chickasaw children also attended classes. In addition, Sunday services were held in the same building. The curriculum largely consisted of daily Bible instruction, but math and social studies were also taught. The female students adopted as their motto "For Jesus." Mary Dawes wrote that when Dawes Academy opened in the little log church, she had fourteen pupils. By 1891 a larger building was under construction and enrollment reached ninety-four, with twenty student boarders. Mary continued as principal until the school closed in 1899 with an enrollment at that time of 134 students.[17]

Missionary schooling was not the only alternative for the education of freedwomen. In the four nations that adopted their former slaves as citizens, limited public schooling was initially available to them. By 1888 the Creek Nation provided ten neighborhood day schools for the black Creeks. Writing about the freedmen, the historian Gary Zellar wrote, "African Creek children were the most schooled African Indian population in the Indian Territory." Many of the Creek and Seminole regular schools were integrated throughout most of the territorial period. In the Seminole Nation a total of only five day schools, two boarding schools, and two academies were established between the Civil War and Oklahoma statehood. Shortly before Seminole lands were incorporated into the state of Oklahoma, only two schools, Tidmore and Wewoka, were specifically designated as black schools. According to Mulroy, for the Seminoles, the desire for traditional education continued to outweigh the desire for white education.[18]

The Cherokees were perhaps the best at providing schools for the

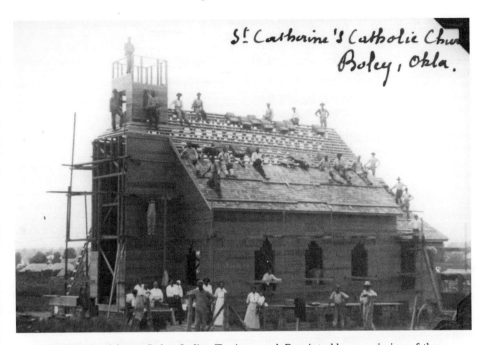

*St Catherine's Catholic Chur*
*Boley, Okla.*

Church raising at Boley, Indian Territory, n.d. Reprinted by permission of the Western History Collections, University of Oklahoma Libraries, Sooner Catholic Magazine Collection, 3.

freedmen children. By 1870 two segregated schools were added for their former slaves. In 1875 schools for black children had increased to seven, and by 1885 they numbered fourteen. These opportunities should not be exaggerated, however, because when attendance dropped below twenty-five, the schools closed. Consequently schools existed only in areas with significant population. In addition, the length of the school terms continued to be erratic because of the necessity for child labor during planting and harvest time. The freedmen schools also received teachers and equipment inferior to that of the Cherokee schools.[19]

The Cherokee Nation opened a high school to provide secondary education for black youths near Tahlequah in 1890. The handsome, three-story brick boarding school, known as the Cherokee Colored High School, operated for the next twenty years, but it rarely functioned on a high school level. The Cherokee Board of Education neglected to adopt a graded course of study in English, history, math, and science until 1899.

Teachers seldom numbered more than three. In order to keep the average attendance to at least twenty-five students, the school recruited primary-level students who had never attended school. Most of these students had their tuition paid by Cherokee Nation funds. Inasmuch as the Cherokee Nation did not admit black children to its orphan asylum, this school was a location where they could be placed. George Nave, steward of the school in 1899, reported fifteen orphans on the rolls with no means of support.[20]

The Chickasaw Nation provided no schools for their freedmen because they did not recognize them as citizens, and the government had not fulfilled its promise to remove them from Chickasaw lands. Sporadic efforts by the U.S. government and Baptist, Presbyterian, and Methodist missionary organizations attempted to establish schools at locations where communities of freedmen existed. In the 1870s the minister George W. Dallas pleaded with the commissioner of Indian affairs, Edward P. Smith, "Will your Honor, as much as it is in your power, give my poor, ignorant and neglected race, schools for the education of the youth?" In his travels throughout the Choctaw and Chickasaw Nations Dallas had encountered widespread "ignorance, poverty, and destitution." The Office of Indian Affairs arranged with the Protestant denominations to provide facilities for freedmen schools in the Choctaw and Chickasaw Nations if the churches would provide the teachers. A missionary doctor, Taylor F. Ealy, arrived with his wife, Mary, in 1874 at the ramshackle buildings of the abandoned Fort Arbuckle. Even though Chickasaw Governor Cyrus Harris had updated the officer quarters for the Ealys to use, it was an inhospitable beginning. Even before their arrival, the Ealys had been warned that "if anybody went to teach those niggers at Fort Arbuckle, they would kill him."[21]

The Ealys recruited students from as far north as the Canadian River and south to the Red River and opened the doors of the school to all ages and racial mixtures. Students were as old as seventy and as young as four; many had never had a book before. The Ealys and their assistant teacher, Miss Forbes, taught every day except Saturday; on Sunday they taught from the Bible. The entire community helped to support the school. Parents brought fresh pork and milk cows to the school. Many black women came to cook and clean the boarding houses and to nurse the students through a measles epidemic. At sundown the whole school assembled for chapel services. Years later Ealy remembered, "To hear those old colored women start off on the familiar hymns was sublime. Their voices were like the sound of a bugle." In 1876 schooling for the freed people at Fort Arbuckle was transferred to the Baptists, and the Ealys were reassigned to the Southwest. In the 1880s small schools such as the Blue Branch School, directed by Georgianna Reeves, and Colbert Station, taught by Ruth Young, continued the work of teaching the children of the freed people and increasing the number who could read and write English. The efforts to establish consistent schools for the Chickasaws, however, failed, largely, as the historian Daniel F. Littlefield, Jr. writes, because of "bureaucratic blunders, incompetence, poor management, and denominational struggles." In 1884 the appropriations for freedmen education ended, having produced only minimal results for the children of the Chickasaw freed people.[22]

The desire for schools for their children was so powerful that, whenever possible, the freedmen built neighborhood subscription schools and employed their own teachers. One black leader, quoted in the *Cherokee Advocate*, explained, "It is our own ignorance now, that is the barrier to social and political consequence today, and if we sit still and do nothing, our children will, when they grow up, labor under the same disadvantage." Often the demand became so great and the resources remained so small that the rural schools struggled to survive. Buck Colbert Franklin wrote about the Chickasaw Nation subscription school near his parents' ranch. His mother was the sole teacher. In the fall of 1885 the enrollment at the little school grew so large that the one room could not hold all of the students, and his mother could not adequately teach all of the children. Franklin's father had indebted himself to pay for the original building, and he decided that another member of the school board, Manuel Williams, should call a meeting of the community. Ninety percent of the parents arrived the next day. Williams explained the situation and asked for cash donations to build another room onto the schoolhouse and to hire an additional teacher. Milley Franklin told the crowd that she would forgo back salary owed to her if they would just find an assistant to help her manage all of the pupils. No money was raised at the meeting. David Franklin gathered estimates for building costs, but barely a quarter of the original group returned for a second meeting, and only a handful of these volunteered to haul the building materials. David gave his word that the additional debt would be paid. By Thanksgiving a second room was completed, and Pleasant Shoals, Milley's cousin, had been hired as an assistant. Milley separately organized the mothers to raise money to equip the second classroom. Only a few of the patrons were able to contribute to the cost of the building, and the Franklins eventually assumed the whole debt. Milley retired from teaching the following year.[23]

Subscription schools, often transient, undersupplied, and poorly taught, had mixed results. Tuition costs and the value of a child's labor in the cotton and corn fields, no matter how small, often limited the ability of black families to keep their children in any school on a regular basis. The narrative of Johnson Thompson, the freedwoman Phyllis Petite's brother, told a familiar story. "I went to a subscription school for a little while, but didn't get much learning," he said, "Lots of the slave children didn't ever learn to read or write." When school attendance dropped even in the all-black communities during harvest time, the editors of black town newspapers wrote intimidating editorials to black parents. The *Boley Progress* blasted, "Our watch word at this time is [to] see that your child is in school . . . the first day and every day up to the last day. Let no excuse keep you from doing your full duty to your children." Still, more freedwomen than freedmen seized any opportunity available for education for themselves and their children. Even a little education allowed freedwomen to secure employment that paid better than domestic service. Mary Grayson proudly remembered that she had attended a "little school called Blackjack School." She recalled that her first teachers were Cherokee women and white women. Over time all of these efforts toward establishing the first schools for freed people in Indian Territory contributed to improved literacy among black children. The rate of illiteracy for black children between ten and fourteen years old in 1900 was 30.7 percent. By 1910 this rate had dropped to 6.2 percent, the lowest for this age group of any southern state.[24]

Schools and churches became the nuclei of the all-black communities in Indian Territory. They were where black agency and independence could most often be exercised. Freedwomen especially found an acceptable medium in which to play a major role in community affairs through these institutions. The number of all-black communities increased toward the end of the territorial period. Tullahassee had been in existence before the Civil War, and Creek freedmen developed many more communities immediately after, such as North Fork Colored, Arkansas Colored, and Canadian Colored. Their combined population grew to more than 4,000 by 1891. Some of the towns also came together because of opportunities created by railroad expansion. Two towns with distinctly different reputations, Gibson Station and Wybark, can be traced back to railroad construction camps in the 1870s. Gibson Station was described by one historian as a place where "the scum of the frontier collected." Wybark and Lincoln, later renamed Clearview, became known early as reputable towns exclusively managed by blacks.[25]

The creation of Rentiesville, not far from both Tulsa and Muskogee, emerged from a meeting at the Paradis Baptist Church in 1903. Rev. N. A. Robinson conferred with William Rentie, W. D. Robinson, I. J. Foster, and Rev. David Green, and the five men organized a town site company. Mrs. Phoebe McIntosh and the William Rentie family each donated twenty acres of land. By 1904 the new town had five businesses, a church, a school, and a post office. Robinson, the Townsite Company's president, told the company meeting that year, "As we assemble in this splendid hall, it reminds us that education and high civilization is the watch word at Rentiesville." Buck C. Franklin would leave his family's ranch in the Chickasaw Nation and, following his education, establish his own family in Rentiesville, serving as postmaster in 1914. Even the Chickasaw Nation had black towns at Bailey and at Tatums, named for Mary Tatums, one of its earliest settlers. Large concentrations of Chickasaw and Choctaw freed people also developed in Pauls Valley and in Stonewall, where the black population outnumbered the Chickasaws. All told, twenty-five all-black communities existed in Indian Territory. These towns swelled in size as new black families migrated to the less repressive and more multiracial environment of Indian Territory. Boley and Clearview became the largest and most well-known of the Indian Territory black towns.[26]

The year 1889 was pivotal. The U.S. government opened an area of land in the center of Indian Territory to white settlement. Westward-moving immigrants early on recognized the value of the excellent farmland in Indian Territory. The "Boomers," as they became known, had been agitating for the release of these lands since 1872, when a Cherokee attorney, Elias C. Boudinot, publicized this area as public lands, not assigned to any of the Indian tribes. The journey for most immigrants from the North, East, and South to the "Unassigned Lands" was through Indian Territory. On April 22, 1889, the first famous Land Run brought thousands of home-seekers into the opened area. The following year Congress created the Oklahoma Territory, with its capital at Guthrie. Subsequent land runs added additional land to Oklahoma Territory and brought many more immigrants. Some of these were freedwomen from Indian Territory. The Creek freedwoman Mamie Elizabeth Crew was one of these. Her father was a successful rancher who had been murdered in Texas in a robbery attempt. At seventeen, she made the land run into the Cherokee Strip on foot and staked a claim in what became Perry, Oklahoma. Her mother followed her, driving a wagon full of tents and household goods. Additional all-black towns such as Langston and Liberty immediately sprang up in the new territory.[27]

By this time the racial composition of Indian Territory had changed dramatically since the Civil War. African Americans represented 10.3 percent (18,636) of the population, and Native Americans 28.5 percent (51,279). Both of these groups were already overwhelmed by the white residents, who amounted to 61.2 percent (110,254) of the population. With the existence of Oklahoma Territory, pressure on the Five Nations to surrender communal ownership of land and to allot their lands into parcels for individual ownership became overwhelming. Originally excluded from the 1887 Dawes Act, this action became obligatory with the enactment of the Curtis Act of 1898, and the Five Nations' governments and courts were effectively abolished. The Dawes Commission proceeded to override the Indians' sovereignty, to determine who was a citizen of the individual nations, and to draw up the allotment rolls. The way was almost clear for the conversion of Indian Territory and Oklahoma Territory into the forty-sixth state.[28]

It is nearly impossible to gauge the feelings of the freedwomen about these political decisions. They had no vote and little voice in the conduct of these public affairs. Those with substantial ties to their Indian families may have felt relief that their names would appear on the official Dawes roll documents and that they would have legal title to their lands. Others

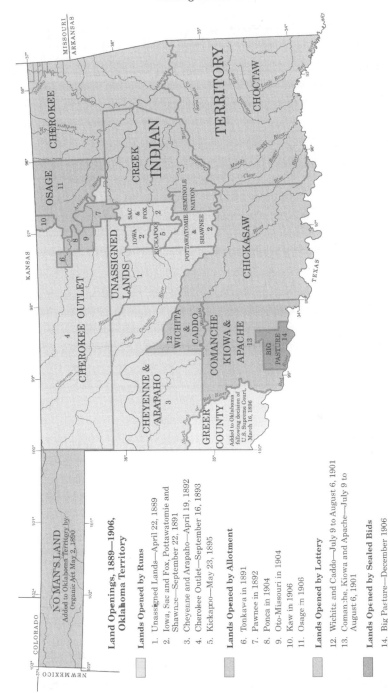

**Land openings, 1889–1906, Oklahoma Territory. Courtesy of the University of Oklahoma Press © 2006.**

Land Openings, 1889–1906, Oklahoma Territory

**Lands Opened by Runs**

1. Unassigned Lands—April 22, 1889
2. Iowa, Sac and Fox, Pottawatomie and Shawnee—September 22, 1891
3. Cheyenne and Arapaho—April 19, 1892
4. Cherokee Outlet—September 16, 1893
5. Kickapoo—May 23, 1895

**Lands Opened by Allotment**

6. Tonkawa in 1891
7. Pawnee in 1892
8. Ponca in 1904
9. Oto-Missouri in 1904
10. Kaw in 1906
11. Osage in 1906

**Lands Opened by Lottery**

12. Wichita and Caddo—July 9 to August 6, 1901
13. Comanche, Kiowa and Apache—July 9 to August 6, 1901

**Lands Opened by Sealed Bids**

14. Big Pasture—December 1906

may have believed, as their Indian neighbors did, in the old way, that communal land ownership provided better protection of their rights from whites. Some may have encouraged their husbands to reject the allotments altogether or to fight against them in organized fashion with the Creek Chitto Harjo's warriors in what became known as the Crazy Snake Rebellion. Still others, who had been abandoned once after the Civil War, could hardly hope that they would not be abandoned again when it came to the distribution of lands. What ultimately became apparent, however, was that white homesteaders and political leaders, now in the majority, respected neither their Indian cultural heritage nor their claims to property. So once again freedwomen sought safety in all-black enclaves and communities.[29]

Many national black leaders, such as Edward P. McCabe, argued for the creation of an all-black state. He publicized the Oklahoma lands across the United States as a place of promise, freedom, and self-determination. The *Boley Progress* newspaper chose young black women to act as agents for the newspaper and to spread the news about the advantages in Oklahoma. To the young woman with the highest number of year-long cash subscriptions greater than 100, the newspaper promised to provide for her education for one year at a school of her choice. Emma Marriott Menser's brother, living in Texas, sent her a copy of the *Boley Progress* and advised her and her husband, Julius, that Boley held far more advantages for their nine children than they would ever have in Louisiana. The large family and all of their possessions filled an entire railroad car to make their way to Boley. Not all of the migrants were as successful as the Mensers. Weary black home seekers from southern states responded to the publicity and sacrificed to make their way into these black towns. Even though the black town newspapers cautioned the arrivals about the scarcity of resources available in the towns, hundreds suffered severe privation upon their arrival. The *New York Times* reported, "Many have gone to that territory with nothing except the rags they wore, but they have never become public charges. They have been cared for by persons of their own race until they were in such condition that they could help themselves and help others."[30]

Oklahoma Territory in 1890 contained 78,475 settlers, and among these were approximately 3,000 blacks, or less than 4.1 percent of the total. A little more than 13,000 Indians resided there. Within the two territories combined there were approximately 2,700 foreign-born white persons, largely concentrated in the mining regions of Indian Territory. The majority of these came from Germany, Russia, and Austria-Hungary. As the century came to an end, neither the white majorities in Oklahoma and Indian Territories nor the political leaders of the United States and the Five Nations had any intention of allowing the creation of an all-black state.[31]

Indian freedwomen recognized that their cultural connections and history of cohabitation with the people of the Five Nations had been thoroughly repudiated. For years, as the historian Barbara Krauthamer asserts, freedmen and -women "assessed the extent of their freedom primarily in relation to their status as recognized citizens of these Indian nations." The Dawes rolls designated the groups as "Indian" and "Freedmen." With allotment, those long-standing connections were officially severed. Black women who were new to Indian Territory and older residents there since before the Civil War bore the same stigma and unequal status of "outsiders."[32]

The unstable conditions in Indian Territory that resulted from the influx of newcomers—black, white, and foreign-born—the rapid transition from Indian nations to twin territories, a fragmented law enforcement system, and the political upheaval of allotment led to another era of violence. Attacks on the freed people came in many forms: whites against freedmen, Indians (both from the Five Nations and from Plains tribal groups) against freedmen, and men against women. Especially violent areas were in the Creek lands where many all-black communities existed. Since the 1880s Creek freedmen had petitioned their government to take action against the Cherokee marauders who attacked their homes and communities. Twelve freedmen leaders appealed to Creek Chief Samuel Checote after months of violence against their people. The most recent attack had included injury to a female child. "We can bear this no longer," they wrote in their petition for action. After many assaults and deaths, they explained: "Nothing done. 'Tis niggers.' We cry for justice. In one accord, 'Give us Justice.'"[33]

All-black communities in Cherokee, Chickasaw, and Choctaw lands also experienced attacks. Settlements along the Red River were particularly susceptible. The Choctaw and Chickasaw Nations passed "Black Codes" and organized "Vigilance Committees" that raided the colonies, whipped the settlers, and drove them off the lands. One of the earliest Oklahoma historians, Joseph Thoburn, described the efforts of the vigilance committees to rid their lands of black communities. He wrote that their methods were "simple and severe." A "ghostly visitor" appeared "in the dark hours of the night" and ordered the blacks to move out on a specific date and time. If they refused to leave, the committee members returned and fired bullets into their cabin until the desired result was achieved. Some of the violence was directed specifically against familial freedwomen. A Choctaw freedwoman reported to a WPA fieldworker that both her daughters had been murdered by their husbands; one was stabbed to death and the other was shot. Interracial marriages that were acceptable earlier might now be considered unsuitable. In addition, bands of Comanche, Kiowa, and Kiowa-Apache raided the homesteads of black families in the Chickasaw Nation for cattle and horses, kidnapping and killing blacks in the process. Sometimes integrated gangs of Plains Indians and blacks terrorized more peaceful white and black homesteaders. Violent deaths might occur from many circumstances in Indian Territory.[34]

Across Oklahoma there were approximately 106 recorded lynching deaths between 1885 and 1907, but the peak years were 1893–95. Most of the reported murders prior to statehood were of whites; after statehood, the number of black murders rose substantially. By 1930 approximately fifty black people had been recorded killed by lynching. This does not account for likely dozens more that went unrecorded. In addition to lynching, public whippings also provided a means for whites and Indians to express social control over the freed people.[35]

An incident on Montford Johnson's Chickasaw lands illustrates how the "law of flight," ended the lives of some black citizens. Johnson, a rancher, received word that some of his horses had been stolen and that the wife of one of his renters had been attack and raped by a member of an all-black settlement. He took some of his "trusted cowboys" and went to investigate. When the woman identified her attacker, Johnson turned him over to two of his men with instructions to deliver him to the nearest marshal at Stonewall, in spite of onlookers' demands that he lynch the accused on the spot. The horse thieves were summarily shot. The following day the cowboys returned to the ranch and reported that they had shot the man when he attempted to escape. Rumor circulated that one of the men just didn't want to make the long ride out and back, so he executed his captive. Johnson gave safe harbor to the killer for years. Eventually a black deputy marshal, Bass Reeves, followed up on the incident, captured the gunman, and took him to Fort Smith, Arkansas, the seat of Judge Isaac Parker's court. He died there awaiting trial. Freedwomen and their children lived in the most vulnerable of positions. When husbands, fathers, and brothers died violently, in addition to the private pain, their physical and economic status altered dramatically for the worse. They were victims of the crossfire among the competing legal and extralegal interests seeking control of Indian Territory.[36]

Indian freedwomen and immigrant freedwomen in Indian Territory who resided in all-black communities and in towns with large black populations joined together to establish the framework for their future in this uncertain and sometimes violent racial milieu. The wives of prominent businessmen and landholders and female schoolteachers set the standard for black females. They followed the example and advice of prominent national black female leaders who set about to improve the status and reputation of all black women in America. After 1889 black women in Indian Territory with a long history among the peoples of this future state also reached across the geographic line to black women newly arrived in Oklahoma Territory in discussions of race, education, violence, women's rights, appropriate conduct, cultural development, and home improvement.

The growth of the black communities in territorial Oklahoma coincided with the emergence of a national black women's movement in the 1890s. The National Federation of Afro-American Women, led by Josephine St. Pierre Ruffin, and the Washington, D.C., National League of Colored Women, under the direction of Mary Church Terrell, merged in 1896 to form the National Association of Colored Women (NACW). Ruffin and Terrell had both experienced rebuffs in their dealings with the leadership of the white General Federation of Women's Clubs as well as racist white press coverage that characterized all black women as liars, thieves, and prostitutes. Ruffin, Terrell, Margaret Murray Washington

(Mrs. Booker T. Washington), Fannie Barrier Williams, and Ida Wells-Barnett joined forces to develop the NACW, an organization largely composed of middle-class women and designed to create an honorable national reputation and to address the needs of black women in the United States. In less than twenty years, the NACW represented more than 50,000 women in twenty-eight federations and over 1,000 clubs.[37]

Hundreds of women's groups organized in Indian Territory before and immediately after statehood in the all-black towns and in areas with a sizable black population. They accepted Margaret Murray Washington's challenge to work for social, economic, and moral reform for "enlightened motherhood, intellectual development, individuality and with all a steady growth of the development of noble womanhood." Some of the groups had specific economic and political goals and activities; others were strictly social in nature; and many, like the Boley Ladies Industrial Club, performed a variety of services. Black newspapers celebrated the accomplishments of the members as not only economically productive but contributing to the improvement of the cultural life of the community. The Boley Women's Club emerged in 1906, and many of its first meetings were devoted to gathering and sharing information about the activities of clubs in other cities. O. H. Bradley, the editor of the *Boley Progress*, encouraged women to organize and to join local clubs. Bradley saw the advantages of these women's clubs and the potential for using them for town improvement projects. He suggested that they organize a "Boley Beauty Club" to make the town more attractive. They would be responsible for street trash cleanup, whitewashing fences and outhouses, and planting flowers and shrubs around town. He had previously scolded men for failing to do this kind of work. He also encouraged the women to form a group to support the "discipline, management, and general progress of the school." The Ladies' Industrial Club founded the Boley Public Library, assisted in local relief, and introduced newcomers and young single women into society. Members functioned as the arbiters of manners and morals, but they also stimulated financial growth through the investment of their time and labor. Men and women alike recognized the value of female support to community institutions and upkeep.[38]

Several female organizations, such as the Order of the Eastern Star and Daughters of Tabor, lent support to male fraternal lodges. The Sisters of Ethiopia functioned as the female auxiliary of the Patriarchs of America in Clearview. They were dedicated to improving conditions for the black race through economic and political unity, claiming that men always worked harder in a cause when they were joined "heart and hand" by women. Also in Clearview were the Alpha Club, the Self-Enterprising Club, and a social club led by the prominent matrons Neva Thompson and Bessie Warren for "ladies of good moral standing," organized to encourage, "literary, social and industral [sic] attainment." Beneath the formation of these groups lay a complex motivation. Unity, cooperation, and activism set a standard of racial advancement. Women's clubs laid the foundation for the elevation of both race and sex. As Margaret Murray Washington wrote, "We accept only the theory that we are inferior in opportunity, and not in capacity or ability. The American colored woman is not going to live beside the American white woman and remain any the less a woman."[39]

Some of these clubs antedate by more than a decade the formal incorporation of Oklahoma Clubs with the National Association of Colored Women. Oklahoma clubs did not formally affiliate with the NACW until 1910, although territorial women sent representatives from the Oklahoma Territory Guthrie Women's Club to the national conventions as early as 1896. Lois Perdue developed the first local clubs in Muskogee with the Francis Harper No. One in 1908. This group was later joined by the Matrons Mutual Improvement Circle, Royal Arts, and Mary Church Terrell clubs. When the Oklahoma Federation of Colored Women's Clubs organized in 1910, the offices of first vice president and treasurer were held by Muskogee women. By 1920 Boley, Eufaula, Tulsa, and McAlester had also joined. Within the first ten years the number of Oklahoma clubs had tripled and the number of members quadrupled. The NACW adopted as its own the official emblem and motto of the Oklahoma Federation, "Lifting As We Climb."[40]

The local clubs organized programs around civil rights issues. Some of these included an examination of women's property rights, the endorsement of woman suffrage after 1914, and work on community development, juvenile delinquency, and education. The meetings went beyond a sharing of information and encouragement of benevolent activities; the clubs promoted political activism by lobbying and petitioning for the economic and social advancement of all blacks in Oklahoma. The federation founded and supported two seminaries for black girls, located at McAlester and Sapulpa, and facilities for delinquent boys at Boley and girls at Taft. They created rural health clinics and developed mothers' clubs to disseminate information about better child care. They also organized fund drives for playground equipment, parks and cemetery beautification, and hospital furnishings and equipment. The club women kept alive a continual negotiation of racial issues that reinforced the legal challenges that black male leaders pursued through the courts under the direction of the Oklahoma branch of the National Association for the Advancement of Colored People. They launched legislative letter-writing campaigns for citizenship rights and for full integration into American life. They also provided financial support to the Oklahoma NAACP and to the Constitution League, a lobby working for state legislation on behalf of black citizens. Indian freedwomen and immigrant black women had united their voices to improve circumstances for themselves and their families in the new state of Oklahoma.[41]

By statehood, the transformation of enslaved women into freedwomen and then into free black women had been won. They had capitalized on every possible opportunity for the improvement of their own lives and those of their children. Membership in Christian churches was a training ground for cooperative community building. There they acquired the tools to meet together openly, discuss their problems, and plan strategies for stabilizing their society. Education, so important to success, had faced enormous obstacles. Religious denominations had been largely responsible for providing what little schooling was available to the freedwomen. When this was lacking, they lobbied the Indian governments to provide them schools or created their own subscription schools to educate their young. The entrance of immigrant freed people, Plains Indians, whites, and foreign-born arrivals changed the social dynamic of their lives. The decisions of the federal government to end communal land ownership and convert the Twin Territories into a state terminated their connection with the people of the Five Nations. In many cases they bore the brunt of violence rampant in Indian Territory. It was in the all-black communities and enclaves that they experienced a modicum of safety and the opportunities to accomplish their goals. Indian freedwomen and black female immigrants joined in union through a variety of clubs and organizations to work together to support their families and their towns in securing freedom and prosperity in this western space that became the state of Oklahoma.

# Epilogue

n rural places far off the main roads of Oklahoma one can find the remains of the numerous communities that the freedwomen inhabited well into the twentieth century. They are mostly overgrown cemeteries and abandoned buildings. The staff of the Oklahoma History Center and the descendants of the freedmen have actively worked to reconstruct the history of African Americans in the state and to educate those who want to hear it. But the stories of the Indian Territory freedwomen have been largely forgotten. At one end of the former Indian Territory near Keystone Lake the shell of what was once a very fine house stands as testament to its owner, the Creek freedwoman Elizzie Redmond Davis. She was born sometime around 1865, the daughter of Mose Redmouth and Annie Martin, her parents enslaved by two different men. She had four children, and she died in 1909, not long after filing for a mortgage on the allotment she had received. There are rumors that she gave hospitality to outlaws and sold illegal liquor to Tulsans. The only evidence supporting this is a small room behind a double wall with a door that can be easily concealed. Her success in navigating the fortunes of Indian Territory is evident in the crumbling remains of her house, but little else about her life is known.[1]

At the other end of Indian Territory, a few miles south and west of Ada, Oklahoma, the Athens Cemetery survives. At one time a small community of Choctaw and Chickasaw freed people lived in the area. There was once a school and a church; now only the silent graves remain. Among the headstones are those of Ella Albert, a Chickasaw freedwoman, Nellie Barnett, a Creek freedwoman, and Betty Franklin, a Choctaw freedwoman, their status confirmed by the existence of their allotment card numbers. For a long time the cemetery was overgrown with weeds, tall grasses, bushes, and tree seedlings. Renewed interest from the descendants of the Athens pioneers and local residents have led to a revival of the burial ground and the creation of a photographic record of the headstones. If written narratives had survived, what would Elizzie, Ella, Nellie, and Betty tell us about their lives in Indian Territory? Would their life stories reflect the accounts told by others? We can only speculate that they would have had similar things to say, though their individual journeys would have been marked by differences.[2]

African American women and black Indian women accompanied the forced migration of the Five Tribes to Indian Territory in the early nineteenth century. Their lack of choice in removal had a double meaning. Except for the small group who had intermarried with members of the Five Tribes and had become acceptable to them, nearly all of them came as enslaved people. They were deported at the order of both the federal government and their masters. By the 1850s their labor had contributed to the building up this beautiful but undeveloped area into a showplace of homes, small farms, plantations, and prosperous communities. Slavery in Indian Territory had many variations depending on the history and culture of each of the tribal groups, the level of acculturation and psychological makeup of individual slaveholders, and the economic resources at hand. It could be as harsh and brutal as the worst examples in the southern states or exist as a more independent, tributary form of servitude. Even so, it was ownership of human beings as property.

The right to keep enslaved women and men in Indian Territory came into question during the decade as conflict over the issue of slavery intensified in the rest of the United States. Religious denominations split over whether Christianity condones human bondage. Family membership divided over the inclusion of African Americans as kin. The constitutional governments of the Five Nations passed legislation to codify and restrict the freedom, movement, and identity of enslaved peoples. In each of these circumstances enslaved women lost position and recognition in tribal societies that had functioned along matrilineal kinship lines. Members of the different tribal groups quarreled among themselves about how to proceed in their interactions with the federal government should there be what seemed an inevitable national schism. So too did enslaved families debate their options. In spite of intentional efforts by the Five Nations to remain outside of the conflict, Indian Territory found itself philosophically, economically, and geographically caught between the Union and the Confederacy. When war came, it forever changed the lives of all who lived there.

The war in Indian Territory was cruelest to the most vulnerable groups there, the women and children. Even before the beginning of hostilities, enslaved women saw their families being separated by slave sales, harassment and sometimes death at the hands of patrollers, and the actions of their husbands and male relatives who seized the opportunity created by the turmoil to run away. When the first military action occurred in 1861, it took the form of a devastating attack on a group of fleeing civilians. Black women and children struggled alongside the Indian population to get to Union safety in Kansas. Their sojourn there had tragic consequences. Before they could safely return to Indian Territory, they saw hundreds of their relatives die from hunger, disease, and exposure in the poorly provisioned camps.

Confederate slaveholders broke up black families as well. Some family members were left on slaveholders' property, while others helped the Indian families retreat from the battle zones. Since the slaves were a valuable commodity and a source of revenue, the slaveholders directed an exodus away from the homelands to areas under Confederate control and into southern-held states. Some enslaved people of both sexes and all ages were sold; others were hired out to work in places far from their families. Husbands and wives, mothers and children became separated. Many of the husbands of the enslaved women fought on the Union side as free men or in Confederate companies alongside their masters. Often they died in battle, their loved ones never to know what happened to them. Along with the material destruction in Indian Territory, the war carried with it the physical, mental, and emotional anguish of a shattered society.

When the war ended, most freedwomen found themselves far from home and bereft of any means of support. In some cases they did not even know for months after the war that they were now free, and they continued to live in servitude. Some relied on their former Indian masters or kin to return them to the Territory. With only minimal resources others struggled to find transportation back to the only homes they had ever known. Uppermost in their minds was the hope of finding loved ones alive. Single parents, mothers, and children searched for each other in order to reconnect the broken family ties. Government officials instituted new rules regarding the marriages of freedwomen and -men. Federal oversight attempted to divest them of plural marriages that had been acceptable under the Indian governments. Once reunited, black families faced the animosity of the defeated Confederate Indians and a stubborn resistance to the acceptance of their rights imposed by the federal government under the peace treaties of 1866. In some cases freedwomen found themselves entirely alone and took action to make their own way in the confusing turmoil of the reconstruction of Indian Territory.

The transition from familial work in slavery to paid work in the new economy of Indian Territory required great dexterity. Since freedwomen had performed many kinds of labor before, they found that they could now barter those skills for money or goods. Cooking, cleaning, child care, and gardening had always been a woman's prerogative. Women alone and with their husbands performed heavy agricultural work on the farms and ranches. If they were married, however, government officials again intervened to regulate the productivity of freedwomen through their husbands. Contracts for their labor and wages paid to the freedwomen were mandated to be under the authority of their husbands. Given the disarray of conditions and the breadth of the Territory, it is unlikely that this arrangement was effectively carried out. More significant impediments for the freedwomen were their ignorance of the many types and values of money circulating in Indian Territory, their lack of literacy, and their ignorance of the culture and English language used by the newcomers to the area. All of these handicaps were compounded, however, when necessity demanded the labor of even the youngest girls in the family.

Freedwomen also provided a valuable service to all residents, no matter race or color, in their facility with homeopathic medicine. They were frequently called into service for childbirth, injury, and serious illness. Even after trained doctors began to arrive in Indian Territory, black women continued to administer folk medicine and to be employed at nursing the sick. Except for the religious rites, they also assumed responsibility in preparing bodies for funeral services. Women with literacy in English and some education occupied the most prestigious of positions, that of teacher. The freedwomen knew that the way for advancement for their children lay in education. Young men could obtain good wages without much education, but the deliverance of their daughters from back-breaking agricultural labor lay in sacrificing to prepare them for teaching.

Most freedwomen labored both privately within the home and on their lands and publicly in their communities. As time passed, the indigenous freedwomen were joined by immigrant freedwomen, and all-black colonies and communities swelled in size. This created a triangulated social fabric that sometimes brought jealousy and violence. Indian freedwomen found themselves outnumbered by noncitizen black women with no knowledge of or connection to the Five Nations. The Indian peoples resented the privileges given to their freed people but became even more angered by the intrusion of other African Americans migrating into their lands. They passed Black Codes in an attempt to regulate the freedoms of these new arrivals and applied them to their freed people as well. Noncitizen black women, however, frequently brought new capital for female-run businesses, experience with white culture, and more education, leading to expanded employment and educational opportunities. The need for protection, mutual economic interests, and a shared desire to build a new and secure future home motivated the Indian freedwomen and immigrant black women to work together.

Since the end of the Civil War, the freedwomen's overwhelming desire for education for themselves and their children had benefited from the unqualified opening to blacks of the mission field in Indian Territory. Presbyterian, Methodist, and Baptist hierarchies sent missionaries not just to the Indian peoples but to the freed people as well. These missionaries not only started churches but trained black ministers and opened schools for the black children. Toward the end of the nineteenth century, many white female missionary teachers were sent into areas with all-black populations. The response of the freedwomen in support of the churches and schools was overwhelming, but the efforts to build these mission stations required economic resources and an ironclad constitution that often broke under the immense labor required. Indian freedwomen carried within themselves a synergistic combination of African, Indian, and white American Protestant religious beliefs that gave them direction and helped them to make sense of their lives. In the churches they gained the experience of leadership and community development; for instance, Rentiesville became a town because of the dedication of the male and female members of the Paradis Baptist Church.

The Indian nations themselves offered to a greater or lesser degree some schooling for the children of the freed people. The Cherokee and Creek Nations provided the strongest support for these schools, even establishing secondary education programs. When Indian nation schools were lacking, black communities pooled whatever resources they could to keep subscription schools operating. Black women such as Milley Franklin led the way not only in teaching but in organizing groups of women to provision the schools with necessary supplies. The combined efforts of religious institutions, Indian governments, and individual initiative produced dramatic results in increasing the level of literacy among the black population in Indian Territory.

As the last decades of the nineteenth century arrived, the freed people in Indian Territory experienced the waning days of their ties to the Five Nations. The new environment included the arrival of not only black immigrants but Plains Indian tribal groups and massive numbers of white people now familiar with the wealth in land and natural resources available in the area. The white population overwhelmed the numbers of Indian and black residents. Black leaders across the United States saw the opportunity for the creation of a black state and encouraged the growth of the all-black communities. In reaction white politicians and some Indian leaders began to demand the transformation of Indian Territory into a white state. The 1889 Land Run and the creation of Oklahoma Territory in 1890, located right in the heart of Indian Territory, rapidly moved that possibility forward. As the numerous groups competed for control, violence directed primarily at the freed people escalated. The limited law enforcement in Indian Territory made it a primary location for illegal activities and outlaws. Black women were caught in the vortex of this violence in which their lives and those of their children and husbands were at risk.

The freedwomen were not without resources or courage, however. The turbulence in the Territory took place at the same time that other black women in the United States proclaimed their demand to end the violence and denigration toward black women. The organizing principles of the National Association of Colored Women reached the women in Indian Territory. Hundreds of female groups came together to serve the needs of the black population. Some were adjuncts of male lodges, some social and beautification clubs, and some supported educational and cultural advancement in the communities. Joining together the imperatives of elevating both race and sex, these women found strength in numbers. Through political activism they worked for improvement in civil rights issues, community social centers, health clinics, and training centers for delinquent youths. Not long after statehood, the Oklahoma Federation of Colored Women's Clubs affiliated with the national organization.

In the end, the federal government rejected the sovereignty of the Indian nations and moved to allot the Indian lands into private ownership and to convert Oklahoma Territory and Indian Territory into one state. The freedwomen of Indian Territory had navigated many difficult trails to reach this moment. They had traversed the multiple intersections of place, gender, race, and culture to create for themselves and their children viable lives as free people. They had known slavery as it developed into diverse forms as bondswomen of the Five Nations in their new homeland of Indian Territory. The Civil War had brought as much suffering, dislocation, and hardship to them as to any other civilians in the Territory or the United States. In the aftermath of the war, they came together in strengthened families. They devoted their lives to build new homes and communities in freedom against an array of impediments. They struggled alone and side by side with their husbands to educate their children and to develop prosperous farms and businesses. When their safety and very lives were threatened by the violence against them, they organized themselves to create a united front and to protect and preserve what they had built. As the historian Karen Anderson has written, these women negotiated "the contradictions and fault lines of domination" to enable "the material and psychological survival of their families." The freedwomen of Indian Territory deserve recognition among the now celebrated Indian and white pioneers. The state of Oklahoma in fair measure is the result of the "lived presence" of the enslaved women who became freedwomen who became free black women over the history of the second half of the nineteenth century.[3]

# Notes

## Introduction

1. In addition to numerous articles, Littlefield's early books include *Africans and Seminoles*, *The Cherokee Freedmen*, *Africans and Creeks*, and *Chickasaw Freedmen*. David A. Y. O. Chang, "Where Will the Nation Be at Home? Race, Nationalism, and Emigration Movements in the Creek Nation," in Miles and Holland, *Crossing Waters, Crossing Worlds*, 81.
2. Piker, "Indians and Race in Early America."
3. Gibson, *Oklahoma,* 4, 64–65; Chavez, "Freedmen Vow to Continue Fighting Cherokee Nation for Their Rights."
4. Perdue, *Slavery and the Evolution of Cherokee Society* and *Cherokee Women.*
5. Walker, *Anything We Love Can Be Saved,* 89–90, 100. For a discussion of blood quantum, see Schmidt, "American Indian Identity and Blood Quantum in the 21st Century."
6. Perdue, "Indians in the Segregated South."
7. Bunn and Bunn, *Constitution and Enabling Act of the State of Oklahoma,* 123.

## Chapter 1

1. Gibson, *The American Indian*, 309–20. See also Baird and Goble, *The Story of Oklahoma*, 125–147; Gibson, *Oklahoma*, 53–70; Foreman, *Indian Removal*, best covers the African Americans held by the Five Tribes during this removal process.
2. Gibson, *The American Indian*, 320–23; Foreman, *Indian Removal*, 229–312.
3. Gibson, *The American Indian*, 323–24, 327–28; Foreman, *Indian Removal,* 19–104, 193–226.

4. Gibson, *The American Indian,* 325–27; Foreman, *Indian Removal,* 107–90.

5. Gibson, *The American Indian,* 328–29; Foreman, *Indian Removal,* 315–86.

6. Gibson, *Oklahoma,* 84–97; Baird and Goble, *The Story of Oklahoma,* 151–69.

7. Perdue, "People without a Place," 31–37; Mulroy, *The Seminole Freedmen,* 5–7; Sweetie Ivery Wagoner in Baker and Baker, *The WPA Oklahoma Slave Narratives,* 442; Halliburton, "Origins of Black Slavery among the Cherokees," 483–96. The *WPA Oklahoma Slave Narratives* (hereafter *Oklahoma Slave Narratives*) must be used with care. There is, of course, the problem of confusion in memory resulting from the advanced age (seventy-three to ninety) of the informants. In addition, inexperienced interviewers sometimes pursued question lines related to their own interests and perspectives and attempted to capture the colloquialism of the informant's speech. The interviews provide fascinating insight and surprisingly candid information, however. The publication of the Baker and Baker book added thirteen previously unpublished interviews that had been unexamined since the 1930s; they are located in the archives of the Oklahoma Historical Society. Narratives taken from the Indian Pioneer History Collection at the University of Oklahoma will be noted by informant name, IPH, volume, and page number.

8. Perdue, "People without a Place," 31–37; Halliburton, "Origins of Black Slavery among the Cherokees," 483–96; McReynolds, *The Seminoles,* 143.

9. Doran, "Negro Slaves of the Five Civilized Tribes," 337; Merrell, "The Problem of Slavery in the Cherokee Culture," 509–14; Halliburton, "Origins of Black Slavery among the Cherokees," 486; Perdue, "Cherokee Planters, Black Slaves, and African Colonization," 329; Perdue, *Slavery and the Evolution of Cherokee Society.* By far the most work on Indian slaveholding until recently has focused on the Cherokee Nation. The early literacy of the Cherokees, the abundant availability of English print sources, and the fact that the Cherokees were the largest slaveholders in Indian Territory make a broader analysis possible. Claudio Saunt makes the argument in *Black, White, and Indian* that the transition years from the East to the circumstances of Indian Territory contributed to Creek racial inflexibility that both received and inflicted cruelty on multiracial Creek families.

10. Miller, "Frontier Freedom," 82; John Armstrong, quoted in May, *African Americans and Native Americans in the Cherokee and Creek Nations*, 60–61, from an interview in the Doris Duke Oral History Collection, Western History Collections, University of Oklahoma. Although there is little documented evidence for slave attachment to Indian removal groups, it is also mentioned in Gaskin, *Black Baptists in Oklahoma,* 82–85; Littlefield and Littlefield, "The Beams Family," 26, 28. The Choctaw leader Tandy Walker used words almost identical to those of Douglas Cooper in the discussion of the new Constitution of 1858, cited in Kidwell, *The Choctaws in Oklahoma,* 46. Ella Coody Robinson, IPH 77: 97–98.

11. Doran, "Negro Slaves of the Five Civilized Tribes," 336–41.

12. Saunt, *A New Order of Things,* 111–35 139–63. Theda Perdue presents a much more balanced gender relationship among the Cherokees in *Cherokee Women.* McLoughlin, "Red Indians, Black Slavery and White Racism," 368.

13. May, *African Americans and Native Americans in the Cherokee and Creek Nations,* 19–21; Debo, *The Road to Disappearance,* 3–36, 68. See also Searcy, "The Introduction of African Slavery into the Creek Indian Nation," 21–32; Braund, "The Creek Indians, Blacks, and Slavery," 601–636.

14. Gibson, *The American Indian,* 289; Nichols, *American Indians in U.S. History,* 98; Owsley, "The Fort Mims Massacre," 192–204. See also Waselkov, *A Conquering Spirit.*

15. Zellar, *African Creeks, Estelvste and the Creek Nation,* 32–39; May, *African Americans and Native Americans in the Cherokee and Creek Nations,* 41–44; Edwards, photocopy of IPH Narrative, 192; Nellie Johnson, in *Oklahoma Slave Narratives,* 225–26; Debo, *Road to Disappearance,* 115–16.

16. Mulroy, *The Seminole Freedmen,* xxi–xxxii. Mulroy disagrees with Daniel Littlefield's interpretation of the history of the Seminole freedmen by relating them directly to descendants of the maroon communities; see Littlefield, *Africans and Seminoles,* 3–13. In 2005 Susan A. Miller published a lengthy article denouncing the claims of freedmen to Seminole Nation membership status and stating that use of the term *estelusti* represented an invented "Black Indian" identity. See Miller, "Seminoles and Africans under Seminole Law," 23–47. For an early collection of primary document commentary on Seminole intermarriage among all racial groups, see Krogman, "The Racial Composition of the Seminole Indians of Florida and Oklahoma," 412–30.

17. Doran, "Negro Slaves of the Five Civilized Tribes," 347, 348; Sweetie Ivery Wagoner, in *Oklahoma Slave Narratives,* 442; Naylor, *African Cherokees in Indian Territory,* 88. See also Doran, "Population Statistics of Nineteenth Century Indian Territory," 492–515; McFadden, " The Saga of 'Rich Joe' Vann," 68–79.

18. Pascoe, *What Comes Naturally,* 1, 21–22; Halliburton, "Black Slave Control in the Cherokee Nation," 23–35; McLoughlin, "Red Indians, Black Slavery and White Racism," 381; Yarbrough, *Race and the Cherokee Nation,* 39–55.

19. Johnston, "Documentary Evidence of the Relations of Negroes and Indians," 41; Jeltz, "The Relations of Negroes and Choctaw and Chickasaw Indians," 31–32; Smith, "The Oppressed Oppressors," 246, 250. For a review of other Choctaw legislation, see Knight, "Fifty Years of Choctaw Law," 76–95.

20. Littlefield, *Africans and Seminoles,* 80–81.

21. Littlefield and Underhill, "Slave 'Revolt' in the Cherokee Nation," 121–31; Littlefield, *Africans and Seminoles,* 80; Naylor, *African Cherokees in Indian Territory,* 44–46; Betty Robertson, in *Oklahoma Slave Narratives,* 356.

22. Littlefield, *Africans and Seminoles*, 81; Naylor, *African Cherokees in Indian Territory*, 47.

23. Ella Coody Robinson, IPH, 77: 112; McLoughlin, "Indian Slaveholders and Presbyterian Missionaries," 535–51.

24. McLoughlin, "Indian Slaveholders and Presbyterian Missionaries," 535–51; Mahnken, "Old Baptist Mission and Evan Jones," 174–93. See also McLoughlin, *After the Trail of Tears*, 121–52; Baird and Goble, *The Story of Oklahoma*, 172.

25. For a study of the work of Evan and John Jones and the Keetoowah Society, see Minges, *Slavery in the Cherokee Nation*; David B. Rollin, in *Baptist Missionary Magazine*, 16 (Boston), in IPH, 13: 289; Polly Colbert, in *Oklahoma Slave Narratives*, 89; Chaney Richardson, in *Oklahoma Slave Narratives*, 351; Betty Robertson, in *Oklahoma Slave Narratives*, 356.

26. Lucinda Vann, in *Oklahoma Slave Narratives*, 439–40; Phoebe Banks, in *Oklahoma Slave Narratives*, 31; Sweetie Ivery Wagoner, in *Oklahoma Slave Narratives*, 443; Nancy Rogers Bean, in *Oklahoma Slave Narratives*, 49.

27. Polly Colbert, in *Oklahoma Slave Narratives*, 86–87; Chaney Richardson, in *Oklahoma Slave Narratives*, 350; Matilda Poe, in *Oklahoma Slave Narratives*, 325–26.

28. Jane Davis Ward, IPH: 11, 196; Frances Banks, in *Oklahoma Slave Narratives*, 28. The original draft of Banks's interview was altered in pencil and never sent to Washington with the other Oklahoma slave narratives. Based on additional information in her narrative, it is likely that Banks was the slave of Choctaw Chief Allen Wright and the nanny of his granddaughter, the Oklahoma historian Muriel Wright. See *Oklahoma Slave Narratives*, 29nn1, 5; Polly Colbert, in *Oklahoma Slave Narratives*, 88.

29. Polly Colbert, in *Oklahoma Slave Narratives*, 88; Phoebe Banks, in *Oklahoma Slave Narratives*, 30; Charlotte Johnson White, in *Oklahoma Slave Narratives*, 464–65; R. C. Smith, in *Oklahoma Slave Narratives*, 399–400.

30. Patsy Perryman, in *Oklahoma Slave Narratives*, 315; Phyllis Petite, in *Oklahoma Slave Narratives*, 317; Kiziah Love, in *Oklahoma Slave Narratives*, 259–61.

31. Kiziah Love, in *Oklahoma Slave Narratives*, 261–62; Charlotte Johnson White, in *Oklahoma Slave Narratives*, 465.

32. Lucinda Vann, in *Oklahoma Slave Narratives*, 436–37.

33. Foreman, *The Five Civilized Tribes*, 393; Miles, *Ties That Bind*, 162–78; Celia Naylor, *African Cherokees in Indian Territory*, 66–72.

34. Sarah Wilson, in *Oklahoma Slave Narratives*, 493–95.

35. Sarah Wilson, in *Oklahoma Slave Narratives*, 496.

36. See Saunt, *Black, White, and Indian.* For additional works on George Washington Grayson, see Baird, *A Creek Warrior for the Confederacy*; Warde, *George Washington Grayson and the Creek Nation.*

37. Sarah Wilson, in *Oklahoma Slave Narratives,* 493; Mary Grayson, in *Oklahoma Slave Narratives,* 171–72; "Native American Herbal Remedies."
38. Nellie Johnson, in *Oklahoma Slave Narratives,* 225–27; Betty Robertson, in *Oklahoma Slave Narratives,* 355.
39. Henry Henderson, in *Oklahoma Slave Narratives,* 196; Adeline Collins, IPH 20: 280–81.
40. Charlotte Johnson White, in *Oklahoma Slave Narratives,* 465; Sarah Wilson, in *Oklahoma Slave Narratives,* 494–95.
41. Phyllis Petite, in *Oklahoma Slave Narratives,* 319; Sarah Wilson, in *Oklahoma Slave Narratives,* 494; R. C. Smith, in *Oklahoma Slave Narratives,* 398.
42. Anna Colbert, IPH 20: 169; Betty Robertson, in *Oklahoma Slave Narratives,* 355–56; Matilda Poe, in *Oklahoma Slave Narratives,* 325; Sarah Wilson, in *Oklahoma Slave Narratives,* 494; Mary Grayson, in *Oklahoma Slave Narratives,* 171–72.
43. Patsy Perryman, in *Oklahoma Slave Narratives,* 314; Mary Lindsay, in *Oklahoma Slave Narratives,* 247–48.

## Chapter 2

1. Morris Sheppard, in *Oklahoma Slave Narratives,* 378–79; Chaney Richardson, in *Oklahoma Slave Narratives,* 349.
2. Kiziah Love, in *Oklahoma Slave Narratives,* 262; Littlefield, *Africans and Seminoles,* 173; Polly Colbert, in *Oklahoma Slave Narratives,* 89; Matilda Poe, in *Oklahoma Slave Narratives,* 325.
3. Mary Grayson, in *Oklahoma Slave Narratives,* 173–74.
4. Woodward, *The Cherokees,* 253–89; McLoughlin, *After the Trail of Tears,* 153–70; Halliburton, *Red over Black,* 107–21; Foreman, *Journal and Letters of Stephen Foreman,* 33; Chaney Richardson, in *Oklahoma Slave Narratives,* 348–49; Morris Sheppard, in *Oklahoma Slave Narratives,* 378; Bonnifield, "The Choctaw Nation on the Eve of the Civil War," 392–93.
5. Baird and Goble, *The Story of Oklahoma,* 170–81; Gibson, *Oklahoma,* 117–29; Fischer, "United States Indian Agents to the Five Civilized Tribes," 34–83; Mulroy, *Seminole Freedmen,* 161–64.
6. Debo, *The Road to Disappearance,* 143–76; Zellar, *African Creeks, Estelvste and the Creek Nation,* 41–76; Warde, "Now the Wolf Has Come," 64–87; McReynolds, *The Seminoles,* 189–312; Trickett, "The Civil War in Indian Territory, 1861," 315–27.
7. Zellar, *African Creeks,* 45; Phoebe Banks, in *Oklahoma Slave Narratives,* 31; Warde, "Now the Wolf Has Come," 69; Trickett, "The Civil War in Indian Territory," 266–80.

8. Phoebe Banks, in *Oklahoma Slave Narratives,* 31–32; Jackson, "Political and Economic History of the Negro in Indian Territory," 71. There is disagreement among authors about the number of casualties. At least part of the confusion may be due to counting only combatants and not the civilian women and children. Many more died as the group fled north without supplies. Trickett, "Civil War in Indian Territory," 270; Banks, "Civil War Refugees from Indian Territory in the North," 286–98.

9. George Collamore quoted in Johnston, "'The Panther's Scream Is Often Heard,'" 84–107; William G. Coffin quoted in Banks, "Civil War Refugees from Indian Territory in the North," 289; Mulroy, *The Seminole Freedmen,* 169–71.

10. Banks, "Civil War Refugees from Indian Territory in the North," 296; Danziger, "The Office of Indian Affairs and the Problem of Civil War Indian Refugees in Kansas," 257–75.

11. Phoebe Banks, in *Oklahoma Slave Narratives,* 32; Banks, "Civil War Refugees from Indian Territory in the North," 294; Gibson, *Oklahoma,* 122–23; Baird and Goble, *The Story Oklahoma,* 175; Abel, *The American Indian under Reconstruction,* 292; Neeley B. Jackson, "Political and Economic History of the Negro in Indian Territory," 73–74.

12. Wrone, "The Cherokee Act of Emancipation," 87–90.

13. Chaney McNair narrative, in Rawick, *The American Slave,* 216. McNair's narrative is more extensive in this publication than in Baker and Baker, *The WPA Oklahoma Slave Narratives.* Eliza Hardwick, in Neilson, "Indian Masters, Black Slaves," 44; Hannah Worcester Hicks, quoted in Naylor, *African Cherokees in Indian Territory,* 143.

14. Rampp, "Negro Troop Activity in Indian Territory," 531–59; Baird and Goble, *The Story of Oklahoma,* 175–77; Jackson, "Political and Economic History of the Negro in Indian Territory," 78; Zellar, "Occupying the Middle Ground," 48–71.

15. R. C. Smith, in *Oklahoma Slave Narratives,* 400–401; Danziger, "The Office of Indian Affairs and the Problem of Civil War Indian Refugees in Kansas," 271–72.

16. Warde, "'Now the Wolf Has Come,'" 64–87; Banks, "Civil War Refugees from Indian Territory in the North," 297–98; Henry Smith quoted in Danziger, "The Office of Indian Affairs and the Problem of Indian Civil War Refugees," 270; James Harlan quoted in Abel, *The American Indian and the End of the Confederacy,* 312–13; McLoughlin, *After the Trail of Tears,* 209–10; Wardell, *A Political History of the Cherokee Nation,* 175–76.

17. Mary Grayson, in *Oklahoma Slave Narratives,* 174; Rochelle Allred Ward, in *Oklahoma Slave Narratives,* 447; James Harlan cited in Danziger, "The Office of Indian Affairs and the Problem of Indian Civil War Refugees," 274; Neilson, "Indian Masters, Black Slaves," 48.

18. Jim Tomm, IPH, reproduced in Teall, *Black History in Oklahoma,* 68; Naylor, *African Cherokees in Indian Territory,* 146; Chaney Richardson, in *Oklahoma Slave Narratives,* 349–50.

19. Lucinda Davis, in *Oklahoma Slave Narratives,* 112–15.

20. Chaney Richardson, in *Oklahoma Slave Narratives,* 349–50; Ashcroft, "Confederate Indian Department Conditions in August, 1864," 270–85.

21. Ashcroft, "Confederate Indian Department Conditions in August, 1864," 278, 282, 277; Sarah C. Watie letter to Stand Watie, September 4, 1864, in Dale and Little, *Cherokee Cavaliers,* 188.

22. LaVere, *Contrary Neighbors,* 174–75.

23. LaVere, *Contrary Neighbors,* 181–99; Johnson and Kingsley, *Chickasaw Rancher,* 51–55; John Criner, IPH 2:323–24.

24. Halliburton, *Red over Black,* 130–31; Washington, *Historical Development of the Negro in Oklahoma,* 17; Chaney Richardson, in *Oklahoma Slave Narratives,* 350; Morris Sheppard, in *Oklahoma Slave Narratives,* 380; Victoria Taylor Thompson, in *Oklahoma Slave Narratives,* 424; Henry Henderson quoted in Neilson, *Indian Masters, Black Slaves,* 48. See also Robinson, "The Sexual Color Line in Red and Black," 453.

25. Chaney McNair, quoted in Rawick, *American Slave,* 12:217; J. W. Stinnett, in *Oklahoma Slave Narratives,* 410.

26. Charlotte Johnson White, in *Oklahoma Slave Narratives,* 466; Sarah Wilson, in *Oklahoma Slave Narratives,* 497; Patsy Perryman, in *Oklahoma Slave Narratives,* 315–16; Phyllis Petite, in *Oklahoma Slave Narratives,* 319.

27. Lucinda Davis, in *Oklahoma Slave Narratives,* 115, 108.

28. Sarah Wilson, in *Oklahoma Slave Narratives,* 497–98. See Naylor, *African Cherokees in Indian Territory,* 158.

29. Mary Grayson, in *Oklahoma Slave Narratives,* 176-177.

30. Phyllis Petite, in *Oklahoma Slave Narratives,* 319–20; Phoebe Banks, in *Oklahoma Slave Narratives,* 33; Milley Fish Gilroy, IPH 26:64–65. Gilroy does not provide the race of the two girls, but she does not include them in the list of descendants as she does other stepchildren of the family of Siah Barnett.

31. Frances Banks, in *Oklahoma Slave Narratives,* 28; Chaney Richardson, in *Oklahoma Slave Narratives,* 350; Rochelle Allred Ward, in *Oklahoma Slave Narratives,* 446.

## Chapter 3

1. Jim Tomm, IPH, reproduced in Teall, *Black History in Oklahoma,* 68; Chaney Richardson, in *Oklahoma Slave Narratives,* 349–50.

2. Mary Lindsay, in *Oklahoma Slave Narratives,* 251–52; R. C. Smith, in *Oklahoma*

*Slave Narratives,* 400–401; U.S. Bureau of the Census, *Compendium of the Ninth Census of the United States,* 20–21; Doran, "Negro Slaves of the Five Civilized Tribes," 347.

3. Sanborn, "Hd. Quarters Commission for regulating relations between Freedmen of the Indian Territory and their former masters." Also quoted in Bailey, *Reconstruction in Indian Territory,* 49.

4. A thorough discussion of the Fort Smith negotiations is in Abel, *The American Indian and the End of the Confederacy,* 219–67.

5. Numerous articles have been written discussing the postwar treaty-making process with the Five Nations. See Grinde, and Taylor, "Red vs. Black," 211–29; Andrews, "Freedmen in Indian Territory," 367–76; Willson, "Freedmen in Indian Territory During Reconstruction," 230–44.

6. Eliza Daniel Strout, IPH 88:181–82.

7. Warner, *Generals in Blue,* 418–19; "Memorial Addresses in Honor of General John B. Sanborn" James Harlan, quoted in Abel, *The American Indian and the End of the Confederacy,* 275.

8. Sanborn, "Hd. Quarters Commission for regulating relations between Freedmen of the Indian Territory and their former masters." Also quoted in Bailey, *Reconstruction in Indian Territory,* 47–49.

9. John B. Sanborn, quoted in Abel, *The American Indian and the End of the Confederacy,* 284.

10. U.S. Commissioner of Indian Affairs, *Report,* 84.

11. Victoria Taylor Thompson, in *Oklahoma Slave Narratives,* 424.

12. John B. Sanborn, quoted in Abel, *The American Indian and the End of the Confederacy,* 292; Patsy Perryman, in *Oklahoma Slave Narratives,* 316.

13. Nancy Roger Bean, in *Oklahoma Slave Narratives,* 48–49.

14. Yarbrough, *Race and the Cherokee Nation,* 8. Yarbrough develops a thorough assessment of the Cherokee legislation regarding intermarriage and sexual relations between African Americans and whites.

15. Rachel Aldrich War, in *Oklahoma Slave Narratives,* 445; Lucinda Vann, in *Oklahoma Slave Narratives,* 440; Patsy Perryman, in *Oklahoma Slave Narratives,* 314.

16. Morton, "Reconstruction in the Creek Nation," 177, quoting the *Second Annual Report of the Board of Indian Commissioners to the Secretary of the Interior,* 1870, 138; Abbott, "The Race Question in the Forty-sixth State," 206–7; May, *African Americans and Native Americans in the Cherokee and Creek Nations,* 171, 178. For a thorough challenge to all previous research on mixed relationships between the Seminoles and African Americans, see Miller, "Seminoles and Africans under Seminole Law," 23–47.

17. Mulroy, *The Seminole Freedmen,* 266.

18. Mulroy, *The Seminole Freedmen,* 246–47, 256–64.

19. Mulroy, *The Seminole Freedmen,* 247–48, Heniha Mikko quoted on 248.

20. Mulroy, *The Seminole Freedmen,* 248–56.

21. Mulroy, *The Seminole Freedmen,* 264–66.

22. Porter, *The Negro on the American Frontier,* 79; Douglas H. Johnston, Chickasaw governor, quoted in Jeltz, "The Relations of Negroes and Choctaw and Chickasaw Indians," 37; Franklin, *My Life and an Era,* 1–25; Grinde and Taylor, "Red vs. Black," 217; Littlefield, *Chickasaw Freedmen,* 92–94, 83; Johnston, "Documentary Evidence of the Relations of Negroes and Indians," 40–41.

23. May, *African Americans and Native Americans in the Cherokee and Creek Nations,* 176–77; Robinson, "The Sexual Color Line in Red and Black," 450–75; Aldrich, *Black Heritage of Oklahoma,* 54–55. See also Pascoe, *What Comes Naturally,* 115, 136.

24. Sarah Wilson, in *Oklahoma Slave Narratives,* 498; Johnson Thompson, in *Oklahoma Slave Narratives,* 421; Phyllis Petite, in *Oklahoma Slave Narratives,* 320; Polly Colbert, in *Oklahoma Slave Narratives,* 89; Betty Robertson, in *Oklahoma Slave Narratives,* 357; Lucinda Vann, in *Oklahoma Slave Narratives,* 440.

25. Betty Robertson, in *Oklahoma Slave Narratives,* 367; Patsy Perryman, in *Oklahoma Slave Narratives,* 316; letter to author, November 25, 2003. I cannot verify the specific authenticity of this story except to say that a mixed-blood relationship existed in this family based on evidence from the *Oklahoma Slave Narratives.* I respect the request from the family member relating the story to remain anonymous.

26. May, *African Americans and Native Americans in the Cherokee and Creek Nations,* 193–200.

27. Wright, "Old Boggy Depot," 12–13.

28. Rampp, "Negro Troop Activity in Indian Territory," 531–59; Leckie, *The Buffalo Soldiers,* 68–69, 245–46; Richard C. Rohrs, "Fort Gibson, Forgotten Glory," in Faulk et al., *Early Military Forts and Posts in Oklahoma,* 27–38; McCombs, "Intruders in the Cherokee Nation"; Sober, *The Intruders*; Savage, "The Role of Negro Soldiers in Protecting the Indian Territory from Intruders," 25–34.

29. Katz, *Black Indians,* 158–62; R. C. Smith, in *Oklahoma Slave Narratives,* 402.

30. Gibson, *Oklahoma,* 131–34; Littlefield and Underhill, "Negro Marshals in the Indian Territory," 77–87; Williams, "Black Men Who Wore White Hats," 4–13; Williams, "Black Men Who Wore the Star," 83–90.

31. Littlefield and Underhill, "Negro Marshalls in the Indian Territory," 77–87. See also Burton, *Black, Red, and Deadly.* Additional lists of black law men are at "The Black Men Who Rode for Parker" and Burton, "Oklahoma's Frontier Indian Police."

32. Baird and Goble, *The Story of Oklahoma*, 190; R. C. Smith, in *Oklahoma Slave Narratives*, 401; Goins and Goble, *Historical Atlas of Oklahoma*, 116–17. See also Porter, "Negro Labor in the Western Cattle Industry," 346–74; Savage, *The Cherokee Strip Livestock Association*.

33. Johnson and Kingsley, *The Chickasaw Rancher*, 57–58.

34. Baird and Goble, *The Story of Oklahoma*, 191–93; U.S. Bureau of the Census, *Extra Census Bulletin*, 4.

35. Baird and Goble, *The Story of Oklahoma*, 194; Gibson, *Oklahoma,* 132–33; Savage, "The Role of Negro Soldiers in Protecting the Indian Territory from Intruders," 31; Morgan and Strickland, *Oklahoma Memories*, 43–44; Travis, "Life in the Cherokee Nation a Decade after the Civil War," 18–19.

36. Andrews, "Freedmen in Indian Territory," 372–73; Grinde and Taylor, "Red vs. Black," 218–19; Christensen, "J. Milton Turner," 1–19; Franklin, *Journey toward Hope*.

37. Fischer, "Oklahoma Territory," 3–8; Gibson, *Oklahoma,* 173–90; U.S. Bureau of the Census, *Extra Census Bulletin*, 4.

38. Grinde and Taylor, "Red vs. Black," 218–19; Alafair Carter Adams, quoted in Pew, "Boley, Oklahoma, Trial in American Apartheid," 17.

39. Rachel Aldrich Ward, in *Oklahoma Slave Narratives*, 448; May, *African Americans and Native Americans in the Cherokee and Creek Nations*, 196–202, 177–78.

40. Littlefield, *The Cherokee Freedmen*, 60–63.

41. Aaron Grayson, IPH, quoted in Teall, *Black History in Oklahoma*, 76–77.

## Chapter 4

1. John B. Sanborn, "Commission for Regulating Relations between Freedmen of the Indian Territory and Their Former Masters, 27 January, 1866," quoted in Abel, *The American Indian and the End of the Confederacy*, 291. Abel reproduces Circular Number 4.

2. Sanborn, "Commission for Regulating Relations between Freedmen of the Indian Territory and Their Former Masters, 27 January, 1866," 292. Theda Perdue maintains that Cherokee women resisted the efforts of the male economic elite to break the power of the matrilineal clans. They continued to preserve a communitarian ethic that competed with patriarchal individualism. Black Cherokee women, even though of unequal status, may have recognized the strength in this model. See Perdue, *Cherokee Women*.

3. Mary Lindsay, in *Oklahoma Slave Narratives*, 251; Chaney Richardson, in *Oklahoma Slave Narratives*, 350.

4. Betty Robertson, in *Oklahoma Slave Narratives*, 355; Patsy Perryman, in *Okla-*

*homa Slave Narratives,* 315.

5. Sarah Wilson, in *Oklahoma Slave Narratives,* 496. See also Travis, "Life in the Cherokee Nation a Decade after the Civil War," 21.

6. For typical explanations of work, see Mary Grayson, in *Oklahoma Slave Narratives,* 177; Nellie Johnson, in *Oklahoma Slave Narratives,* 227.

7. Polly Colbert, in *Oklahoma Slave Narratives,* 89. On Bloomfield Academy, see Mitchell and Renken, "The Golden Age of Bloomfield Academy in the Chickasaw Nation," 412–26; Cobb, *Listening to Our Grandmothers' Stories.*

8. Huggard, "Culture Mixing," 438, 445; Baker and Henshaw, *Women Who Pioneered Oklahoma,* 167–69.

9. Chaney McNair, in Rawick, *American Slave,* 12: 217–18.

10. Alice Douglass, in Rawick, *American Slave,* 7: 74; Current-Garcia and Hatfield, *Shem, Ham and Japheth,* 104–5; Zellar, *African Creeks,* 119.

11. Lucinda Davis, in *Oklahoma Slave Narratives,* 109–10; Patsy Perryman, in *Oklahoma Slave Narratives,* 87–88; Victoria Taylor Thompson, in *Oklahoma Slave Narratives,* 423; Phyllis Petite, in *Oklahoma Slave Narratives,* 319.

12. Nancy Rogers Bean, in *Oklahoma Slave Narratives,* 49; Rachel Ward, IPH 11:206.

13. Richard C. Rohrs, "Fort Gibson: Forgotten Glory," in Faulk et al., *Early Military Forts and Posts in Oklahoma,* 35, 26–38; Wickett, *Contested Territory,* 148–50; Gibson, *Oklahoma,* 132; Logsden, n.d. Although prostitution is briefly mentioned in many sources on Indian Territory, there has been no definitive study of it. Fort records are incomplete, as many forts were occupied sporadically, rarely had substantial numbers of occupants, and changed from U.S. to Confederate forts during the Civil War, and as the settlement line moved westward those related to the Five Tribes were closed down.

14. Allen, *Grandmothers of the Light;* Perone et al., *Medicine Women, Curanderas, and Women Doctors;* Crockett, "Health Conditions in the Indian Territory from the Civil War to 1890," 38; Ross, "Retrospection of a Pioneer Doctor's Wife," 6; Hayes, "Leroy Long," 342–60. See also Welton, "Frontier Doctors in Indian Territory Oklahoma."

15. Crockett, "Health Conditions in the Indian Territory from the Civil War to 1890," 32–33, 36–37.

16. Nancy Grayson Barnett, IPH 13:392–93. In "Power, Danger, and Control," Elizabeth D. Blum discusses how enslaved women used the knowledge of their environments in the provision of medicine, food, and shelter.

17. Polly Colbert, in *Oklahoma Slave Narratives,* 88; Rochelle Ward, in *Oklahoma Slave Narratives,* 448; Kiziah Love, in *Oklahoma Slave Narratives,* 259; Jane Davis Ward, IPH 11:196–97. See Crockett, "Health Conditions in the Indian Territory

from the Civil War to 1890," 21–39.

18. Frances Banks, in *Oklahoma Slave Narratives,* 28–29. According to Banks's narrative, she was clearly the caregiver for the famed Oklahoma historian Murial Wright. Wright altered the original draft of the narrative in pencil (5n), and the typed copy was never sent to Washington with the other freedmen's narratives (1n).

19. Blum, "Power, Danger, and Control," 247–66.

20. Johnson and Kingsley, *Chickasaw Rancher,* 63–64.

21. Lucinda Davis, in *Oklahoma Slave Narratives,* 110–11; Lucinda Vann, in *Oklahoma Slave Narratives,* 440; Betty Robertson, in *Oklahoma Slave Narratives,* 357; *Boley Progress,* 1905–15; Mrs. Essie B. Williams, letter to author, November 13, 1987.

22. U.S. Congress, Senate, *Reports of the Assistant Commissioner, Bureau of Refugees, Freedmen, and Abandoned Lands of Missouri, Arkansas, and Indian Territory,* 24; Franklin, *My Life and an Era,* 12–13.

23. Patsy Perryman, in *Oklahoma Slave Narratives,* 315; Elzora Lewis, IPH 33:342–43; Zellar, *African Creeks,* 120; Ballenger, "The Colored High School of the Cherokee Nation," 454–62.

24. Betty Robertson, in *Oklahoma Slave Narratives,* 356–57; Travis, "Life in the Cherokee Nation a Decade after the Civil War," 21; Morris Sheppard, in *Oklahoma Slave Narratives,* 380.

25. Fite, "Development of the Cotton Industry by the Five Civilized Tribes in Indian Territory," 342–53; Katz, *The American Negro,* 528, Table 21. The figures in Katz's table include both Indian Territory and Oklahoma Territory. An excellent study of woman and modern cotton agriculture in Texas is Sharpless, *Fertile Ground, Narrow Choices.*

26. Staniford, "Harrison to Celebrate 100th Birthday." In "Social Change and Sexual Inequality," Susan Archer Mann maintains that the position of freedwomen improved subjectively and objectively in the transition from slavery to share-cropping In her study, *Labor of Love, Labor of Sorrow,* Jacqueline Jones argues that at a time when industrialization was creating a male-female division of the labor system, black sharecropping families struggled to create patterns of joint, complementary work in spite of economic adversity and without the institutional supports given to white farm families (79–109). In Indian Territory institutional reinforcements were there for the Native peoples, but not for the freedmen. See also Brown, "Black Women in American Agriculture," 202–12.

27. *Senate Document,* 54th Congress, 1st Session, 182, 111, quoted in Littlefield, *The Chickasaw Freedmen,* 80–81.

28. Donald A. Grinde and Quintard Taylor, "Slaves, Freedmen, and Native Americans in Indian Territory (Oklahoma), 1865–1907," in Chan et al., *Peoples of Color*

*in the American West,* 290; Bogle, "On Our Way to the Promised Land," 173–74.

29. Kiziah Love, in *Oklahoma Slave Narratives,* 257–62; Mary Lindsay, in *Oklahoma Slave Narratives,* 252.

30. Mary Lindsay, in *Oklahoma Slave Narratives,* 249–50.

31. Franklin, *My Life and an Era,* 22–25.

32. Tolson, *The Black Oklahomans,* 93, 97; Gray, "Taft," 430–47.

33. Alafair Carter Adams, quoted in Pew, "Boley, Oklahoma, Trial in American Apartheid," 17; Bittle and Geis, "Racial Self-Fulfillment and the Rise of an All-Negro Community in Oklahoma," 249–50, quotation from Sameth, "Creek Indians," 56; Crockett, *The Black Towns,* 28, 68. On black town promotion, see Hamilton, *Black Towns and Profit.*

34. Essie B. Williams to author, November 13, 1987. Mrs. Williams's letter included a list of Boley pioneer women and identified those who were both native-born and immigrant. Harshbarger, "Our Boley"; *Boley Progress* and *Boley Informer,* 1905–15.

35. *Clearview Tribune* and *Clearview Patriarch,* 1905–15; *Boley Informer,* May 10, 1911. Bonnie Thornton Dill argues in "Our Mothers' Grief" that racial-ethnic women worked both in the public (productive) and private (reproductive) spheres in order to sustain and stabilize their families, and that the contradiction between the prevailing domestic ideology and the reality of their lives created conflicts and stereotypes. In the all-black Oklahoma communities, this duality strengthened and nurtured self-esteem and worth, as men and women were committed to a higher communal goal of economic independence and racial example.

## Chapter 5

1. Gaskin, *Black Baptists in Oklahoma,* 85, 92; *Baptist Missionary Magazine* 16 (Boston, 1836), in IPH 13:289–90.

2. L. W. Marks quoted in Gaskin, *Black Baptists in Oklahoma,* 95; Baptist Missionary and Educational Convention of Oklahoma and Indian Territories, Annual Report, 1891, quoted in Gaskin, *Black Baptists in Oklahoma,* 95.

3. McLoughlin, "Indian Slaveholders and Presbyterian Missionaries," 551; Franklin, *My Life and an Era,* 14–18. Buck Colbert Franklin's grandfather bought his family out of slavery. His father fought for the Union in the Civil War, and his mother was a Black Choctaw. Buck Franklin is the father of renowned American historian John Hope Franklin.

4. Flickinger, *The Choctaw Freedmen and the Story of Oak Hill Industrial Academy,* 17, 25–26.

5. Flickinger, *The Choctaw Freedmen and the Story of Oak Hill Industrial Academy,* 17–19, 24, 91–93.

6. Victoria Taylor Thompson, in *Oklahoma Slave Narratives*, 424; Betty Robertson, in *Oklahoma Slave Narratives*, 356; Charlotte Johnson White, in *Oklahoma Slave Narratives*, 466; Phyllis Petite, in *Oklahoma Slave Narratives*, 320.

7. Chaney McNair, in *Oklahoma Slave Narratives*, 275–76; Kiziah Love, in *Oklahoma Slave Narratives*, 261; Frances Banks, in *Oklahoma Slave Narratives,* 28. It is obvious that some of the responses by the freedwomen about ghost or spirits were deliberately elicited by the leading questions of the fieldworkers.

8. Betty Robertson, in *Oklahoma Slave Narratives*, 357; Kiziah Love, in *Oklahoma Slave Narratives*, 261; Matilda Poe, in *Oklahoma Slave Narratives*, 325.

9. Dennis Vann, IPH 11:63–64.

10. Eliza Hartford letter, quoted in Flickinger, *The Choctaw Freedmen and the Story of Oak Hill Industrial Academy,* 115–16; Littlefield, *The Chickasaw Freedmen,* 89–90.

11. Chaney Richardson, in *Oklahoma Slave Narratives,* 351; Mulroy, *The Seminole Freedmen,* 259.

12. Flickinger, *The Choctaw Freedmen and the Story of Oak Hill Industrial Academy,* 101–4; Jeltz, "The Relations of Negroes and Choctaw and Chickasaw Indians," 35.

13. Flickinger, *The Choctaw Freedmen and the Story of Oak Hill Industrial Academy,* 105–13, 117.

14. Flickinger, *The Choctaw Freedmen and the Story of Oak Hill Industrial Academy*, 123, 146–54. For a narrative by a Choctaw/Chickasaw freedwoman who attended Oak Hill Academy, see Baker and Henshaw, *Women Who Pioneered Oklahoma,* 192–94.

15. Bass, *The Story of Tullahassee,* 262–69; Zellar, *African Creeks,* 31.

16. Debo, *The Road to Disappearance,* 249; Zellar, *African Creeks,* 135–36, 177–80; John P. Lawton Report, 1883, in Teall, *Black History in Oklahoma,* 88; Phoebe Banks, in *Oklahoma Slave Narratives,* 33.

17. Gaskin, *Black Baptists in Oklahoma,* 255–57.

18. Zellar, *African Creeks,* 176–77; Mulroy, *Seminole Freedmen,* 259–60; McReynolds, *The Seminoles,* 356.

19. Littlefield, *The Cherokee Freedmen,* 52–58.

20. Ballenger, "The Colored High School of the Cherokee Nation," 454–62.

21. Littlefield, *The Chickasaw Freedmen,* 119-120; Bender, "'We Surely Gave Them an Uplift,'" 184.

22. Bender, "'We Surely Gave Them an Uplift,'" 186–89, 187; Littlefield, *The Chickasaw Freedmen,* 112–39, 134.

23. *Cherokee Advocate,* September 9, 1876, quoted in Littlefield, *Cherokee Freedmen,* 52; Franklin, *My Life and an Era,* 12–13.

24. Johnson Thompson, in *Oklahoma Slave Narratives,* 421; Mary Lindsay, in *Oklahoma Slave Narratives,* 177; "Opening of the Public School," *Boley Progress,* September 14, 1905; Katz, *American Negro,* 386, diagram 4, 415, Table 19.

25. Franklin, *The Blacks in Oklahoma,* 99.

26. Franklin, *The Blacks in Oklahoma,* 97–104. See also Hamilton, *Black Towns and Profit;* Crockett, *The Black Towns.*

27. Fischer, "Oklahoma Territory," 3–8; Gibson, *Oklahoma,* 173–90. See also Colbert, "Elias Cornelius Boudinot," 249–59. Crew, photocopy of IPH interview; Tolson, *The Black Oklahomans,* 69–89; Franklin, *The Blacks in Oklahoma,* 6–8.

28. Gibson, *Oklahoma,* 193–95.

29. See a discussion of Chitto Harjo and Native resistance in Baird and Goble, *The Story of Oklahoma,* 314–19.

30. "To Make a Negro State," *New York Times,* February 28, 1890; Littlefield, "Black Dreams and 'Free' Homes," 341–57; *Boley Progress,* July 20, 1905; Harshbarger, "Our Boley," 35; *Langston City Herald,* November 17, 1892, 20 October 1894; Hamilton, "The Origin and Early Developments of Langston, Oklahoma," 270–87; "The Blacks in Oklahoma," *New York Times,* April 9, 1891.

31. Tolson, *The Black Oklahomans,* 54; Hale, "European Immigrants in Oklahoma," 182–83.

32. Barbara Krauthamer, "In Their 'Native Country': Freedpeople's Understandings of Culture and Citizenship in the Choctaw and Chickasaw Nations," in Miles and Holland, *Crossing Waters,* 100.

33. Teall, *Black History in Oklahoma,* 98. See Grinde and Taylor, "Red vs. Black," 211–29. In *The Color of the Land,* David A. Chang documents the culmination of factors that led to a transition in definitions of race and citizenship in the Indian nations.

34. Thoburn, *A Standard History of Oklahoma,* 345–47. Thoburn describes the communities of blacks as "intruding negroes" with "shiftless dispositions" who "resorted to stealing" from the Indians to support themselves. Baker and Henshaw, *Women Who Pioneered Oklahoma,* 148; Johnson and Kingsley, *The Chickasaw Rancher,* 52–53. Wickett, *Contested Territory,* 145–46; LaVere, *Contrary Neighbors,* 180–83.

35. Everett, "Lynching."

36. Johnson and Kingsley, *Chickasaw Rancher,* 121 23.

37. The founding of the black women's club movement is discussed in Giddings, *"When and Where I Enter,"* 75–117. The importance of the direction of Mary Church Terrell, who served as the first NACW president, is outlined in Jones, "Mary Church Terrell and the National Association of Colored Women," 20–33. Rosalyn Terborg-Penn addresses the discrimination against black women in

"Discrimination against Afro-American Women in the Women's Movement, 1830–1920," in Harley and Terborg-Penn, *The Afro-American Woman,* 17–27. An excellent analysis of the "True Womanhood" concept and of the racist sympathies of white suffrage leaders is developed by Barbara Hilkart Andolsen in *"Daughters of Jefferson, Daughters of Bootblacks."*

38. Margaret Murray Washington, "National Federation of Afro-American Women," reprinted in *Langston City Herald,* October 26, 1895; *Boley Progress,* December 10, 1908; "Mothers Club for Boley City School," *Boley Progress*, November 24, 1910; Mrs. Essie B. Williams, letter to author, November 13, 1987. See also Harshbarger, "Our Boley." The historical invisibility of these organizations as well as the central role they played in the creation of the black communities are discussed in Scott, "Most Invisible of All," 3–22.

39. *Clearview Patriarch,* August 1, 1912, March 23, 1911; "Timely Suggestions by a Woman of the Race," *Oklahoma Guide* (Guthrie), July 23, 1903.

40. Strong, "The Origin, Development, and Current Status of the Oklahoma Federation of Colored Women's Clubs," 45, 57, 59, 64, 62, 87–88.

41. Strong, "The Origin, Development, and Current Status of the Oklahoma Federation of Colored Women's Clubs," 83, 115–68.

## Epilogue

1. Roberts, "Ruins Still Standing at Keystone Lake."

2. Walton, "Find a Grave Memorial." The information and photographed headstones were contributed by Susie Moore.

3. Anderson, *Changing Woman,* 13.

# Bibliography

## Books

Abel, Annie H. *The American Indian and the End of the Confederacy, 1863–1866.* Lincoln: University of Nebraska Press, 1993.

———. *The American Indian under Reconstruction.* Cleveland, Ohio: Arthur H. Clark, 1925.

Aldrich, Gene. *Black Heritage of Oklahoma.* Edmond, Okla.: Thompson, 1973.

Allen, Paula Gunn. *Grandmothers of the Light: A Medicine Woman's Sourcebook.* Boston: Beacon Press, 1991.

Anderson, Karen. *Changing Woman: A History of Racial Ethnic Women in Modern America.* New York: Oxford University Press, 1996.

Andolsen, Barbara Hilkart. *"Daughters of Jefferson, Daughters of Bootblacks": Racism and American Feminism.* Macon, Ga.: Mercer University Press, 1986.

Bailey, M. Thomas. *Reconstruction in Indian Territory,: A Story of Avarice, Discrimination, and Opportunism.* Port Washington, N.Y.: Kennikat Press, 1972.

Baird, W. David., ed. *A Creek Warrior for the Confederacy: The Autobiography of Chief G. W. Grayson.* Norman: University of Oklahoma Press, 1988.

Baird, W. David, and Danney Goble. *The Story of Oklahoma.* Norman: University of Oklahoma Press, 1994.

Baker, T. Lindsey, and Julie P. Baker. *The WPA Oklahoma Slave Narratives.* Norman: University of Oklahoma Press, 1996.

Baker, Terri M., and Connie Oliver Henshaw. *Women Who Pioneered Oklahoma: Stories from the WPA Narratives.* Norman: University of Oklahoma Press, 2007.

Bass, Althea. *The Story of Tullahassee.* Oklahoma City: Semco Color Press, 1960.

Brooks, James, ed. *Confounding the Color Line: The Indian-Black Experience in North America.* Lincoln: University of Nebraska Press, 2002.

Bunn, Clinton O., and William C. Bunn, compilers. *Constitution and Enabling Act of the State of Oklahoma, Annotated and Indexed.* Ardmore, Okla.: Bunn Brothers, 1907.

Burton, Arthur T. *Black, Red, and Deadly: Black and Indian Gunfighters of the Indian Territory.* Waco, Texas: Sunbelt Media, 1994.

Chan, Sucheng, Douglas Henry Daniels, Mario T. Garcia, and Terry P. Wilson, eds. *Peoples of Color in the American West.* Lexington, Mass.: D. C. Heath, 1994.

Chang, David A. *The Color of the Land: Race, Nation, and the Nature of Landownership in Oklahoma, 1832–1929.* Chapel Hill: University of North Carolina Press, 2010.

Cobb, Amanda. *Listening to Our Grandmothers' Stories: The Bloomfield Academy for Chickasaw Females, 1852–1949.* Winnipeg, Canada: Bison Books, 2007.

Crockett, Norman L. *The Black Towns.* Lawrence: Regents Press of Kansas, 1979.

Current-Garcia, Eugene, and Dorothy B. Hatfield, eds. *Shem, Ham and Japheth: The Papers of W. O. Tuggle, Comprising His Indian Diary, Sketches and Observations, Myths and Washington Journal in the Territory and at the Capital, 1879–1882.* Athens: University of Georgia Press, 1973.

Debo, Angie. *The Road to Disappearance: A History of the Creek Indians.* Norman: University of Oklahoma Press, 1941.

Faulk, Odie B., Kenny A. Franks, and Paul F. Lambert, eds. *Early Military Forts and Posts in Oklahoma.* Oklahoma City: Oklahoma Historical Society, 1978.

Flickinger, Robert Elliott. *The Choctaw Freedmen and the Story of Oak Hill Industrial Academy.* Berwyn Heights, Md.: Heritage Books, 2002.

Foreman, Grant. *The Five Civilized Tribes.* Norman: University of Oklahoma Press, 1934.

———. *Indian Removal: The Emigration of the Five Civilized Tribes of Indians.* Norman: University of Oklahoma Press, 1932.

Franklin, Jimmie Lewis. *The Blacks in Oklahoma.* Norman: University of Oklahoma Press, 2011.

———. *Journey toward Hope: A History of Black in Oklahoma.* Norman: University of Oklahoma Press, 1982.

Franklin, Buck Colbert. *My Life and an Era: The Autobiography of Buck Colbert Franklin.* ed. John Hope Franklin and John Whittington Franklin. Baton Rouge: Louisiana State University Press, 1997.

Gaskin, J. M. *Black Baptists in Oklahoma.* Oklahoma City: Messenger Press, 1992.

Gibson, Arrell M. *The American Indian: Prehistory to the Present.* Lexington, Mass.: D. C. Heath, 1980.

———. *Oklahoma: A History of Five Centuries.* 2nd edition. Norman: University of Oklahoma Press, 1981.

Giddings, Paula J. *"When and Where I Enter": The Impact of Black Women on Race and Sex in America.* New York: William Morrow, 1984.

Goins, Charles Robert, and Danney Goble. *Historical Atlas of Oklahoma.* 4th edition. Norman: University of Oklahoma Press, 2006.

Halliburton, R., Jr. *Red over Black: Slavery among the Cherokee Indians.* Westport, Conn.: Greenwood Press, 1977.

Hamilton, Kenneth M. *Black Towns and Profit: Promotion and Development in the Trans-Appalachian West, 1877–1915.* Urbana: University of Illinois Press, 1991.

Harley, Sharon, and Rosalyn Terborg-Penn, eds. *The Afro-American Woman: Struggles and Images.* Port Washington, N.Y.: Kennikat Press, National University Publications, 1978.

Johnson, Neil R., and C. Kingsley, eds. *The Chickasaw Rancher.* Boulder: University Press of Colorado, 2001.

Jones, Jacqueline. *Labor of Love, Labor of Sorrow: Black Women, Work, and the Family from Slavery to the Present.* New York: Basic Books, 1986.

Katz, William Loren, ed. *The American Negro: His History and Literature.* New York: Arno Press, 1968.

———. *Black Indians: A Hidden Heritage.* New York: Athenaeum Press, 1986.

Kidwell, Clara Sue. *The Choctaws in Oklahoma: From Tribe to Nation, 1855–1870.* Norman: University of Oklahoma Press, 2007.

LaVere, David. *Contrary Neighbors: Southern Plains and Removed Indians in Indian Territory.* Norman: University of Oklahoma Press, 2000.

Leckie, William H. *The Buffalo Soldiers: A Narrative of the Negro Cavalry in the West.* Norman: University of Oklahoma Press, 1967.

Littlefield, Daniel F., Jr. *Africans and Creeks: From the Colonial Period to the Civil War.* Westport, Conn.: Greenwood Press, 1979.

———. *Africans and Seminoles: From Removal to Emancipation.* Jackson: University Press of Mississippi, 1977.

———. *The Cherokee Freedmen: From Emancipation to American Citizenship.* Westport, Conn.: Greenwood Press, 1978.

———. *Chickasaw Freedmen: A People without a Country.* Westport, Conn.: Greenwood Press, 1980.

May, Katja. *African Americans and Native Americans in the Cherokee and Creek Nations, 1830s–1920s: Collision and Collusion.* New York: Routledge, 1996.

McLoughlin, William G. *After the Trail of Tears: The Cherokees' Struggle for Sovereignty, 1839–1880.* Chapel Hill: University of North Carolina Press, 1994.

McReynolds, Edwin C. *The Seminoles.* Norman: University of Oklahoma Press, 1957.

Miles, Tiya. *Ties That Bind: The Story of an Afro-Cherokee Family in Slavery and Freedom.* Berkeley: University of California Press, 2006.

Miles, Tiya, and Sharon P. Holland, eds. *Crossing Waters, Crossing Worlds: The African Diaspora in Indian Country*. Durham, N.C.: Duke University Press, 2006.

Minges, Patrick M. *Slavery in the Cherokee Nation: The Keetoowah Society and the Defining of a People 1855–1867*. New York: Routledge, 2003.

Morgan, Anne Hodges, and Rennard Strickland, eds. *Oklahoma Memories*. Norman: University of Oklahoma Press, 1981.

Mulroy, Kevin. *The Seminole Freedmen: A History*. Norman: University of Oklahoma Press, 2007.

Naylor, Celia. *African Cherokees in Indian Territory: From Chattel to Citizens*. Chapel Hill: University of North Carolina Press, 2008.

Nichols, Roger L. *American Indians in U.S. History*. Norman: University of Oklahoma Press, 2003.

Pascoe, Peggy. *What Comes Naturally: Miscegenation Law and the Making of Race in America*. New York: Oxford University Press, 2009.

Perdue, Theda. *Cherokee Women: Gender and Culture Change*. Lincoln: University of Nebraska Press, 1998.

———. *Slavery and the Evolution of Cherokee Society, 1540–1860*. Knoxville: University of Tennessee Press, 1979.

Perone, Bobette, H. Henrietta Stockel, and Victoria Krueger. *Medicine Women, Curanderas, and Women Doctors*. Norman: University of Oklahoma Press, 1989.

Porter, Kenneth W. *The Negro on the American Frontier*. New York: Arno Press, 1971.

Rawick, George P., ed. *The American Slave: A Composite Autobiography*. Westport, Conn.: Greenwood Press, 1977.

Saunt, Claudio. *Black, White, and Indian: Race and the Unmaking of the American Family*. New York: Oxford University Press, 2005.

———. *A New Order of Things, Property, Power, and the Transformation of the Creek Indians, 1733–1816*. New York: Cambridge University Press, 1999.

Savage, William W., Jr. *The Cherokee Strip Livestock Association*. Norman: University of Oklahoma Press, 1968.

Sharpless, Rebecca. *Fertile Ground, Narrow Choices: Women on Texas Cotton Farms, 1900–1940*. Chapel Hill: University of North Carolina Press, 1999.

Sober, Nancy H. *The Intruders: The Illegal Residents of the Cherokee Nation, 1866–1907*. Ponca City, Okla.: Cherokee Books, 1991.

Sturm, Circe. *Blood Politics: Race, Culture, and Identity in the Cherokee Nation of Oklahoma*. Berkeley: University of California Press, 2002.

Teall, Kaye M. *Black History in Oklahoma: A Resource Book*. Oklahoma City: Oklahoma City Public Schools, 1971.

Thoburn, Joseph B. *A Standard History of Oklahoma*. Vol. 1. Chicago: American Historical Society, 1916.

Tolson, Arthur L. *The Black Oklahomans: A History, 1541–1972*. New Orleans: Edwards, 1972.

Walker, Alice. *Anything We Love Can Be Saved: A Writer's Activism*. New York: Ballantine Books, 1998.

Warde, Mary Jane. *George Washington Grayson and the Creek Nation, 1843–1920*. Norman: University of Oklahoma Press, 1999.

Wardell, Morris L. *A Political History of the Cherokee Nation*. Norman: University of Oklahoma Press, 1938.

Warner, Ezra J. *Generals in Blue: Lives of the Union Commanders*. 1964; Baton Rouge: Louisiana State University Press, 1992.

Waselkov, Gregory A. *A Conquering Spirit: Fort Mims and the Redstick War of 1813–1814*. Tuscaloosa: University of Alabama Press, 2006.

Wickett, Murray R. *Contested Territory: Whites, Native Americans and African Americans in Oklahoma, 1865–1907*. Baton Rouge: Louisiana State University, 2000.

Woodward, Grace Steele. *The Cherokees*. Norman: University of Oklahoma Press, 1963.

Yarbrough, Fay. *Race and the Cherokee Nation: Sovereignty in the Nineteenth Century*. Philadelphia: University of Pennsylvania Press, 2007.

Zellar, Gary. *African Creeks, Estelvste and the Creek Nation*. Norman: University of Oklahoma Press, 2007.

## Articles

Abbott, L. J. "The Race Question in the Forty-sixth State." *Independent,* July 25, 1907, 206–7.

Andrews, Thomas F. "Freedmen in Indian Territory: A Post–Civil War Dilemma." *Journal of the West* 4 (July 1965): 367–76.

Ashcroft, Allan C. "Confederate Indian Department Conditions in August, 1864." *Chronicles of Oklahoma* 41 (Autumn 1963): 270–85.

Ballenger, T. L. "The Colored High School of the Cherokee Nation." *Chronicles of Oklahoma* 30 (Winter 1952–53): 454–62.

Banks, Dean. "Civil War Refugees from Indian Territory in the North, 1861–1864." *Chronicles of Oklahoma* 41 (Autumn 1963): 286–98.

Bender, Norman J. "'We Surely Gave Them an Uplift': Taylor F. Ealy and the Mission School for Freedmen." *Chronicles of Oklahoma* 61 (Summer 1983): 180–84

Bittle, William E., and Gilbert Geis. "Racial Self-Fulfillment and the Rise of an All-Negro Community in Oklahoma." *Phylon* 18 (1957): 247–60.

Bogle, Lori. "On Our Way to the Promised Land: Black Migration from Arkansas to Oklahoma, 1889–1893." *Chronicles of Oklahoma* 72 (Summer 1994): 160–74.

Bonnifield, Paul. "The Choctaw Nation on the Eve of the Civil War." *Journal of the West* 7 (1973): 386–402.

Blum, Elizabeth D. "Power, Danger, and Control: Slave Women's Perceptions of Wilderness in the Nineteenth Century." *Women's Studies* 31 (2002): 247–66.

Braund, Kathryn E. Holland. "The Creek Indians, Blacks, and Slavery." *Journal of Southern History* 57 (November 1991): 601–36.

Brown, Minnie Miller. "Black Women in American Agriculture." *Agricultural History* 50 (January 1976): 202–12.

Christensen, Lawrence O. "J. Milton Turner: An Appraisal." *Missouri Historical Review* 70 (1975): 1–19.

Colbert, Thomas Bernell. "Elias Cornelius Boudinot: The Indian Orator and Lecturer." *American Indian Quarterly* 13 (Summer 1989): 249–59.

Crockett, Bernice Norman. "Health Conditions in the Indian Territory from the Civil War to 1890." *Chronicles of Oklahoma* 36 (Winter 1958): 21–38.

Danziger, Edmund J., Jr. "The Office of Indian Affairs and the Problem of Civil War Indian Refugees in Kansas." *Kansas Historical Quarterly* 35 (Autumn 1969): 257–75.

Doran, Michael F. "Negro Slaves of the Five Civilized Tribes." *Annals of the Association of American Geographers* 68 (September 1978): 335–50.

———. "Population Statistics of Nineteenth Century Indian Territory." *Chronicles of Oklahoma* 53 (Winter 1975–76): 492–515.

Fischer, LeRoy H. "Oklahoma Territory, 1890–1907." *Chronicles of Oklahoma* 53 (Spring 1975): 3–8.

———. "United States Indian Agents to the Five Civilized Tribes." *Chronicles of Oklahoma* 51 (Spring 1973): 34–83.

Fite, Gilbert C. "Development of the Cotton Industry by the Five Civilized Tribes in Indian Territory." *Journal of Southern History* 15 (August 1949): 342–53.

Gray, Linda C. "Taft: Town on the Black Frontier." *Chronicles of Oklahoma* 66 (Winter 1988–89): 430–47.

Grinde, Donald A., Jr., and Quintard Taylor. "Red vs. Black: Conflict and Accommodation in the Post Civil War Indian Territory, 1865–1907." *American Indian Quarterly* 8 (Summer 1984): 211–29.

Hale, Douglas. "European Immigrants in Oklahoma: A Survey." *Chronicles of Oklahoma* 53 (Summer 1975): 179–83.

Halliburton, R., Jr. "Black Slave Control in the Cherokee Nation." *Journal of Ethnic Studies* 3 (Summer 1975): 23–35.

———. "Origins of Black Slavery among the Cherokees." *Chronicles of Oklahoma* 52 (1974–75): 483–96.

Hamilton, Kenneth M. "The Origin and Early Developments of Langston, Oklahoma." *Journal of Negro History* 62 (March 1977): 270–87.

Hayes, Basil A. "Leroy Long: Teacher of Medicine." *Chronicles of Oklahoma* 20 (December 1942): 342–60.

Huggard, Christopher J. "Culture Mixing: Everyday Life on Missions among the Choctaws." *Chronicles of Oklahoma* 70 (Winter 1992–93): 432–45.

Jeltz, Wyatt F. "The Relations of Negroes and Choctaw and Chickasaw Indians." *Journal of Negro History* 33 (January 1948): 24–37.

Johnston, Carolyn Ross. "'The Panther's Scream Is Often Heard': Cherokee Women in Indian Territory During the Civil War." *Chronicles of Oklahoma* 78 (Spring 2000): 84–107.

Johnston, J. H. "Documentary Evidence of the Relations of Negroes and Indians." *Journal of Negro History* 14 (January 1929): 21–43.

Jones, Beverly W. "Mary Church Terrell and the National Association of Colored Women, 1896 to 1901." *Journal of Negro History* 67 (Spring 1982): 20–33.

Knight, Oliver. "Fifty Years of Choctaw Law, 1834–1884." *Chronicles of Oklahoma* 31 (Spring 1953): 76–95.

Krogman, Wilton Marion. "The Racial Composition of the Seminole Indians of Florida and Oklahoma." *Journal of Negro History* 19 (October 1934): 412–30.

Littlefield, Daniel F. "Black Dreams and 'Free' Homes: The Oklahoma Territory, 1891–1894." *Phylon* 34 (December 1973): 341–57.

Littlefield, Daniel F., Jr., and Mary Ann Littlefield. "The Beams Family: Free Blacks in Indian Territory." *Journal of Negro History* 61 (January 1976): 17–35.

Littlefield, Daniel F., Jr., and Lonnie E. Underhill. "Negro Marshals in the Indian Territory." *Journal of Negro History* 56 (April 1971): 77–87.

Littlefield, Daniel F., Jr., and Lonnie E. Underhill. "Slave 'Revolt' in the Cherokee Nation, 1842." *American Indian Quarterly* 3 (Summer 1977): 121–31.

Mahnken, Norbert R. "Old Baptist Mission and Evan Jones." *Chronicles of Oklahoma* 67 (Summer 1989): 174–93.

McFadden, Marguerite. "The Saga of 'Rich Joe' Vann." *Chronicles of Oklahoma* 61 (1983): 68–79.

McLoughlin, William G. "Indian Slaveholders and Presbyterian Missionaries, 1837–1861." *Church History* 42 (December 1973): 535–51.

———. "Red Indians, Black Slavery and White Racism: America's Slaveholding Indians." *American Quarterly* 26 (October 1974): 367–85.

Merrell, James H. "The Problem of Slavery in the Cherokee Culture." *Reviews in American History* 7 (December 1979): 509–14.

Miller, Diane. "Frontier Freedom: Seeking the Underground Railroad in Indian Territory." *Chronicles of Oklahoma* 87 (Spring 2009): 76–93.

Miller, Susan A. "Seminoles and Africans under Seminole Law: Sources and Discourses of Tribal Sovereignty and 'Black Indian' Entitlement." *Wicazo Sa Review* 20 (Spring 2005): 23–47.

Mitchell, Irene E., and Ida Belle Renken. "The Golden Age of Bloomfield Academy in the Chickasaw Nation." *Chronicles of Oklahoma* 49 (Winter 1971–72): 412–26.

Morton, Ohland. "Reconstruction in the Creek Nation." *Chronicles of Oklahoma* 9 (June 1931): 171–77.

Neilson, John C. "Indian Masters, Black Slaves: An Oral History of the Civil War in Indian Territory." *Plains-Panhandle Historical Review* 65 (1992): 40–51.

Owsley, Frank L., Jr. "The Fort Mims Massacre." *Alabama Review* 3 (1971): 192–204.

Perdue, Theda. "Cherokee Planters, Black Slaves, and African Colonization." *Chronicles of Oklahoma* 60, no. 3 (1982): 322–29.

———. "People without a Place: Aboriginal Cherokee Bondage." *Indian Historian* 9 (Summer 1976): 31–37.

Pew, Thomas W., Jr. "Boley, Oklahoma: Trial in American Apartheid." *American West* 17 (July 1980): 14–21, 54–56, 63.

Porter, Kenneth W. "Negro Labor in the Western Cattle Industry, 1866–1900." *Labor History* 10 (Summer 1969): 346–74.

Rampp, Lary C. "Negro Troop Activity in Indian Territory, 1863–1865." *Chronicles of Oklahoma* 47 (Spring 1969): 531–59.

Roberts, Paula. "Ruins Still Standing at Keystone Lake." *Tulsa District Record*, Department of the Army, Tulsa District, Oklahoma, Corps of Engineers, January/February 2002, 1.

Robinson, Charles F., II. "The Sexual Color Line in Red and Black: Anti-miscegenation and the Sooner State." *Chronicles of Oklahoma* 82 (Winter 2004–5): 450–75.

Savage, W. Sherman. "The Role of Negro Soldiers in Protecting the Indian Territory from Intruders." *Journal of Negro History* 36 (January 1951): 25–34.

Scott, Anne Firor. "Most Invisible of All: Black Women's Voluntary Associations." *Journal of Southern History* 56 (February 1990): 3–22.

Searcy, Martha Condray. "The Introduction of African Slavery into the Creek Indian Nation." *Georgia Historical Quarterly* 66 (Spring 1982): 21–32.

Smith, C. Calvin. "The Oppressed Oppressors: Negro Slavery among the Choctaw Indians of Oklahoma." *Red River Valley Historical Review* 2 (1975): 240–53.

Travis, V. A. "Life in the Cherokee Nation a Decade after the Civil War." *Chronicles of Oklahoma* 4 (March 1926): 16–30.

Trickett, Dean. "The Civil War in Indian Territory, 1861" (part 1). *Chronicles of Oklahoma* 17 (September 1939): 315–27.

———. "The Civil War in Indian Territory, 1861" (part 2). *Chronicles of Oklahoma* 18 (September 1940): 266–80.

Warde, Mary Jane. "Now the Wolf Has Come: The Civilian Civil War in Indian Territory." *Chronicles of Oklahoma* 71 (Spring 1993): 64–87.

Williams, Nudie E. "Black Men Who Wore White Hats: Grant Johnson, United States Deputy Marshal." *Red River Valley Historical Review* 5 (1980): 4–13.

———. "Black Men Who Wore the Star." *Chronicles of Oklahoma* 59 (1981): 83–90.

Willson, Walt. "Freedmen in Indian Territory During Reconstruction." *Chronicles of Oklahoma* 49 (Summer 1971): 230–44.

Wright, Murial. "Old Boggy Depot." *Chronicles of Oklahoma* 5 (March 1927): 4–17.

Wrone, David. R. "The Cherokee Act of Emancipation." *Journal of Ethnic Studies* 1 (Fall 1973): 87–90.

Zellar, Gary. "Occupying the Middle Ground: African Creeks in the First Indian Home Guard, 1862–1865." *Chronicles of Oklahoma* 76 (Spring 1998): 48–71.

## Archival Material

Dale, Edward E., and Gaston Little, eds. *Cherokee Cavaliers: Forty Years of History as Told in the Correspondence of the Ridge-Watie Family.* 1939. Western History Collections, University of Oklahoma Library, Norman.

Doris Duke Oral History Collection. Western History Collections, University of Oklahoma Library, Norman.

Foreman, Stephen. *Journal and Letters of Stephen Foreman, Cherokee Minister.* Norman: Western History Collections, University of Oklahoma Library.

Indian Pioneer History. Western History Collections, University of Oklahoma Library Norman.

Ross, Maude Barnes. "Recollections of a Pioneer Doctor's Wife." Typescript. Ross Collection, Western History Collections, University of Oklahoma, Norman.

Washington, Nathaniel J. *Historical Development of the Negro in Oklahoma.* 1948. Archive Paper, Oklahoma State University, Tulsa.

## Internet Sources

Burton, Art T. "Oklahoma's Frontier Indian Police." 1996. http://www.coax.net/people/lwf/FIP_PT5.HTM, accessed May 1, 2011.

Chavez, Will. "Freedmen Vow to Continue Fighting Cherokee Nation for Their Rights." Cherokee Phoenix.Org, August 30, 2011. http://www.cherokeephoenix.org/Article/Index/5449, accessed March 7, 2012.

Crew, Mamie Elizabeth. Photocopy of interview with Carl R. Sherwood, Indian Pioneer History Collection, University of Oklahoma. May 18, 1937. http://www.thecreekfreedmen.com/id7.html, accessed April 7, 2011.

Edwards, Elsie. Photocopy of interview 192 with Billie Byrd, Indian Pioneer History Collection, University of Oklahoma. July 17, 1937. http://www.thecreekfreedmen.com/id7.html, accessed April 19, 2011.

Everett, Dianna. "Lynching." Oklahoma Historical Society's *Encyclopedia of*

*Oklahoma History and Culture*. http://digital.library.okstate.edu/encyclopedia/entries/L/Ly001.html, accessed March, 25, 2011.

Logsden, Guy. "Choc Beer." *Encyclopedia of Oklahoma History and Culture,* http://digital.library.okstate.edu/encyclopedia, accessed December 5, 2012.

"Memorial Addresses in Honor of General John B. Sanborn: At the Monthly Meeting of the Minnesota Historical Society." October 10, 1904. http://archive.org/stream/sanbornmemorial00minnrich, accessed December 5, 2012.

"Native American Herbal Remedies." Cherokee Messenger. 1996. www.powersource.com/cherokee/herbal.html, accessed June 30, 2008.

Piker, Joshua. "Indians and Race in Early America: A Review Essay." *History Compass* 3 (December 2005). Wiley Online Library, http://onlinelibrary.wiley.com/doi/10.1111/j.1478-0542.2005.00129.x/full, accessed December 5, 2012.

Sanborn, John B. "Hd. Quarters Commission for regulating relations between Freedmen of the Indian Territory and their former masters." Freedmen's Bureau Online, January 5 and 8, 1866, http://freedmensbureau.com/arkansas/indian-territory.htm, accessed June 22, 2009.

Schmidt, Ryan W. "American Indian Identity and Blood Quantum in the 21st Century: A Critical Review." *Journal of Anthropology* 2011. http://www.hindawi.com/journals/janth/2011/549521/, accessed March 15, 2012.

Staniford, Mile. "Harrison to Celebrate 100th Birthday." *Oklahoma Eagle*, November 3, 1988. http://www.nathanielturner.com/harrison100.htm, accessed July 21, 2009.

"The Black Men Who Rode for Parker." Angelfire.com. http://www.angelfire.com/ar/freedmen/lwmen.html, accessed May 1, 2011.

Walton, Ronald. "Find a Grave Memorial." (Search Athens Cemetery, Pontotoc County, Oklahoma.) http://www.findagrave.com/cgi-bin/fg.cgi?page=gsr&GScid, accessed December 5, 2012.

Welton, Will. "Frontier Doctors of Indian Territory Oklahoma." Summary. AuthorsDen.com. http://www.authorsden.com/visit/viewwork.asp?id=29364, accessed July 18, 2009.

## Theses and Dissertations

Jackson, Neeley Belle. "Political and Economic History of the Negro in Indian Territory." MA thesis, University of Oklahoma, 1960.

McCombs, Virginia. "Intruders in the Cherokee Nation: 1865–1907." MA thesis, University of Oklahoma, 1973.

Sameth, Sigmund. "Creek Indians: A Study of Race Relations." MA thesis, University of Oklahoma, 1940.

Strong, Willa Allegra. "The Origin, Development, and Current Status of the Oklahoma Federation of Colored Women's Clubs." PhD dissertation, University of Oklahoma, 1957.

## Government Documents

U.S. Bureau of the Census. *Compendium of the Ninth Census of the United States, 1870*. Washington, D.C.: Government Printing Office, 1872.
————. *Extra Census Bulletin: The Five Civilized Tribes*. Washington, D.C.: Government Printing Office, 1894.
U.S. Commissioner of Indian Affairs. *Report, 27 January 1866*. Washington, D.C.: Government Printing Office, 1866.
U.S. Congress, Senate. *Reports of the Assistant Commissioner, Bureau of Refugees, Freedmen, and Abandoned Lands of Missouri, Arkansas, and Indian Territory*. 39th Congress, 2nd Session, 1866, 24.

## Newspapers

*Boley (Okla.) Informer*. 1905–15.
*Boley (Okla.) Progress*. 1905–15.
*Clearview Patriarch*. 1905–15.
*Clearview Tribune*. 1905–15.
*Langston City Herald*. 1895.
*New York Times*. 1890–91.
*Oklahoma Guide* (Guthrie). 1903.

## Miscellaneous Papers

Dill, Bonnie Thornton. "Our Mothers' Grief: Racial Ethnic Women and the Maintenance of Families." Research Paper 4, Center for Research on Women, Memphis, Tennessee, 1986.
Harshbarger, Mary. "Our Boley: Picture Book with Stories of Some of Boley's Pioneers." Boley, Okla.: Dawn, 1984.
Mann, Susan Archer. "Social Change and Sexual Inequality: The Impact of the Transition from Slavery to Sharecropping on Black Women." Working Paper 3, Center for Research on Women, Memphis, Tennessee, 1986.
Perdue, Theda. "Indians in the Segregated South." Keynote address delivered at the Mid America Conference on History, Tulsa, Oklahoma, 2007.

# Index

Page numbers in *italics* refer to figures. Entries with two first names separated by a semicolon (;) indicate kinship and are cited on the same page.

Abbott, L. J., 76
abolition, 23, 26–27
Adair, William Penn, 52
Adams, Alafair Carter, 87, 109
African Americans: all-black communities, 86, 108–111, *109*, 113, 128–34, 136, 138, 145–46; citizenship, 6, 34, 68–69, 83, 90, 106, 138; construction/home production skills, 21; cowboys, 84; immigrant, 110; language, 21; law officers, 83–84; military units, 52–53, 67, 81–82; subservient class, 8–9; women's clubs, 135–38
Aikens, Maggie, 111
Albert, Ella, 142
Allen Seminary (TX), 122
allotment process, 9, 130, 132, 133, 141–42, 147
Alpha Club, 137

American Baptist Home Mission Society, 123
American Baptist Missionary Union, 27
American Board of Commissioners for Foreign Missions (ABCFM), 26, 27
Anderson, Karen, 148
Apache Tribe, 59, 134
Arkansas Colored (Indian Territory), 109, 129
Armstrong, John, 18
Armstrong, Mrs. Mattie, 102
Armstrong Academy, 78, 102
Ashley, Mary Reynolds, 111
Atoka (Choctaw Nation), 115, 117
"Aunt" designation, 101
Averall, William W., 45

Bacone College, 103
Bailey (Chickasaw Nation), 129
Banks, Frances, 30, 64, 100, 119, 152n28
Banks, Phoebe, 28, 31, 48, 51, 64, 124
Baptist, 16, 27, 115–16, 120, 126, 127, 145
Baptist and Educational Convention, 116
*Baptist Missionary Magazine*, 28, 115

Barnett, Nancy Grayson, 64, 155n30, 99
Barnett, Nellie, 142
Barnett, Patsy, 64, 155n30
Barnett, Siah, 155n30
Barnett family, 99
Bean, Nancy Rogers, 28–29, 39–40, 74, 97, 114
Beck, Joe, 54
Beloved Woman. *See* Ward, Nancy
Berry, Francis B., 111
Black Codes, 134, 145
Blackjack School, 128
blood quantum, 7–8
Bloomfield Academy, 94–95, 122
Blue Branch School, 127
Blue Lodge, 45
Blunt, James G., 52, 53
Boggy Depot (Indian Territory), 16, 30
Boley, OK, 110–11, 129, 137
*Boley Informer*, 112
Boley Ladies Industrial Club, 112, 136
*Boley Progress*, 128, 132, 136
Boley Women's Club, 136
"boomers," 129–30
Boots, Doll, 5, 33–34
Boots, Elizabeth, 34
Boots, Polly, 34
Boots, Shoe, 5, 33–34
Boots, William, 34
Boudinot, Elias C., 86, 130
Bowlegs, Billy, 14
Bradley, Mrs. O. H., 102
Bradley, O. H., 136
Breiner, Henry, 99
Bridges, Jeanne Rorex, *Trail Sisters,* 3, 10
Brooks, James, 4
Brown, Eliza, 84, 101
Brown, Jack, 84, 101
Brown, Mrs. M. W., 111
Burial and Funeral Association of Boley, 101
Butler, Benjamin, 18–19

Cabin Creek, Battle of, 53, 81
Campbell family, 101
camp meetings, 119–20
Canadian Colored (Indian Territory), 109, 129
Carter, Hannibal, 86
Catholic, *125*
cattle ranches, 84
Caty (slave woman), 17
Celia (slave cook), 27
Chang, David A., 4
Checote, Samuel, 133
*Cherokee Advocate*, 34, 127
Cherokee Colored High School, 125
Cherokee Female Seminary, 122
Cherokee Nation: Canadian District, 70; citizenship, 6, 7, 34, 69–70, 106; Civil War, 42–43, 46, 51, 53, 55, 57, 59; Colored High School, 103–4; communities, 129; education, 16, 24, 64, 102–4, 122, 125–26, 146; free people, 5–6, 24, 69–71; Indian Territory population, 16, 23; intertribal factionalism, 45; kinship norms, 5, 158n2; post-Civil War treaty, 68; race-culture characteristics, 6; removal treaty, 12; resistance, 7; slave revolt, 25–26; slavery, 5, 6–7, 16–18, 19, 24, 26, 27, 36–40, 45, 56, 150n7; sovereignty, 5; written language, 5–6. *See also* Five Tribes
Cherokee Teachers Institute, *103*
*Chicago Times*, 86
Chickasaw Nation: citizenship, 68–69, 83, 106, 126; Civil War, 46, 53, 57; education, 27, 94–95, 122, 124, 126, 127; free people, 71; Indian Territory population, 16, 23; post-Civil War treaty, 68; racial purity, 78; removal process, 13; slavery, 18, 19, 22, 24–25, 29, 32, 39–40, 45, 67–68; tribal raids, 58. *See also* Five Tribes
childbearing decisions, 5

childbirth services, 100–101, 145

child caregivers (occupation), 31–33, 112, 144

Chisholm, Jessie, 58, 84

Chisholm Trail, 84

Choctaw Nation: citizenship, 68–69, *69*, 83; Civil War, 46, 53, 57; education, 27, 78, 95, 102, 120–22, 126; free people, 71; Indian Territory population, 16; Mississippi Choctaws, 13; post-Civil War treaty, 68; removal process, 13; slavery, 18, 19, 22, 24–25, 39, 67–68; tribal raids, 58. *See also* Five Tribes

Chupco, John, 77

Church, Ebenezer, 115

churches. *See* religion

Civil War, 42–67

Clearview, OK, 110–11, 129

*Clearview Patriarch*, 111

Cline, Johnson; Malvina, 80–81

Coffin, William G., 50, 54

Cohee, Ed, 84

Colbert, Anna, 39

Colbert, Betsy, 29, 31

Colbert, B. R., 83

Colbert, Buck, 32, 37–38, 44

Colbert, Frank, 107

Colbert, Holmes, 29

Colbert, Julie, 107

Colbert, Polly, 28, 29, 30–31, 43, 79, 99–100

Colbert, Tim, 78

Colbert, Winchester, 68, 78

Colbert family, 39, 94–95

Colbert Station (school), 127

Cole, Henry, 84

Collins, Adeline, 38

Colored Methodist Episcopal Church (CME), 116

Comanche Tribe, 58–59, 134

Constant School, Mrs. D. C., *123*

Constitution League, 138

Coody, Elizabeth Fields; William Shorey, 19

cooking occupation, 97–98, 112, 144

Cooper, Douglas, 19, 46, 50

Cowan, Mrs. Annie, 111

Cowskin Prairie (Indian Territory), 51

Crazy Snake Rebellion, 132

Creek Nation: citizenship, 106; Civil War, 46–48, 53, 55, 57, 64; Council, 46–47; education, 103, 123–24, 146; free people, 4, 71; Indian Territory population, 16, 108; land ownership, 131–33; links to Seminoles, 22–23; Lower Creeks, 13, 46; Muscogee, 5, 21, 61, 109; post-Civil War treaty, 68; Red Stick warriors, 22; removal process, 13–14; slave revolt, 25; slavery, 5, 17, 21–22, 25, 35–37; Upper Creeks, 13, 14, 46, 47. *See also* Five Tribes

Crew, Mamie Elizabeth, 130

Culckeeeshowa, 17

Cummings, Amanda (Mrs. J. H.), 111

Curtis Act, 130

Cushing, Caleb, 19

Dallas, George W., 126

Daniel family, 70

Daughters of Tabor, 136

Davis, Elizzie Redmond, 141

Davis, Jefferson, 45–46

Davis, Lucinda, 56–57, 61, 97

Davis, Reverend, 116

Dawes, Mary Allen; Hiram, 124

Dawes Academy, 124

Dawes Act, 130, 133

Doaksville, Treaty of, 13

domestic service, 95–97, 112, 144

Doran, Michael, 18, 19, 24

Downing family, 75

Drew, John, 25–26

Ealy, Mary; Taylor F., 126–27
East Shawnee trail, 84
economic status, 3, 76–78, 91–113
education, 3, 138: missionary, 16, 27,
    103, 113, 120–27, 146; subscription,
    127–28, 138, 146; teaching
    occupation, 102–4, 111, 145. *See
    also specific Native American nation*;
    freedmen/freedwomen; slaves
Edwards, Elsie, 22
Edwards, James, 25–26
Edwards, John, 27
emancipation, 5, 7, 51–52, 60, 63, 88,
    *89*, 90
Emancipation Proclamation, 52, 60–61
*estelusti*, 23, 151n16
Eufaula, OK, 137
Evangel Mission, 103

Fanny (runaway slave), 19
farming occupation, 104–8, 144
Five Nations. *See* Five Tribes
Five Tribes: civilized tribes, 9; Civil War,
    42–67, 143; family reconstruction,
    66–90; intertribal factionalism, 45;
    kinship norms, 5, 7, 17, 33, 85, 142–
    43, 158n2; Reconstruction treaties,
    83, 114; removal process, 11–16,
    18–19, 26, 142, 150n10; status,
    32–33. *See also* Cherokee Nation;
    Chickasaw Nation; Choctaw Nation;
    Creek Nation; intermarriages;
    Seminole Nation
Florida, removal process, 14
Forbes, Miss, 126
Foreman, Stephen, 45
Fort Arbuckle (Oklahoma), 59, 126–27
Fort Gibson (Indian Territory), 14, 25,
    51, 53–57, 63, 81–82, *82*, 98
Fort Mims (Alabama), 22
Fort Scott (Kansas), 51, 52
Fort Smith (Arkansas), 63, 68, 83

Fort Sumter (South Carolina), 45
Fort Washita (Oklahoma), 57, 63
Foster, I. J., 129
Four Mile Creek (Indian Territory), 63
Francis Harper No. One, 137
Franklin, Betty, 142
Franklin, Buck Colbert, 108, 116, 127,
    129, 161n3
Franklin, David, 78, 102, 108, 116–17,
    127–28
Franklin, Dolores, 108
Franklin, Milley, 78, 102, 108, 116–17,
    127–28, 146
Franklin, John Hope, 161n3
freedmen/freedwomen: business
    initiatives, 109–13; citizenship, 6,
    68–70, *69*, 106; designator, 4, 67;
    domestic skills, 9; economic stability,
    74–76; education, 9, 112; family
    stability, 73, 74–76; homesteading,
    73, 85; Indian connections, 73–74;
    Indian territory settlements, 67–90;
    transition to paid work, 91–113, 144.
    *See also specific Native American
    nation*
funeral services, 101–2, 145

Garrett, John, 83
gender roles, 7, 8, 21, 102, 113
General Federation of Women's Clubs,
    135
Georgia, removal process, 12, 13
Gibson Station, OK, 129
Gilroy, Milley Fish, 64
Goen, Mrs. B., 111
Goldsby, Crawford; Ellen Beck; George,
    82–83
Grayson, Aaron, 88, 90
Grayson, Elizabeth, 36
Grayson, George Washington, 36
Grayson, Judah, 36
Grayson, Katy, 5, 35–36

Grayson, Mary, 36–37, 40, 44, 63–64, 107, 128
Grayson, Rebecca, 111
Grayson, William, 5, 35–36, 44
Grayson family, 99
Green, Rev. David, 129
Grierson, Benjamin, 81
Grierson, Robert, 5, 35–36
Grierson, Sinnugee, 5, 35–36
Guerring, Matt, 34
Guthrie (Oklahoma Territory), 130, 137

Halfbreed, Pigeon, 34
Halleck, Henry, 70
Halliburton, R., 18
Harjo, Chitto, 132
Harlan, James, 54, 55, 70
Harlin, Justin, 54
Harnage, John, 39
Harris, Cyrus, 126
Harrison, Benjamin, 87
Harrison, Emma Rentie, 105–6
Harrison, Rebecca, 106
Hartford, Eliza, 120, 121, *122*
Hawkins, Benjamin, 21
Hayes, Rutherford B., 85
Haymaker, Priscilla, 121, *122*
Hector (M. Perryman's slave), 37, 44
Henderson, Henry; Mollie, 59
Herriford, Miss Scott, 111–12
Hicks, Hannah Worcester, 52
Hodges, Celestine, 122
homesteading, 73, 85, 106, 130, 132
Honey Springs, Battle of, 52, 55, 56, 61, 81
Horseshoe Bend, Battle of, 22

immigration society, 86
Indian Expedition, 51
Indian Removal Act, 12
Indian Springs, Treaty of, 13–14
Indian Territory, 12, 16: Civil War,

42–67; communal land, 130, 132, 138, 147; federal sovereignty, 68; incorporation of freedmen, 68–70; lawlessness, 83; orphans, 64; population, 23, 110, 113, 130; settlements, 15, 19, 61–65, 67–90, 108–11, 113, 129, 142; slavery, 8, 16–17, 19, 23–24, 29–30, 142; tribal raids, 58–59; tribal unification, 68
intermarriage, 5–6, 9, 22–25, 33–40, 71–88, 134, 144, 150n9
Islands, Harry, 116

Jack (African American pastor), 115
Jackson, Andrew, 12, 22
Jacob (M. Perryman's slave), 37, 44, 51
Jefferson, Edward D., 83
Jefferson, Thomas, 11–12
Jimboy, Tustenugge, 22
Jim Crow law, 22, 115
Johnson, Adeline; Annie, 34–35
Johnson, Ben, 32, 34, 36, 37–38, 60–61, 63
Johnson, Charlotte, *62*
Johnson, Grant, 83
Johnson, Hagar; Jackson, 37
Johnson, Lottie; Ned, 34–35
Johnson, Montford, 84, 101, 134–35
Johnson, Nellie, 22, 37
Johnson family, 39, 101
Jones, Evan, 27
Jones, John B., 27
Jones, Maymie Morris, 111
Jones, Wilson N., 84
Joss, John, 83
Jubilee Singers, 117

Kansas, 43, 45, 50–51
Keetoowah Society, 27, 45
Kemp, Mr. and Mrs. Jackson, 38
kinship lineage, 5, 7, 17, 33, 85, 142–43, 158n2

Knights of the Golden Circle, 45
Kingsbury, Cyrus, 121
Kiowa Tribe, 58–59, 134
Krauthamer, Barbara, 133

land ownership, 130, *131*, 132, 138.
  *See also* allotment process;
  homesteading
Landrum, Charles, 34
Land Run, 130, 146
Langston, OK, 130
language differences, 95–96, 112, 144
LaVere, David, 58
Lawton, John P., 123
Lee, R. W., 57
Leslie, Nellie Ann; Robert A., 96, 103
Lewis, Mr. and Mrs. David, 115
Lewis, Elzora, 103
Liberty, OK, 130
Lighthorse, 83
Lincoln, Abraham, 47, 55, 60, 63
Lincoln, OK. *See* Clearview, OK
Lindsay, Henry, 107
Lindsay, Mary (elder); William, 40
Lindsay, Mary (younger), 40, 67, 92–93,
  107
Little Arkansas Treaty, 58
Littlefield, D., 3–4, 23, 26, 83, 127
Locust Grove, Battle of, 51
Loughbridge, Robert, 28
Love, Franklin "Bruner," 67
Love, Isaac, 38, 39
Love, Kizah, 32, 43, 44, 55, 100, 107,
  118–19
Love, Isom, 107
Love, Robert, 83
Love, Sam, 107
Love, Sobe, 40, 93
Love family, 39, 93
*Lucy Walker* (steamboat), 26
lynching, 134–35

"mammy" designation, 101
maroon, 23, 77, 151n16
Martin, Annie, 141
Matrons Mutual Improvement Circle,
  137
May, Katja, 76, 80, 88
McAlester, OK, 137, 138
McBride, Mr.and Mrs. James, 121
McCabe, Edwin P., 86, 132
McIntosh, Phoebe, 129
McIntosh, Roley, 22, 37
McIntosh, William, 13–14
McIntosh family, 39, 44, 48
McLoughlin, William, 21
McNair, Caney, 52, 60, 91, 96, 118
medicine, practice of, 30–32, 98–101,
  112, 138, 144–45
Menser, Emma Marriott; Julius, 132
Menser, Julius, 132
Merrell, James H., 18
Methodist, 16, 116–17, 126, 145, 145
*mikko*, 77
Mikko, Heniha, 46, 77
Miles, Tiya, 4, 5
miscarriage, 101
mission work, 16, 26, 115–22, 145. *See
  also* education, missionary
Mississippi, removal process, 13
MK&T (Katy) Railroad, 85, 86
money, 93–94, 112, 144
Monroe, James, 12
Mulroy, Kevin, 76–77, 120, 124
Murrow, J. S., 103
Muskogee, OK, 137

National Association for the
  Advancement of Colored People,
  138
National Association of Colored
  Women (NACW), 135, 137, 147
National Federation of Afro-American
  Women, 135

National League of Colored Women, 135
Nave, George, 126
Naylor, Celia, 4, 6–7, 26
*New York Times*, 132
Nicks, Crowder, 83
North Fork Church, 116
North Fork Colored (Indian Territory), 109, 129

Oak Hill Church (Valiant, OK), 120
Oak Hill Industrial Academy, 121–22, *122*
Oberlin College, 96
Ohopeyane, 58
Oklahoma Federation of Colored Women's Clubs, 137–38, 147
*Oklahoma Eagle*, 105
Oklahoma statehood, 130
Oklahoma Territory, 87, 108–12, 130, 132–33, 146
O'Neal, Mrs., 74
Opothleyoholo, 14, 46–48
Order of the Eastern Star, 136
Osage Tribe, 57
Osceola, 14

Paradis Baptist Church (OK), 129, 146
Parker, Isaac, 83, 135
Pascoe, Peggy, 24
Patriarchs of America in Clearview, 137
patrollers, 43–44, 143
Pauls Valley, OK, 129
Payne's Landing, Treaty of, 14
Pegg, Thomas, 51
Perdue, Lois, 137
Perdue, Theda, 7, 8, 16, 18, 158n2
Perry, OK, 130
Perryman, Jim, 37
Perryman, Mose, 31, 37, 44, 54, 63
Perryman, Patsy, 29, 32, 40, 61, 66, 73–74, 76, 80, 97, 102–3

Perryman, Randolph, 80
Perryman family, 28, 48
Petite, George, 79
Petite, Phyllis, 32, 39, 61, 79, 97, 118, 128
Phillips, Martha, 55
Phillips, William A., 51, 53
Pike, Albert, 46, 48
Piker, Joshua, 4
Pin Indians, 45. *See also* Keetoowah Society
Plains Indians, 58, 58, 65, 134, 146
Poe, Matilda, 29, 38, 39, 44, 119
polygyny, 71–72, 144
Pontotoc, Treaty of, 13
Prairie Indians, 58
Presbyterian, 16, 26–27, 117–18, 120, 126, 145
Presbyterian Board of Foreign Missions (PBFM), 26
Presbyterian Board of Missions for Freedmen, 117, 121
Price, Sterling, 70
prostitution, 98, 159n13

racial etiquette, 96–97
racism, 4–5
rag-head, 87
railroads, 85–86, 98, 129
ranching occupation, 104–8
Reconstruction, 66–90, 114
Red River War, 59
Redmouth, Mose, 141
Reece, Betsy; John, 18–19
Reeves, Bass, 83, 84, 135
Reeves, Georgina, 127
Reid, Rev. Alexander, 117
religion, 3, 27–29, 16, 116–28, 138, 142. *See also specific religion*
removal process, 11–16, 18–19, 26, 142, 150n10
Rentie, William, 129

Rentiesville, OK, 129, 146

Richardson, Chaney, 28, 29, 43, 45, 56, 57, 59, 64, 66, 93, 120

Ridge, John, 34

Robertson, Ann Eliza Worchester, 122

Robertson, Betty, 28, 37, 39, 79–80, 93, 104, 118, 119

Robertson, William Schenck, 122–23

Robinson, Ella Coody, 26

Robinson, Mollie, 111

Robinson, N. A.; W. D., 129

Roebuck, Dick, 83

Rogers, Charlie, 43

Rogers, Isaac, 83

Rogers plantation, 29, 56

Rollin, David B., 28, 115

Rose Cottage (Indian Territory), *47*

Ross, Hannah, 56, 64, 93

Ross, John, 46, *47*, 51

Ross, Lelia Sweptson, 104

Rouce, James; Queenia Z., 106

Round Mountain, Battle of, 48, 51

Royal Arts (club), 137

Ruffin, Josephine St. Pierre, 135

Sac and Fox Tribe, 50

Sanborn, John, 67–68, 70–71, 81, 92

Sapulpa, OK, 138

Saunt, Claudio, 4–5

schools. *See* education

Scotia Seminary (North Carolina), 122

Scott, Susie Bruner, 103

sectionalism, 23

Self-Enterprising Club, 137

Seminole Nation: citizenship, 106; Civil War, 46–48, 53, 57; education, 77; free people, 26, 71; Indian Territory population, 16, 108; links to Creeks, 22–23, 25; membership status, 151n16; post-Civil War, 68, 76–78; raids, 58; Red Stick warriors, 22; removal process, 13–14, 23; slavery, 16–17, 19, 21–23, 25, 26, 37, 43. *See also* Five Tribes

Sequoyah, 5

sharecropping, 160n26

Sheppard, Morris, 42–43, 45, 59

Sheppard, Wash, 59

Shoals, Pleasant, 128

Sisters of Ethiopia, 136–37

slavery: abolition, 68; Civil War, 42–67, 143; cohabitation provisions, 25; living in, 11–41; neutrality position, 26–27; transition to paid work, 91–113, 144; variations, 142–43. *See also* emancipation; *specific Native American nation*

slaves: abandoned, 59–60; daily life, 29–30; designators, 16–17, 23; education, 25, 27–28, 144; firearm ownership, 25; intermarriages, 33–41; property ownership, 25; religion, 27–28, 142; runaway, 17, 18–19, *20*, 21, 23, 25, 38–39, 59–60

Smith, Edward, 106, 126

Smith, Henry, 54

Smith, Presley, 31

Smith, R. C., 31, 53, 67, 84

Smith, Silas, 87

Spelman College, 7

Spencer Academy, 27, 95, 117, 121

Sprague, J. W., 102

Starr, 35

state Negroes. *See* freedmen/ freedwomen

St. Catherine's Catholic Church (Boley, OK), *125*

Stephenson, Mrs. A. E., 111

Stewart, Bettie, 121

Stewart, Charles W., 117, 120–21, 122

Stidham, George W., 55, 84

Stidham plantation, 66

Stinnett, J. W., 60

Stonewall, OK, 129

Strout, Eliza Daniel, 70
Sturm, Circe, 4, 6
subscription schools. *See* education

Taft, OK. *See* Twine
Tahlequah (Indian Territory), 16, 51
Tatums, Mary, 129
Tatums (Chickasaw Nation), 129
Taylor, Hilliard, 111
Taylor, Judy, 40
Taylor family, 32
teaching. *See* education, teaching
    occupation
Terrell, Mary Church, 135, 137
Thoburn, Joseph, 134
Thompson, Johnson, 128
Thompson, Neva, 137
Thompson, Victoria Taylor, 59, 73–74,
    97, 118
Tidmore School (OK), 124
Tieuel, Mrs. Nodie, 111
Tomm, Jim, 54, 66
Trail of Tears, 12
Tuggle, W. O., 96
Tullahassee, OK, 109, 129
Tullahassee Freedmen's School, *104*
Tullahassee Mission and Manual Labor
    School, 122, 123–24
Tulsa, OK, 137
Tulwa Tustanagee, 35
Turner, California Taylor, 111
Turner, James Milton, 86
Tuskaya-hiniha, 61
Twine (Oklahoma Territory), 109

Underhill, Lonnie, 26, 83

Van Buren, Arkansas, 43
Vann, Clara, 103–4
Vann, Dennis, 119–20
Vann, Jim, 32–33
Vann, Joseph, 24, 25–26, 37, 93, 104,
    118

Vann, Lucinda, 28, 32–33, 75, 79
Vann, Martin, 59
Vann family, 28, 39, 64, 75, 93
Vicksburg, Battle of, 70
"Vigilance Committees," 134

Wagoner, Sweetie Ivery, 16–17, 28
Walker, Alice, 7
Walker, Emily, 51
Wapanucka Female Seminary, 27
Ward, Jane Davis, 29
Ward, Nancy, 17
Ward, Rachel Aldrich, 54, 75, 87, 97,
    100
Ward, Rochelle Allred, 64
Warren, Bessie, 137
Washington, Booker T., 111
Washington, Margaret Murray, 135, 137
*Watchina*, 110
Watie, Sarah, 58
Watie, Stand, 46, *47*, 53, 58, 60, 81
Weer, William, 51
Wells-Barnett, Ida, 136
Wesley, John, *75*
Western University, 112
westward expansion, 11, 129–35, 146
Wewoka, OK, 108
Wheelock Seminary (Choctaw Nation),
    27, 121, 122
White, Charlotte Johnson, 31, 32, 38,
    60, 118
white race: definition, 9–10, 79;
    intermarriage, 33–40, 87–88;
    supremacy, justification of, 24
Wildcat, 14
Williams, Clara Boykin, 111
Williams, Fannie Barrier, 136
Williams, James M., 81
Williams, Manuel, 127
Willis, Minerva; Wallace, 117
Wilson, Billy, 25–26
Wilson, Lottie, 36

Wilson, Oliver, 79
Wilson, Sarah, 34–35, 36, 38, 40, 51,
    60–61, 63, 79, 93–94
women's clubs, 135–38, 147
Women's Missionary Societies, 117
Worcester, Samuel Austin, 122
Works Progress Administration (WPA), 6
Wright, Allen, 152n28
Wright, Muriel, 152n28, 160n18
Wright, W. N., 30, 100
Wybark, OK, 129

Yarbrough, Faye, 4, 6, 74
Young, Ruth, 127

Zellar, Gary, 47, 124